OVER TIME

Also by Frank Deford

FICTION
Cut 'n' Run
The Owner
Everybody's All-American
The Spy in the Deuce Court
Casey on the Loose
Love and Infamy
The Other Adonis
An American Summer
The Entitled
Bliss, Remembered

NONFICTION
Five Strides on the Banked Track
There She Is
Big Bill Tilden
Alex: The Life of a Child
The World's Tallest Midget
The Best of Frank Deford
The Old Ball Game

OVER TIME

MY LIFE AS A SPORTSWRITER

FRANK DEFORD

As Told to Frank Deford

Atlantic Monthly Press
New York

Published simultaneously in Canada
Printed in the United States of America

ISBN-13: 978-0-8021-2015-1

Atlantic Monthly Press
an imprint of Grove/Atlantic, Inc.
841 Broadway
New York, NY 10003

Distributed by Publishers Group West

www.groveatlantic.com

12 13 14   10 9 8 7 6 5 4 3 2

CONTENTS

1. A Not Very Bright Boy   1
2. Something of a Vote of Confidence   7
3. In Which I First Encounter Faster Guns   10
4. Roamer   16
5. Granny   20
6. Walking in Place   27
7. Old-Timers   30
8. The Vietnam War Is Finally Over   40
9. Push On   48
10. The Best Advice I Ever Got in My Whole Life   58
11. Scribes for the Cranks and the Fancy   61
12. El Tigre   68
13. In Which I Finally Discover the Difference Between Winning and Losing   83
14. Bawlmer, Merlin, My Hametown   91
15. Gee Whiz   101
16. Beauty and the Beasts   114
17. This Just In: Writing Can Be Fun   125
18. In Which I Happen Upon an Eye-Opener   135
19. Kingsley   141
20. My Damn Name   145
21. It Happens to the Best of Us   152
22. The Way It Was. Really   155
23. The Kid   160
24. Andre   170

25. Mr. King Will See You Now   178

26. Hobey and Danny and Bill   180

27. The Most Amazing Feat in Sport in
    the Twentieth Century   194

28. Hub Tales   205

29. My Man   211

30. Anglophile   219

31. Remember "Consciousness-Raising"?   227

32. Fun in the Sun   232

33. Summer Songs   239

34. Roadie   249

35. With Ease or Angst   256

36. Lost in Translation   267

37. The Anchor Leg   279

38. The Sweetest Thing I Ever Saw an Athlete Do
    for a Member of the Fourth Estate   287

39. You Won't Believe This   289

40. The Most Amazing Thing I Ever Saw an Athlete Do   301

41. Red   311

42. The Amateur Voice   318

43. The Best I Ever Was Fired   328

44. Naked Slept the Commissioner   332

45. Taboo   344

46. Last Call   350

Acknowledgments   353

For
Jerry Downs
and
Nemo Robinson

1

A NOT VERY BRIGHT BOY

*I was still enough of a child to think that anger could best be
expressed with perversity.*

An American Summer, 2002

After my junior year at Princeton, it another desultory academic lay-
by, I decided I might as well go into the army and get it over with. In
those days of the draft a healthy enough American boy had to do that
for at least six months. I chose the least. This was during that peaceful
lull separating Korea from Vietnam, though, so I was but a tweener,
passing through when nothing much was going on in a martial way.

My military highlight, such as it was, came when the sergeant
said to me: "DeFord, you wanna be the guide-on?" I had no idea what
that was, but it sounded OK, so I said, yes, I'd like that. Good answer.
The guide-on, I discovered, is the guy who carries the flag that the
other soldiers follow after. Guide-on would not have been a good job,
say, on Pickett's Charge in 1863, but at Fort Dix in 1961, when no one
was firing live rounds, it was an excellent vocation.

It wasn't even that I had earned the job of guide-on. It was just
that I was the tallest man in my company, so for most of my military
tenure I played retirement ceremonies, just holding a flag and standing tall, which I can do perfectly well. I was no better a soldier than I
was a student. In fact, in some respects I've never grown up. Primarily,
I don't think I've ever learned to do anything new since I was about
nine years old, when I first discovered that I had some facility for

writing and speaking. Well, I did learn about sex later on. But that's instinctive, so I don't think it can necessarily be counted as another arrow in my quiver.

Anyway, as a "returning serviceman," I put mufti back on and reconnoitered Princeton for one last year, there to officially conclude my education and contemplate my future. The main thing was, I wanted to go to New York, which is where I knew writers went to write and live life large. Prefiguring LeBron James, you might say, I decided to take my talents to midtown. But while Gotham beckoned me, I was not the sort of virtuous artiste who was willing to live in a garret and wait tables while I wrote the Great American Something. At a minimum, I needed a comfortable roof over my head and some walking-around money.

Fortuitously, one day I saw a notice that Time Incorporated would be interviewing on campus. The company's celebrated, respectable magazines—*Time, Life,* and *Fortune*—were not, I thought, the right sort of showcase for my presumed ability, but I'd been a reader of *Sports Illustrated* and very much admired the writing in the magazine. Whereas it had a lot of yummy stuff about yachts and show dogs and what tweeds to wear when tailgating at the Yale Bowl, there was, in counterpoint, some awfully good writing in it. I also figured that, as a starter course, a magazine would be a better fit for me than would a newspaper, as I imagined that the larger canvas was better suited for my more expansive, embroidered style.

I bundled up my choice clippings and went to see the interviewer. He was a Mr. Titman—a name Dickens had somehow missed. At first Titman told me that he really wasn't interviewing people who wrote, that he was just after business types—information I found a little disconcerting, coming from a publishing company's talent scout—but as I was about to scoop up my clips and depart, something crossed his mind. Titman was a Princeton man himself, and he recognized me from articles I'd written for the alumni magazine, and so, as a loyal Tiger, he very nicely said he'd go the extra mile and look into getting me an interview. So, there: thanks to Titman, now I was an official cog in the celebrated Old-Boy Network. My vaunted Princeton education—uh, affiliation—had already paid off.

Of course, understand: in 1962 it was hard for someone like me, an Ivy League Wasp, *not* to move to the head of the line, for certain rather prominent subgroups—notably the female gender and all racial and ethnic minorities—were not taken seriously at that time. Diversity was not yet a concept. In many distinguished places of business in New York then, what passed as diversity meant making sure not to hire too many Andover graduates at the expense of Exeter. Plus, I was born at the right time; I was that rare specimen, a Depression Baby. Better yet, I had been conceived early in 1938, at a time when there was *a recession in the middle of the Depression*. Except for my dear parents, almost nobody in America with any sense was having babies around the time I was born. So when I got out of college, there were only a handful of us coming onto the job market in the United States of America. It was actuarial affirmative action. While all those subsequent oodles of War Babies and Baby Boomers would have to go all-out Darwinian all their lives, we Depression Babies got a pass.

Because of this demographic serendipity, it was a seller's market extraordinaire, and I could approach job interviews with aplomb. So it was, on my appointed day, that I took the train into New York and boldly presented myself at the Time Incorporated personnel office.* There, I was handed two things. First, a list of the editors I was scheduled to see. Second, a folder with my name on it: Frank DeFord. I was advised to hand the folder to each big-shot Timeink editor that I met. Now, nobody told me *not* to look inside the folder, but even if anyone had, I would've had to be inhumanly incurious not to. So, first chance I got, I sneaked a peek. Samples of my writing were in there,

---

*Although please understand: nobody who has ever worked there ever has said "Time Incorporated." Never. It is Timeink, which sounds racier, and was, at least during that halcyon era, populated by devil-may-care folk who loved to call themselves "Timeinkers."

but on top was sort of an assessment of who this particular Depression Baby candidate might be, and here were the very first words typed there to sum me up:

"Not very bright . . ."

Now, fair's fair: if it was strictly based on my (ahem, gentleman's) grades at Princeton, this was a perfectly reasonable assessment. Still, talk about carrying your own cross. Sure, the offensive introduction was followed by something like ". . . but perhaps may have a passable way with words . . ." But still: I walk into an office and hand over the folder to Mr. High-and-Mighty Editor behind the desk, and the first thing he sees is "Not very bright . . ." Then he would look up at me, surprised that at least I wasn't drooling.

I remember the man in a backwater Timeink position, he being in command of the company newspaper—which was little more than a mimeographed wraparound for classified ads from one Timeinker to another. After seeing that analysis of my intellect he then allowed, well, maybe if I got some experience out in the hinterlands, maybe . . . maybe there could be a place for me there as an intern in a couple of years, reporting to him on things such as the Timeink blood drive.

Well, let me tell you: there's only so much a Depression Baby will take!

So, rather nicely but firmly, I advised all the editors I met (who didn't want a dummy like me anyway) that I didn't want anything to do with them, either, that I was merely humoring them because the only magazine where I wanted to work in the whole lousy company was *Sports Illustrated*.

This was heresy! Here was this snotty young apostate who actually was giving *Time* and *Life* and *Fortune,* not to mention the crappy company newsletter, the back of his hand. Nobody had ever dared do such a thing in the Time-Life Building.

But, although I certainly wasn't smart enough to have cannily plotted this strategy, this blasphemy made me immensely attractive in the one right place, for somehow this information lasered back to the twentieth floor, to *Sports Illustrated* HQ, and there I became an instant hero. You see, at this point, in the hallowed halls of Timeink, *SI* not only was considered déclassé for its sweaty content but was losing money as well. As a consequence, rude members of the other, fancy-schmancy magazines would, on the elevators, mutter aspersions at random *Sports Illustrated* employees for damaging their profit sharing.

But, one man's meat . . .

So, ipso facto, I suddenly found myself invited up to the elite company dining room for cocktails and lunch with *Sports Illustrated* editors. Moving right ahead at warp speed: I was escorted down to the magazine domain itself, and rushed toward the inner sanctum, the very office of the managing editor, Andre Laguerre, himself. I felt like one of those quarterbacks that the NFL and AFL were fighting over at the time.

I didn't know enough to be nervous. I had no idea that the "managing" editor was the boss editor, that this was *the* guy. I had no idea that Laguerre was an icon who put the fear of God into all and sundry. No, by now, I was just rockin' and rollin'. Watch my smoke. Hey, as Chuck Berry sang: *"Yeah 'n' I'm doin' all right in school. / They ain't said I broke no rule. / I ain't never been in dutch. / I don't browse around too much. . . . Anyway, I'm almost grown."* I was more interested in chatting up Laguerre's pretty secretary, when the great man interrupted my patter, asked me in, and told me he'd heard so much about me and was so pleased to meet me.

Hey, not very bright, my ass.

There was an opening as a researcher in the baseball department, because, of all things, I learned later, on the night during spring training when Laguerre had taken the incumbent researcher out to dinner, the witless lunkhead had written down on his expense account that he had himself entertained some ballplayers. Even at Timeink, where a liberal amount of expense-account fairy taling was accepted, this was beyond the pale. Creativity was one thing, stupidity another. They fired the guy. Hence, a spot on the roster had miraculously opened up. When could I start? Hell, I was ready to roll up my sleeves and pitch in right there, but there was this nasty little detail about finishing certain statutory requirements in order for me to get that precious Princeton diploma. Well, all right, they *would hold the job for me* till I could go through the motions and take my final exams.

I popped up to the Time-Life Building as soon as my last exam was finished, and while that meant I had to miss my graduation, nobody missed me either. And so it was that I got ahead of the curve and was gainfully employed, on my way to becoming a bona fide sportswriter. *"I don't run around with no mob. / Got myself a little job. . . . / Don't bother me, leave me alone. / Anyway, I'm almost grown."*

2

SOMETHING OF A VOTE OF CONFIDENCE

The whole point of man, the essence of us all, is contradictions.
Love and Infamy, 1993

But enough about me.

I have always believed that, ideally, your memoirs should be filled with anecdotes about *other*, more attractive people so that you might improve on the necessarily duller parts of the narrative, i.e., yourself. David Niven, for example, wrote memoir after memoir, because he knew all the stylish folk in the world, and wherever they were together, in the Hamptons or Gstaad or on yachts in the Mediterranean, they all had big names and they absolutely adored lunches, so they ate and drank long, languid midday repasts and threw off priceless bons mots, one after the other, for Mr. Niven to dress up his own memoirs with. Alas, although it was not my life's intention at the time when I chanced to become a sportswriter, I have thereafter mostly remained a sportswriter; and I'm afraid athletes don't traffic in bons mots, whether or not I am in their presence with a notepad.

Also, I have read dreadful memoir-like remembrances of times past by sportswriters, who go after the Great Man in History of Sports, retelling profiles of stars who never said die and had no quit in them. A little of that goes a long way, let alone to read, and certainly to write.

I mentioned this to my wife, Carol. We've been married for forty-six years, after a whirlwind courtship. She was a model, absolutely alabaster gorgeous, but fragile to the naked eye because models had to be frightfully skinny then in order to sell clothes no other women could possibly fit into. My mother made the mistake of reading too much into that. "She's very nice," she said, "but I don't think she looks like she's able to be tough enough on you."

Mothers should know not to judge a book by its cover. Carol has done just fine in the toughness line, thank you. We lost our daughter, Alexandra, to cystic fibrosis, and Carol was the one who was so much better at handling that than I. And she was the one who was smart enough then to say that we had to move ahead and adopt another daughter and get on with it. That turned out to be Scarlet, and she was a gem, and we did get on with it.

Yet for all Carol's innate savvy and sweetness, there are two postnuptial agreements vis-à-vis my work that have kept the marriage intact for these many moons.

1. Whenever I write something, I do not show a word of it to her until it is set in print. It absolutely amazes me when I read how writers explain on page ii of the preface* or foreword how they could not have done this work without the support of their dear, supportive, etc., wife, who advised and typed and proofread and consoled and did God knows what all else. The reason I never show Carol anything I write is that if I do, then:

a. If she says she likes it, I immediately assume she's just saying that to be nice, and I sulk and dislike her for patronizing me. Or:

b. If she says she doesn't like it, I hate her and there go forty-six mostly good years down the drain. Maybe that's—what? Active-passive? Passive-inactive? I don't know. But lose-lose for sure.

Isn't marriage tenuous enough without begging for trouble?

---

*I have never understood why only watch faces, Super Bowl, and book prefaces any longer employ Roman numerals.

2. Carol never has to attend an event where I am speaking, especially if it involves a head table. From her point of view, that's probably more important than item 1.

The only codicil to this will is that when I'm invited to speak on a luxury cruise ship, a package deal which includes her, then Carol must attend my speeches because she dresses up the crowd, and because otherwise the cruise director might say, "Even his wife didn't come to hear him speak"—thereby ruining any chance that I (and, hence, she) will be invited for a return engagement on another luxury cruise.

So, when I told her I didn't plan to accept the offer to write a memoir, she said, "Aw no, you can put in all those things you always say in your speeches." And, she added, ruefully, eyes rolling: "All those stories I've heard you tell guys over drinks."

So, that pushed me over the top, and here we go.

3

IN WHICH I FIRST ENCOUNTER FASTER GUNS

High schools are our commonest common denominator. Good Lord, they even all smell the same, that stale institutional odor that can be disturbed only by another ringing bell. The children fall out into the corridors, moving with a special rhythm, at a pace they will never again employ in life. Nothing else in the human experience resembles the break between classes.

"When All the World Was Young, Lad,"
Sports Illustrated, 1977

Besides prefaces counting their pages in Roman numerals, the other thing about books that always confounds me is that we authors go on and on, tediously, with acknowledgments (see page 353), but we usually make a mystery of our dedication. So, here is who this book is dedicated to: my high school adviser and my high school basketball coach.

You see, since much of this book is about writing and sports, it is especially appropriate to dedicate it to them.

Jerry Downs not only was my adviser but he taught me English, and (although I could've done without the Thomas Hardy) he showed me how to appreciate great writing—Shakespeare in particular, of course—and he wonderfully encouraged my own writing and helped me improve it without ever being pedantic. He also directed me in school plays (struggling mightily with me when I was in my James

Dean period), where I believe I learned to appreciate actors more than athletes. He was everything good that a high school teacher should be, and he was a wonderful influence on me, but, of course I was a teenager then and therefore I didn't let him know that I thought that.

Nemo Robinson—square name: John—was my varsity basketball coach. I had no idea, until forty years later, that he had been a certified hero at the Battle of the Bulge. That was revealed to me only when the History Channel devoted a whole program to a re-creation of his incredible courage, for which he was awarded the Bronze Star with valor. In deep snow, out in the open, Lieutenant Robinson led an assault on an entrenched, well-fortified German position, then crawled back and forth under the enemy machine-gun fire to rescue several of his wounded men, dragging them to safety—even as he suffered a hernia for these extraordinary exertions.

But what did I know when Nemo coached me? If I'd actually known what he'd so bravely achieved against the Germans I would've been too nervous around a truly courageous man like that. Luckily, I just knew Nemo as Coach Robinson, who put up with me.

Because I'm tall, people naturally assume I played basketball. Every tall guy gets that. When people meet Abraham Lincoln in heaven, I'm sure they start off asking him where he played hoops. Unfortunately, I'm not much of an athlete. I have terrible hand-eye coordination. It's so bad that, when operating a computer, for some unknown reason, I hold the mouse backward. Apparently, I alone in the world have this mysterious vertical dyslexia.

Incredibly, though, I could shoot a basketball, and when I was in my senior year at Gilman School, playing for Nemo, and the jump shot was coming into vogue, I just sort of magically started making jump shots. I'd put on a little weight, too, from taking the Charles Atlas course, which cost $30 (an awful lot of money at the time). Mr. Atlas called his secret regimen "Dynamic Tension." You sent away for it through the ads on the back of comic books, where there were panels showing how the erstwhile skinny Charles himself had put on muscle and, thereupon, at the beach, beat up a bully who had kicked sand in his face.

Ideally, you did the exercises naked before a mirror; this gave them more of a hush-hush, even lurid, aspect. When I got my driver's license at sixteen, it listed me at 6 feet 2½ inches, 127 pounds, so I was a wraith. With the help of Charles Atlas, by the time I was a senior I was up to a hefty 150, and I'd grown a couple more inches, too, so I was finally able to muscle up jump shots.

It was all quite amazing; *overnight* I got off the bench and became a star. It absolutely confounded Nemo that I came out of nowhere. But me—I knew, secretly, my success was a fluke. As a precursor to so much in my life, I was just in the right spot. We had a very good center named Tommy Garrett, who was 6 feet 7 inches, so he had to play the oppponent's big man, and by far the best athlete on our team was the point guard, Alan Yarbro, who would bring the ball up court, do all the hard work, then pass me the ball so I could launch my beautiful new jump shot over the poor little shorter guy guarding me.

By coincidence, that season, 1956–1957, was the first time that the Baltimore high school conference, which had been segregated, allowed in the black schools. Promptly, Dunbar easily won the championship. Its star player was named Joe Pulliam. One day, before school, we were sitting around reading the Baltimore papers, both of which, that day, selected me for second-team all-city. Joe Pulliam was one of the five players on the first team. My friend Bob Reiter said, "You know, Frank, whatta shame. The one year the colored boys come in, they have a good basketball team. Otherwise you would have been first-team all-Baltimore."

I said, "Bob, I really don't think this was like a onetime thing for the colored boys in basketball."

It was one of the few predictions in sport I've ever gotten right. Like most sportswriters and, for that matter, like most other people, very few of us ever predict sports correctly. It isn't even worth the effort, and you shouldn't pay any attention to what anyone predicts,* but everybody keeps trying and many people take it seriously.

A few years later, when I was covering basketball for *Sports Illustrated,* I obtained, if secondhand, the definition of basketball, from the very lips of the creator himself. This happened when I interviewed the old retired Kansas coach Phog Allen, who had himself been coached as a Jayhawk by Dr. James Naismith—he who had personally invented basketball. Imagine somebody actually inventing a whole sport. You remember the peach baskets.

It was an even more disorienting conversation for such a young man as I, however, because Allen continually referred to Naismith as "Jim," and to me, this was like talking to someone who had known Edison and kept recalling a chat with "Tom" about working up electricity.

Allen told me Naismith had told him: "Phog, the appeal of basketball is that it is a game easy to play but difficult to master."

And Phog replied: "You mean just like life, Jim?"

And Naismith agreed. "Yes, anybody can piddle at it, but to master it—yes, just like life."

So, there I had basketball straight from the horse's mouth. Really, I had been a piddler. Would that I could do better with life.

Nevertheless, because of that one glorious year in high school, I've always known, from personal experience, exactly what it's like for someone to, as they say, *get hot.* I got hot, and even though I understood it was a mirage, I had the time of my life. It taught me how confidence can transform you, even carry you—well, at least for a while. We had a terrific team, and I broke the school scoring records, and one day Nemo told someone that I was the best "game player" he'd ever coached. Not the best player, you understand—I knew I wasn't even the best player on this one team—but his best "game player." All-time.

---

*Let alone "guarantees." It is the stupidest thing in sports journalism that we actually report it when some player "guarantees" that his team will win. Please.

More than fifty years on, I don't believe I've ever had a compliment
I prized so much.

However, when I went off to college, the Princeton coach, an
old gruff billiard-ball-bald guy named Cappy Cappon, watched me
at practice for a while. Cappy was not long on words or diplomacy.
I was already writing for the college paper, and Cappy came over to
me and said, "You know, DeFord, you write basketball much better
than you play it."

Luckily, I already knew this, and Cappy knew I knew it, so it was
not wounding. Sure, I'd have loved to be Mr. Hotshot Player. Wouldn't
everybody? But I'd had that one freak year, *when I got hot*, and, wow,
that was fantastic, and it taught me so much.

I think of all the boys (and girls now, too) who, as I was, are
good at a sport at some certain level—maybe even really good—but
that's as far as they can go. Sometimes, like me, they're finished after
high school. Sometimes in college. Some players are even absolutely
drop-dead terrific, all-Americans, but they're a total bust in the pros.
Water finds its own level. When I started covering sports, it helped
that, because of my own experience as a glorious flash in the pan, I
understood how hard it was on the ones who thought they were so
good, but found out, no, they were good only up to a point, because
there were faster guns out there, beyond. There's always a faster gun.

But I know it's true that so many grown American men are walking around all the rest of their lives, playing those glory days over,
still hearing the cheers in their inner ear. A lot of them lie about how
good they were, and I think after a while, they come to believe their
own lies. Some of them never get it out of their system, no matter how
long they live or what they do for a living, because in this country,
when you're so damn young and impressionable, it's especially ex-
hilarating, playing for your school, with pretty cheerleaders jumping
up and down and fans yelling for you. Young tits and the roar of the
crowd—all your life, you might never beat that.

The fuss we make over high school sports is probably the main reason so many men in the United States are forever adolescent. High school sports have replaced The Western as the male American lyric.

Anyway, the point is that I wasn't hurt when Cappy Cappon told me I couldn't play basketball very well, because he didn't say just that; he also implied, in counterpoint, that there was something else I *could* do well: I was able to write.

4

ROAMER

But sometimes it isn't that you grow up. Sometimes I think it's just that you've already grown up, only you don't realize it till something faces you down. But, of course, I didn't look back because by then I was looking forward. That's the whole point of growing up, isn't it?

Bliss, Remembered, 2010

So now, let us heat up the cauldron by describing my first nibble at sportswriting.

For a couple of summers, when I was a teenager, I worked as copyboy at the *Baltimore Evening Sun.* It would be my journalistic destiny to serve on two professional newspapers. On one, I was a copyboy. On the other, the *National Sports Daily,* I was the editor in chief. Nothing in between. Despite the huge difference in my particular role on these two newspapers, both went out of business, for, as we know, especially nowadays in journalism, it doth raineth the same upon the high and mighty as it doth upon the low and meek.

In any event, as part of my misspent youth, during one of those summers at the *Evening Sun,* I went out and got a tattoo at an establishment known, directly enough, as Tattoo Charlie's. Understand, that day and age was not like the twenty-first century, when everybody, male and female alike, has tattoos on all and sundry body parts, and prisoners and professional athletes look as if they have turned their epidermis into rough drafts for Willem de Kooning. Back then, only degenerates and sailors got tattoos, so it was an extreme statement for me to join that company.

I'm the soul of moderation, though, even when being extreme, and so the tattoo I got was rather small and in a discreet location, on the underside of my forearm. The impressively muscled patron before me chose M*O*M on a biceps far larger than mine, but I opted for a swordfish. I do not, to this day, know why. I do not much care for swordfish as a foodstuff, and I'd certainly never entertained any thought whatsoever of going *after* swordfish on the open sea. But when Tattoo Charlie asked me what I had in mind, it just popped out that I was opting to spend the rest of my life with a swordfish.

I once did a story on an old country-boy basketball coach in Oklahoma named Abe Lemons, and harking back to his rural upbringing, I asked him if he enjoyed fishing. "No, don't like myself that much," Abe replied.

So, too, me. I'm like Abe, with respect to fishing.

But, notwithstanding, my swordfish served the purpose of giving me something of an exotic aspect—and perhaps a forbidding one, as well, at least upon first impression. In my brief time in the army, some other soldiers took a wide berth of me until they realized the tattoo suggested pretension more than menace. I never had any desire to be rough-and-tumble. I always wanted to be a writer, but the thought of being an intrepid Jack Londonish type never crossed my mind. It is people I've always wanted to write about. Them and, preferably, places fashioned more by man than God.

Now, also when I was a copyboy, a few doors down from Tattoo Charlie's establishment on the notorious Baltimore Street, I would occasionally attend burlesque shows at the Gayety Theatre. Take my word, back in the day it was an honorable profession, to be a stripper; however, if you were never lucky enough to've seen Tempest Storm or Irma the Body remove her long, lovely gloves, slowly, tantalizingly, one after another, you'd have no idea whatsoever. All you'd have as a modern point of reference would be pole dancing, which is raunchy and without any redeeming grace. I mention this because another fifty years from now when some old man says that, back when he was a boy, he'd read sportswriters in newspapers and magazines—that is: in *print*—I hope he speaks kindly of us. Otherwise, no one will appreciate what sportswriting was really like at its apogee. I fear all you'd know would be blogs and/or statistics—the pole dancing of sports journalism.

Also when I was a boy, it was yet another occasional part of my misspent youth to go bet horse races. They'd open the gates at places like Pimlico after the seventh race, and you could walk in free, and although you were supposed to be twenty-one to place a wager, you could bet as long as you could manage to reach up on your tippy-toes and shove two singles toward the man inside the $2 window. Thus, early on, as the wags used to say, I was "an improver of the breed."

So it was that when I was working those summers as a copyboy at the *Evening Sun,* where once giants like H. L. Mencken had stridden the linoleum, I occasionally filled in for Jim M., who was the regular designate in the sports section. It was not a difficult job, copyboy, consisting mostly of responding to urgent cries of "Copy down!" or "Copy over!" or getting drinks and vittles for the reporters and editors, a few of whom still wore suspenders and eyeshades and kept a pint of whiskey in a desk drawer. It was vintage, but fading.

One of the editors on the sports desk was a wavy-haired gentleman named Leonard, who always kept a pipe firmly gripped in his teeth and moved with the greatest deliberation. Besides editing something or other, Leonard had the additional responsibility of picking the local races—just the win/place/show, which would appear in a box alongside the choices of the other, more thorough handicappers. Whereas most handicappers went with the chalk, it was Leonard's job to select mostly long shots. His *nom de tout* was "Roamer."

On those days when I subbed for Jim M. in the sports section, I would occasionally shoot the breeze with Leonard, and he came to realize that, while, to the uninformed, I may have appeared to be a wet-behind-the-ears copyboy, in reality I was wise beyond my years, knowing a thing or two about horseflesh. Thus, to my delight, one day, when Leonard, ever moving slowly, was overwhelmed with deadline chores, he asked me to lighten his burden and, on the q.t., finish picking the horses for him. I became Roamer for a day. *Copy down!*

Looking at the *Evening Sun* the next day, with my selections *in print*, there for all the world to see, I could only imagine certain other improvers of the breed out at Pimlico hurrying to the windows and saying, "Look, Roamer picks so-and-so," and plunking their money down accordingly. It was a feeling of incalculable power which I had never heretofore possessed.

The euphoria of being, temporarily, Roamer, did not, however, seduce me into planning that occupation for eventual grown-up employment. Sportswriters then were not generally held in high regard, and for someone like myself, who yearned to be a "real" writer, sportswriting did not appear to light a noble career path.

That awful term "role model" had not yet come into currency, but even if it had, there certainly were none of the sportswriting ilk in the Land of Mencken. Of the three sports columnists in Baltimore, one restricted himself to clusters of short items, hackneyed vacuity rendered with the most hoary clichés; another was a passionate anti-vivisectionist, who peppered his *sports* column with heart-tugging photographs of endangered puppies and kittens; and the third, personally on view to me at the *Evening Sun,* was also in charge of officiating for the city's high school conference. He would whip off his boring column in jig time, then spend long, thoughtful hours allotting the various referees and umpires to junior varsity lacrosse and baseball games—or "tilts," as they were often referred to then in the sports pages.

5

GRANNY

At sporting events there are three kinds of ovations. The first is the most common, the spontaneous happy roar for the home team. Number two is the studied courtesy cheer reserved for beloved opponents, coaches who field grounders, uninvited dogs, and umpires who either fall down or retrieve errant paper napkins. The third is a special generous cheer, filled with rare, warm appreciation. This type can be detected by the fact that it swells with no pattern. Instead it grows in choppy bursts. Hollering is out of place and people pause from clapping to exchange happy talk with their neighbors. "Isn't that great?" or "Good for him." Stuff like that. Then they clap a little more and pause and smile. It is a tender cheer.

Everybody's All-American, 1981

Had my introduction to sportswriting been limited solely to the hack Baltimore sports editors, I might've been prepared to consider that writing about sports could be a more distinguished genre somewhere out there in the wider world. Unfortunately, however, the *Morning Sun* also carried the weekly column of Grantland Rice, who, my father advised me, was the crème de la crème of the profession—and, sadly, Mr. Rice's sappy prose was barely a step up from the offerings of the local sports scribes.*

Unfortunately, as but a wiseass child, I had no idea what a force Rice had been, how he had affected sportswriting—and, really,

---

*The only journalists ever any longer referred to as "scribes" are sportwriters, but I promise not to do it again, even facetiously.

ultimately, the way so many Americans looked at sports. But at the time I was reading him, in the early 1950s, he was an old man—or, from another awful point of view, just about my advanced age now. The poor senior citizen had been humping heavy typewriter cases up stadium stairs to press boxes for a half a century, and was thus (I like to think) more worn down in his dotage than I am in mine. Also, in those primitive times, Rice was literally mailing it in. Although he had become quite a wealthy man, he saved on postage by mailing batches of his columns out at the same time to his syndicate. As a consequence, the pieces were necessarily vague and invariably out-of-date by the time they eventually appeared in the *Sun* or the myriad other papers that still ran his stuff. Often, too, his columns were chopped up and mangled by insensitive copy editors, who jammed his work in between box scores and the race results.

So, I was certainly not seeing vintage Rice. On the other hand, even in his prime, Rice had not been a superior writer. He was good enough and facile and God knows he was never at a loss for words, but he simply wasn't in the same league as the best columnists who followed him—genuinely fine writers like Red Smith, Jimmy Cannon, Jim Murray, Dave Kindred, or Mitch Albom. In fact, Rice's poetry was much better than his prose, for as had been the custom when he started out, around the turn of the century, he peppered almost every column with homespun verse. He was, in fact, an accomplished acolyte of James Whitcomb Riley, of "The Old Swimmin'-Hole" fame, and if Rice had written nothing else, he would always be remembered for his inspirational athletic couplet:

> *For when the One Great Scorer comes to mark against your name—*
> *He writes—not that you won or lost—but how you played the Game.*

In my attic a while ago, I came across a photograph of me, in tank top, shorts, and sneakers, at summer camp, when I was about twelve, grouped with a bunch of other boys around a large billboard bearing nothing but that quotation, that moral battle cry of Uncle Sam's playing field. Imagine how long ago that was! Vince Lombardi's "Winning isn't the most important thing. It's the only thing" was still out there beyond the crass horizon. And trash-talking—my gracious, not even the One Great Scorer had heard of that yet. Grantland Rice's axiom was then the star we athletes of America were to try and steer by.

But Rice wrote everything about sports—an estimated 67 million words—or 3,500 words for every day of his fifty-three years as a sportswriter. One of his biographers, Charles Fountain, described Rice as "the Matthew, Mark, Luke, and John of American sport." That is certainly fair enough—but only so far as it goes. Rice was not only the one-man gospel of sport for the first half of the twentieth century, but sort of the benevolent godfather of athletics—the beloved, lionized (and so aptly named) Granny.

It is impossible now to understand how this colossus bestrode our games. Certainly, there has never been any one person who occupied such an eminent position in his sector of journalism as did Rice in sports—and for decades. Rush Limbaugh now in politics, Walter Winchell when he was dot-and-dashing gossip for Mr. and Mrs. America and all the ships at sea, Walter Lippmann upon Olympus, Louella Parsons in Hollywood, Walter Cronkite at the end of the workday—whoever in whatever phase of journalism: none approached what Grantland Rice was in sports.

It wasn't just that he was so prodigious at his newspaper day job.* He also was the author of something like a thousand magazine articles, edited a magazine (*American Golfer*), put together book collections of his works, had his own radio show, narrated movie shorts, provided endorsements, and picked the only certified official annual all-American college football team. You simply can't compare any

---

*His personal best—PB, as they say in track and field—fifty thousand words for the *New York Evening Mail* in the nine days of the 1912 World Series.

individual, ever, in American journalism to what Grantland Rice was. The closest analogy in our journalistic history would be to say that ESPN today most approximates him. But ESPN is a whole conglomeration of networks. And there is no poetry in its soul.

As an "evangelist of fun," as he would be eulogized at his funeral, Rice was a whirling dervish. Remember, in those days, to be a sports "expert," a writer had to physically go to the games. Now, you (i.e., me) can watch almost everything on television, alight at only a few preferred events, and still voice opinions with authority. But Rice beamed himself up everywhere —accumulating as many as sixteen thousand miles a year by train alone. It's amazing all the games he saw, never mind that he managed to actually have the time to write about them, as well—and never, it seems, never, without taking off his gray fedora. If he hadn't been so damn well adjusted, you'd say he must have been obsessive.

Rice was, however, well compensated for his extraordinary labors. At the height of his powers, he was making something like $100,000 a year—at a time when a top all-star baseball player might be pulling down $20,000—but on a slow day Rice would slap that fedora on his balding noggin and have his chauffeur drive him out so he might cover some metropolitan women's golf tournament, shoot the breeze with the other reporters, take the air, then bang out some of that 3,500-word daily quota.

He was quite a good athlete himself. This, of course, is unusual among sportswriters. The image (perhaps especially among the athletes we cover) is that we are all uncoordinated wimps who developed a passionate love for all sports as wee tykes, but we all got put out in right field in Little League and certainly couldn't make a varsity team, so we started writing about sports just to get into the locker room. OK, there's probably some truth there. (I also have formed the impression, completely unscientifically, that sportswriters as a group had happier childhoods than other journalists and many athletes. So there.) Whatever, athletes certainly want to think about us as physical flotsam, and they forever love to profess that *if you haven't played the game* you couldn't possibly be wise enough to write about it.

"If that were true," Red Smith opined, "then only dead men could write obituaries."

But Grantland Rice was the real deal afield. He was pigeon-toed, like a lot of great athletes, and in college, he was a good-hitting short-stop, captain of his baseball team at Vanderbilt—promising enough to ponder playing minor-league baseball until his parents told him to get serious and find a real job. He had also played end on the football varsity, even though at that time he carried only 130 pounds on his 6-foot frame. In fact, he only *played* games in college. There is no evidence that he wrote a single word, outside his assigned schoolwork, until, after graduation, when he found work as a sportswriter on a fledgling Nashville newspaper. Even then, he coached college baseball and refereed football games on the side, while developing into a scratch golfer. Granny simply couldn't get enough of sports. All his life, he and his best chums—invariably other sportswriters—would take a break after being stuck together at another Kentucky Derby or another U.S. Open or another all-star game and go off for more bonding on hunting and fishing trips. He played cards at night, bet the ponies by day, and drank lots of whiskey.

And this above all: everybody loved Granny.

I mean: everybody.

I mean: loved him.

It's downright amazing to read the personal testaments to his goodness, goodwill, good fellowship, and good spirits. Guaranteed: the One Great Scorer gave Granny an A+. Although he lived most of his life, happily married, in a Fifth Avenue apartment overlooking Central Park, he was the epitome of the Dixie squire. Grantland Rice, as much as any other southerner, became sort of the twentieth-century extension of the luminous Robert E. Lee. "A virile saint," his buddy

George M. Cohan called Granny. Despite his wealth and fame, he remained unassuming and modest. He would never even so much as call his rhyming "poetry"; instead, he passed it off merely as "verse." Everybody wanted to be his friend, and the wish was easily enough consummated because Granny was ever friendly to everybody who crossed his peripatetic shadow.

And, most significant from a vocational point of view, the gracious gentleman wrote as he lived, always looking to find not just the bright side, but the heroic, the noble. Remember, he was born in Tennessee only fifteen years after Appomattox, and one has to wonder how much he, as a boy, heard tales of his gallant forebears, sallying forth in their butternut uniforms, battling against the odds to fight on for a cause. Hell, I was born seventy-three years after Appomattox, and that's what I still heard from my southern kin.

When President Wilson finally decided that we had to take care of business and show the Hun who was boss, Rice immediately volunteered for the Great War, even though he was thirty-seven and didn't have to serve. When he was commissioned, the army tried to keep him safe behind the lines in France, editing an army newspaper, but First Lieutenant Rice demanded to see action and hiked alone for three days to get to the front, there to join his 115th Field Artillery unit in the Argonne. He would probably have been killed but for the fact that the earth was so soft that German shells that landed near him merely buried themselves in the mushy turf, instead of exploding on impact with the ground. Winter rules.

Sport for Rice was a better war, because it was a safe and fun version of the real thing. Yes, he chose the rose-colored glasses for the arena, but quite purposefully. Another of his biographers, William A. Harper, wrote: "When sport is taken less seriously, more playfully, and, at the same time infused with the standards and duties of chivalrous conduct, it escapes triviality and becomes a significant and dignified culture-bearer."

That counterintuitive attitude was already fading fast in 1954 when Rice collapsed (at his typewriter, of course, batting out the last of his seventeen thousand columns). Thereafter, more sportswriters came to think precisely the opposite, that you must take sport more seriously, less playfully, to make it significant—so that, in tandem, your own work appears more significant, as well. Certainly, once Granny was gone, there were no more poems issued from the press box.

6

WALKING IN PLACE

Those of us in the grandstand seats always want our athletes—the ones who are our age—to quit while they're still on top. That way they won't embarrass us. We then want our heroes to instantly disappear so that we can always remember them (and ourselves) as magnificent and forever green. For it is when our athletes start to go downhill that we are first forced to come to grips with the possibility of our own mortality.

"A Lesson in Mortality," *Sports Illustrated*, 1987

Grantland Rice's autobiography, published posthumously, wonderfully entitled *The Tumult and The Shouting,* pretty much stuck to the shouting; he told fond, hagiographic tales of athletes he knew, rather than saying much about himself. Most of his favorite players were from his salad days, which is not surprising—even for the elderly Rice, who forever received grateful audiences from all living stars (and at a time when none of these heroes had managers or agents or entourages to serve as dry moats for them).

Unfortunately, you see, being a sportswriter is the exact opposite of being Dorian in Oscar Wilde's *The Picture of Dorian Gray.* You age, as all about you the players stay forever young. You stick around the arena while your contemporaries on the field of play grow old in sports years and fade away. "I'm sorry. I'd like to still be your friend," Bill Russell told me when he retired, "but friendship takes a lot of effort if it's going to work. We can still be friendly, but now we're going off in different directions in our lives." Well, he was going off in a different direction; I was pretty much just going to keep walking in place.

So here comes the next cohort of guys in satin shorts, only now they're not your peers and there's less personal connection. Soon, you're a whole generation older than the heroes you're covering. You absolutely know you've arrived in a different cultural universe when you can't stand any of the goddamn music playing in the locker room. About all you share anymore with most of the players is their sport itself—or listening to them talk about themselves. Soon, the coaches and managers are the ones of your vintage. As you grow older, in fact, you gravitate more toward doing stories about coaches—not just because now they're your new contemporaries, but because they've lived longer, more complicated lives. They're simply better stories. After all, most of them failed, in that they couldn't cut it as players. That's why they become coaches.

Coaches are movies. Players are snapshots.

So, the one great irony of writing about sports is that the most important people *in* sports are young and unformed, and, consequently, if through no fault of their own, less interesting. At least back when Granny Rice was cataloging the triumphs of the young Lochinvars, he—like his colleagues—could rave on in his dispatches about their heroics on the field. The Babe wallops another four-master! The Manassa Mauler pummels another challenger! The Four Horsemen are outlined against the sky (even though I'm looking *down* at them from the press box)! But now, with television, everybody with a clicker is privy to seeing the same thing clear as day on HD as are the pros on the scene with media passes, so you have to eschew the games and write about the athletes *as people.*

And that can be a trial. Too often, it's reminiscent of when someone asked Fred Zinnemann, the movie director, what a certain young actress was like, and he replied: "What makes you think she's like *any*thing?"

Therefore, more and more we tend to celebrate the loud-mouths—the highest percentage, it seems, being wide receivers in football—who first make themselves accessible, then voluble, and thereupon qualify as "characters," but who are, really, just so many obnoxious jerks.

Of course, I'm old and cranky, so pay me no mind.

I'm even finally getting tired of Charles Barkley.

7

OLD-TIMERS

There is a moment, somewhere, when the most beautiful and accomplished part of sport turns to art. But athletes are probably wrongly identified as artists. Rather, they are the art, not the author of it.

"When All the World Is Young, Lad,"
Sports Illustrated, 1977

Because athletes are often so young when they are introduced to fans by us in the media, that first image usually captures them for a lifetime. Now, often we observers do indeed get it right and the initial impression is the correct one. There was an old Yankee outfielder, long before my time, named Bob Meusel, who, it seemed, was generally unpleasant. Apparently, when Meusel realized that his days in the spotlight were numbered and he might need a bit more goodwill in his less glamorous upcoming civilian life, he took on a more studied friendly aspect around the press.

Frank Graham, one of the better writers of that era, was not taken in. "Bob only learned to say 'hello,'" he said, "when it was time to say 'good-bye.'"

In any event, fair or not, seldom do we change our opinions about sports stars. They are categorized throughout their lives as lovable or dopey or disagreeable or "controversial," which is the worst tag to be stuck with, even though I've never been quite sure what exactly it means. All I do know is that "controversial" is the cheapest catchall negative in celebritydom, and God help you if you are ever pinned with it, for it will be lint on your jacket forever.

There are a few stars who come on the scene young, who amaze us with their precociousness and thus gain our esteem, and then manage to screw up when they gain their maturity and reveal a more gross adulthood. O. J. Simpson, of course, immediately comes to mind. Tiger Woods and Lance Armstrong are more recent egregious examples. But the other way round is at least as rare: an athlete who is initially portrayed negatively—and certainly as controversial—but then manages to gild his reputation. Usually, in fact, you have to be a Grand Old Man before you can be lucky enough to get a second look. Ted Williams was the best example: the odd one who not only pulled it off but, to some extent, switched images with his presumably dearer alter ego, Joe DiMaggio. But it took some doing, because the Boston reporters—whom Williams cleverly immortalized as the "Knights of the Keyboard"—were initially brutal to him, characterizing him as selfish and uncaring. How dare the sonuvabitch not wear a tie like everybody else?

The first time I, as a kid reporter, had to interview Williams, he was managing the Washington Senators, and I was quaking in my boots as I waited to waylay him in the lobby of his hotel. He was annoyed at the intrusion, but he was obviously cognizant of my nervousness and perhaps sensitive to a callow innocent's jitters. "You're tall for a writer," he assayed. I agreed that that was so. It bemused him. I had known some of the Knights of the Keyboard in their declining years, and they were not men of superior height. "Well, all right," he said, and thereupon answered my questions (whatever they were) directly, with dispatch, if without enthusiasm. Good enough. Thank you, Mr. Williams, and now lemme scram outta your way.

In New York, meanwhile, Joe D, DiMag, the Yankee Clipper, was universally canonized as elegant and polite. Whatever, he certainly was not controversial. Somehow, however, the press missed the rather salient truth that Williams was ebullient, beloved by his teammates, while DiMaggio was, in fact, mostly just a cold fish. Not even his brother Dom, who played outfield for the Red Sox alongside Williams, seemed to care much for the Yankee Clipper. As someone best summed up DiMaggio: "What kind of guy learns to love the most beautiful woman in the world only after she dies?"

Nevertheless, when it comes to Joe and Marilyn, I've always most appreciated the story about how, when he was playing exhibitions in Japan with the Yankees just before he retired, she left him in Tokyo to fly over to Korea to entertain the troops. When Marilyn came back she cooed, "Oh Joe, you just can't imagine what it's like, playing before forty thousand men and all of them cheering for you."

And, apparently expressionless, Joe D just said, "Yes, I can."

But give the devil his due. Maybe that's the best testament ever to what it's like being the athlete as hero.

Mostly, however, it seems that—as Richard Ben Cramer's marvelous biography would eventually show—DiMaggio was simply uncomfortable around people. You never hear any endearing anecdotes about him. You always hear he was at Toots Shor's, which was *the* place to be then if you were in sports, but nobody ever says, "Then there was this one evening at Toots, and good old Joe . . ." He was just *at* places, being himself (or later, as he demanded to be introduced, being "the world's greatest living ballplayer"; just so).

One little revealing anecdote I did hear was told to me by the fabulous sports photographer Neil Leifer. When Neil was young and red-haired, he was hired to shoot the Yankees' team photograph, so, during a game, he was allowed to sit in a special Yankee team box. He was there, by himself, when suddenly DiMaggio, with his usual aplomb and sharkskin gray suit, materialized, coming majestically down the steps, to take another seat in the box. Neil could not believe it. The great Joe D. Himself. The two of them, alone in a crowd.

Then, to Neil's amazement, Joe D actually spoke to him. He asked to look through Neil's telescopic viewfinder in order to check out the stands for good-looking broads. After he found one, his appetite for pulchritude sated, he handed the camera back to Leifer, and this, in his entirety, is what he said: "Getting any puss lately, Reds?"

Leifer was struck dumb. No more conversation ensued. However, DiMaggio remained elegant.

Over the years, however, Williams was that one athlete who was able to see his original public personna in the press turned around, as he became accepted for what he really was, an idiosyncratic, unpredictable enthusiast—Teddy Ballgame. To be sure, he was chronically profane and hopelessly opinionated and could be terribly difficult if you happened to be married to him, but otherwise he was loyal, charming, and wonderful company.

I accepted an invitation to speak on behalf of the sporting press extant when he was honored in Boston on the occasion when the city decided to name a tunnel after him.* By then, the Knights of the Keyboard of his controversial youth had all gone to that great pressbox in the sky, so I was the designated speaker on behalf of sportswriters everywhere, all time, and afterward Williams thanked me for my encomium, being so kind as not to heap the sins of my vocational fathers upon me.

Ted was already failing then, and the last time I saw him, a couple of years later, he was down to maneuvering with a walker. The only thing left of him whole was his great booming voice. Nothing, apparently, could still that. This was at his house on the west coast of Florida, when he was with Bob Feller—Rapid Robert, the greatest baseball phenom of them all. It was a little bit like seeing

---

*Boy, did that piss off Tommy Heinsohn, Bill Russell's former teammate on the Celtics. "So Williams gets a tunnel named after him, and he never even won a championship," he said to me. "Russ won eleven. So what they gonna name after *him*? The whole Mass Pike?"

Achilles and Hector together, had they managed to become senior citizens, for in their prime, Feller and Williams had been the grandest of rivals. Feller told me how they would both just sit alone and contemplate, with utter delight, the joy of facing each other two or three days hence—the greatest hitter versus the greatest pitcher of their time.

Now they were together again, savoring each other's company, going on about the good old days and how in God's name so much had gone to hell in the meantime. Although Williams and Feller were born within weeks of each other in the waning days of World War I, only Feller had remained in superb health—at that time, nearing eighty. But then, he would thrive for another decade, the last surviving great athlete who was already a star previous to World War II. A few years later I'd spend several days at the Indians' spring training base doing a story on Bob. We'd make sure to get to the early-bird dinner seating, and then, after perusing the menu, Bob would, nevertheless, invariably order the liver. "Iron—good for you." Every time.

His wife, Anne, told me food had never been anything but fuel to Bob, and here he was, staring down ninety, still pitching in old-timers' games, signing hours worth of autographs at five bucks a copy, and remaining just as cocksure and ornery as Ted Williams ever was. No wonder they so loved to face each other, horsehide versus ash. "I'm not PC," Bob explains to me, unnecessarily, digging into the liver.

Anne told me that once, after being with him during yet one more public Fellerian outburst, she actually asked her doctor: "Really, is it medically possible to die of embarrassment?"

On another, more recent occasion, in 2008, I sat next to Feller and Monte Irvin at a dinner in Atlantic City. Feller had just turned ninety and Irvin would reach that milestone in three months. You had to understand what history it was having dinner next to me. The two men had played against each other, barnstorming, *before*

Jackie Robinson broke the major-league color line in 1947. Imagine.
It was dear.

As a sportswriter, you get to like the old-timers even better than
you like the coaches.* Whatever else they've forgotten, they remember so much about their games of long ago, and they're grateful for
anybody younger who cares to ask about what it was like when the
One Great Scorer was still paying attention to them, back when they
were in their prime.

But now, back in 1998, when Feller was still a whippersnapper
of seventy-nine, he and Williams were together, bound by an effort
to get Shoeless Joe Jackson eligible for the Hall of Fame. Poor illiterate Shoeless Joe had been the best of the Chicago "Black Sox"
who had taken money to throw the 1919 World Series—although
it's always been dubious quite how much he took or what that he
took he might have kept, or even whether he really tried to lose
(or maybe even understood that that was the idea). After all, he hit
.375 in the series.

In the event, Jackson—"Say it ain't so, Joe"—received a lifetime
ban, and although you could hardly say that either Williams or Feller
was a bleeding-heart softy, both had taken up Shoeless Joe's cause. If
nothing else, as Williams pointed out to me in his most exasperated
fashion, "Only fucking baseball could give someone a lifetime ban
and then keep it going after his fucking lifetime was over." Shoeless
Joe had been dead half a century or so, but baseball was unrelenting
in retaining his exile from what is always called "the shrine."

It's another version of the same distorted logic applied in the
case of Pete Rose, who is denied entrance to the Hall of Fame as a
player for sins he committed *after* he was through playing. Shoeless
Joe got a lifetime ban that has become an eternal ban. Charley Hustle

---

*I don't believe that any people except elderly athletes are any longer referred to as
"old-timers." Everybody else is a senior citizen. Personally, I would prefer to be called
an "old-timer" any day of the week.

got an ex post facto ban that likewise appears to offer no parole, in perpetuity. Let me tell you, when it comes to the Hall of Fame, there are some hard hearts at that ballot box. Come on, the membership is approaching three hundred *immortals* now. Some zip codes are more exclusive. But Shoeless Joe and Charley Hustle must never darken our doors!

Well, say the protectors of shrine purity, Pete lied. And God knows he did, for years. He lied to me, for example, relentlessly, effortlessly, for about an hour when I was interviewing him one fine morning in a hotel room in Kentucky, across the river from Cincinnati. I didn't, however, take it personally, and don't consider his middle-aged prevarication as disqualifying the majestic feats he accomplished in his younger days—especially since it was altogether apparent to me at the time that he was lying to me (and he knew that I knew he was lying to me). Pete wasn't, you see, even a particularly persuasive liar. Sorry, I just tend to believe that, like Shoeless Joe, Rose was more dumb than venal.

In fact, the best assessment of Rose was one given to me by Richie Ashburn, who, by the by, was never controversial and is safely in the Hall of Fame himself. I had first interviewed Whitey, as he was called, when he was finishing out his career with the woebegone new Mets in 1962, and I had just started mine a few weeks before. Ships in the night, passing at the Polo Grounds.

Ashburn retired then, and returned to Philadelphia to be the color announcer for the Phillies, the team he had starred for. One winter's day, about fifteen years later, out of the blue, I got a call from Ashburn. He had heard I was doing research on a story about the late, disgraced Big Bill Tilden, the pedophile tennis champion who was from Philadelphia, and because Ashburn had become a good club tennis player and happened to have come from the town of Tilden, Nebraska, he had always been curious about Bill Tilden.

So—get this—Whitey was calling me to volunteer his services to drive me around the next time I came to town. Naturally, I took him up on the offer, so I had a Hall of Fame driver. Ashburn even looked the part of a genuine chauffeur. He wore a little soft cap and smoked a pipe. He drove me, with consummate care, all over greater Philadelphia, to interviews and points of interest and to Big Bill's grave site. Rich was, however, disturbed when I casually mentioned to him that on my last visit to town, I had been turned away from the Union League, a very fancy Republican redoubt that Tilden's father, a distinguished citizen, had once been president of.

I had learned that there was a portrait of Tilden Senior prominently displayed in the Union League, and I wanted to see it, but when I'd presented myself at the front door and explained my purpose, I was held there in the cold until the manager was fetched. He informed me that certainly I could understand that the press could not just show up and be allowed, indiscriminately, into the hallowed Union League. I promised him that I would not pinch any of the silverware, and would be soiling the premises for only a minute or two, looking respectfully up at Mr. Tilden's portrait. The manager was unmoved; the Union League was as unyielding as the Hall of Fame. I was turned out.

Ashburn was appalled that I had been treated so shabbily in his adopted fair city and wanted to drive me right back downtown to the Union League and, as my advocate, gain me admittance—which I knew he, Whitey, beloved Philly Hall of Famer, certainly could manage. But I had my back up by now, and, honestly, seeing the goddamn portrait of Big Bill's father really wasn't that high up on my wish list. "Rich," I said, "I appreciate the offer, but they made it plain they don't want the press in there—and think about it, you're a member of the press yourself now. To hell with the Union League."

Reluctantly, he bit on his pipe and agreed, steering me safely onto our next rendezvous.

So I wrote about Big Bill, several more years passed, and the next time I saw Ashburn was during spring training of 1979. Rose had come over to the Phillies the season before. He was in the batting cage now, lacing* line drives. I gestured to him. "What's he like, Rich?"

"I'll tell you," Ashburn said. "Pete Rose is the most obsessive person I've ever met in my life. It doesn't matter—baseball, women, gambling—he's obsessed with whatever he's involved with. He doesn't drink, you know." I nodded. "Let me tell you, Frank. If Pete had a drink at lunch, he'd be an alcoholic by the time he went to bed."

It's the best definition I ever heard of Rose, especially since, also, we would discover he could be just as obsessive about lying.** But if Williams and Feller were unforgiving about Rose, they both felt old Shoeless Joe deserved at least the consideration of a review. Good Lord, even living serial murderers get that. The two old heroes were going to plead his case before a crowd of those Sabre people—the statistics nuts. They were all assembled in a hotel conference room near Williams's house, waiting anxiously for Rapid Robert and the Splendid Splinter to appear. Sabreites may be in love with numbers, but they are, foremost, unabashed devotees of the game that, after all, provides them with their inert numbers. So, to actually see two of the grandest flesh-and-blood idols from some Golden Age was more thrilling even than calculating something like road-game on-base percentage with two outs against southpaws in the 1920s. Goose pimples pimpled the room.

And here came Feller through the door, first, erect, striding, surveying the gathering with his usual jaundiced eye. Williams followed with his walker. As he neared the microphone, though, he pushed his assistance device aside and took the last couple of steps by himself. The Sabre people, clutching the statistics of Shoeless Joe to their

---

*God, but that's a great verb for line drives: "lacing."
**He could be straightforward about me, though. When Pete was about to break Ty Cobb's sainted record for most hits, I wrote a column whimsically suggesting that what Rose should do, when he made the hit that tied Cobb, was depart the field, retire, leaving the two men deadlocked through all eternity. When someone asked Pete for his response to my suggestion, this is what he said, in its entirety: "Is DeFord out of his fucking mind?"

bosoms, waited to hear him address them. Williams raised himself up as tall as he could, thrust out his chest, and in that great bombastic voice, this is what he hollered as an introduction: "Are there any fucking Marines in here?"

So, you can well understand how Teddy Ballgame went from youthful ignominy to become beloved. The Knights of the Keyboard blew that one.

8

THE VIETNAM WAR
IS FINALLY OVER

Poor Joe Louis was called America's Guest. Muhammad Ali is America's Honored Guest.

"Who's That with Muhammad Ali?"
Sports Illustrated, 1998

However much the public may have changed its mind about Ted Williams, there was certainly no athlete in my lifetime who provoked so many conflicting attitudes, only, ultimately, to be almost universally accepted (even loved), as Muhammad Ali. He was always either criticized excessively by those who did not like him for being so boastful and/or so ex-Christian and/or simply so different from anyone who had come before; on the other hand, by those who did like him, he was always either forgiven much too easily for his faults or accorded far too much credit for his wit, intelligence, and character. To read some writers, you would've thought Ali's doggerel made him a sort of homespun poet laureate. Even leaving aside the business about Vietnam, which was altogether political, Ali was viewed more like a politician than an athlete. He often seemed to be more a candidate than a boxer.

I never covered any of his fights, because we had boxing specialists to handle that at *Sports Illustrated*—although I did see him win the title from Sonny Liston in Miami when I was down there for spring training. But then, I don't care much for boxing. It's the only traditional sport where the object is to hurt your opponent; boxing really goes against our very Christian-Judaic ethic.

Everybody has always chuckled about how boxers end up on Queer Street; boxing is a really mean exercise, and that, of course, is why mostly only desperately poor people get into the ring. Whereas the children of athletes usually gravitate to their father's (or mother's) sport, rarely will you see a boxer's son take up boxing. Billy Conn, the old light-heavyweight champion, first pointed that out to me. If the father has had any success in the ring, and has somehow kept his wits, then he will not allow his son to follow him.

Now, in the United States, boxing struggles to get good athletes because the big desperately poor people are recruited for football, so they can get their concussions that way.* But I'll say this for the so-called sweet science: boxers tend to be really quite nice people. It's the classic case of hate the sin and love the sinner. And, of course, boxing is a neat, gritty scene, full of earthy "characters," who are either perfect scoundrels or crusty factotums who wrap the boxers' hands and utter the sort of wry, humorous truths that kept columnists in business for decades.

Nevertheless, I spent a rather remarkable train trip with the young Cassius Clay in 1962, when he returned from Albany to New York. He had been dispatched to the Empire State capital, where the honorable legislators were considering the possibility of banning boxing. Clay had become a popular figure at the 1960 Rome Olympics, where he had won a gold medal. For sportswriters, he was then sort of a slightly grown-up version of the cute li'l tykes on the show Art Linkletter emceed called *Kids Say the Darndest Things.* So, in Albany, Clay testified on behalf of boxing, making no real sense, but charming the pols, who, so far as I can recall, soon lost whatever interest they had had in banning boxing, at least until the next fighter was pummeled to death in the ring.

---

*In fact, now I'm starting to hear the same thing from old football players about their sons—that they don't want them to play such a brutal sport.

Being lowest man on the totem pole at the magazine, I had been dispatched to Albany just in case anything of consequence happened, and I rode back with Cassius. Incredibly, he was alone, a fate he despised, and so he settled into the seat next to me, the better to allow me to hear him bloviate. Any port in a storm. Soon, he borrowed my pad and pen and began to draw some sort of solar system (I think that's what it was) with lines and circles indicating descending aliens and something or other about God. But although at first I almost laughed, I then realized that he was obviously deadly serious, so I suppressed all smiles as he went on, the whole way to Grand Central, with this dissertation that was perfectly incomprehensible to me.

I told no one about the episode, because I didn't know what to make of it, and, to my eternal regret, I tossed out the pages of drawings he had made. Later, though, when Cassius became a Muslim, I assumed that, somehow, what he was trying to outline for me back then had something to do with the spiritual exploration that he must have already been in the process of making, hesitantly.

Opinions about Ali (well, at least among white folks) began to diverge even before he became champion. His braggadocio went against everything Grantland Rice had instructed us in. Sportswriters were split regarding him no less than was the general population. There was some resistance even to calling him, in print, by his chosen new name. Dick Young, the prickly and influential columnist for the *New York Daily News,* refused for years to refer to him as anything but "Ali Baby." *Sports Illustrated* was generally supportive, but certainly did not crusade for him, in the sense, say, that Howard Cosell did on ABC—especially after Muhammad was stripped of his title for refusing to be drafted because, as he explained, "I ain't got no quarrel against them Vietcong."

Of course, having Howard as a defender may very well have served to turn even more fans against Ali, because Cosell was most unpopular in precisely those quarters likewise least inclined to cotton to Ali. The two certainly made for an intriguing odd couple, though, and there have been, through the years, all sorts of speculation about the value of the symbiotic relationship that Howard and Muhammad shared. Yes, each man used the other, but benignly, and I always believed there was genuine mutual affection between them.

I was given the greatest assurance of this conclusion the last time I visited Howard in 1994. He was terribly diminished by then, with only a few months left to live. But then, after his wife had died in 1990, he had never really been himself again. Emmy had been Howard's Abie's Irish rose: a Presbyterian from Philadelphia to his Jew from Brooklyn. They absolutely adored each other, and when Emmy left him, you might as well have put Howard in the casket beside her.

Even when he had been at the height of his fame, even when he was Howard Cosell in a crowd, smugly playing a character named Howard Cosell to the assembled, Emmy had been the one person who could put him in his place.

Rolling her eyes: "Oh, Howard, for God's sake, how many times do I have to hear that?"

Meekly: "All right, Emmy." A ducked head, chastised.

But by now, Emmy had taken his spirit with her, and as I tried to make conversation with Howard, he began wandering listlessly around his apartment, picking up objects to show me. It was almost at random—pick this one up, try to think about it, maybe utter a few meaningless words, then lay it back down and cast about for another. Suddenly, though, Howard spied a little statue and moved toward it with what energy was left in him. He picked it up and, tenderly, clasped it to his breast. I hadn't even been sure that he remembered anymore who I was, but now some life came to his eyes, and he even spoke my name. "Frank," he whispered.

"Yes, Howard."

"Frank, Muhammad gave me this," he said, poignantly, gently fondling the statue. "Muhammad Ali. He did. Himself."

Howard almost began to cry, but then he put Muhammad's present back down, and the moment was gone. He tried to remember about other things in the apartment, but he would forget and stumble, and finally he just gave up on me because I became as vague to him as the memorabilia. He went over to a television set, sat down, and watched a game show, vacantly. And I left him that way.

I saw Ali after I spoke at Howard's memorial service. He was already starting to go himself, already getting unsteady.

A quarter century before, back when Ali's exile ended after the Supreme Court ruled he could not be kept out of the ring, he had finally begun to win some true-blue American hearts back simply with his gallant victories. But then, it's also true that so many other black athletes (and some whites, as well) started acting out their anger as the 1960s wore on that it became rather difficult for people to single out Ali to hate. By 1974 he was rehabilitated enough for *Sports Illustrated* to name him Sportsman of the Year,* and the cancel-my-subscription reaction was sufficient to prove that there remained a large segment of the citizenry who would surely never forgive Ali his apostasy.

Then he fought too long and took too many blows, leaning back, doing that insane rope-a-dope, and almost overnight, it seemed, he was, well, used up. All his Muslim pals and the other leeches who had dined out on him had fled. The gorgeous women, assorted wives and mistresses, were no longer, breathless, at his side. He began to shake. Maybe saddest of all, he who had been, after all, the Mouth, began to have trouble speaking. I remember one night, at Gabriel's restaurant in New York, when a bunch of us had dinner with him, and when he could not get into the table chatter, he simply nodded off, almost plopping his head onto the shoulder of my embarrassed wife.

What touched me, in his decline, was that only one of the old entourage did stay loyal to him. He was Howard Bingham, a photographer, a lovely guy who stuttered. All the others had abandoned the old champ when he was no longer a meal ticket. Not Howard. I was so moved by this

---

*And who do you think won it in 1975? Charley Hustle, aka Pete Rose.

enduring affection between two men that I did a story on their friendship. I found that Bingham and Ali called each other Bill. It was a sort of code, their way of saying that, whatever one of them had been to the world, to each other neither was more special than the other. They were just a couple of guys named Bill. "I'm lucky," Muhammad told me. "Did *you* ever have a good friend?" This from the man who was supposed to be the most famous person in the world.

He had a good wife now, too—Lonnie, a plain, sweet woman, who had known him, adoringly, when she was a child down the street in Louisville, and he was already the idol. To Muhammad and Howard, I wrote, Lonnie was like Wendy to the lost boys. But, still, Ali's disease was irreversible, and every time I'd see him again he'd declined some more. Oh, there were moments. Sometimes, although it seemed that he could barely walk, he would, incredibly, out of the blue, launch into the Ali shuffle for a few seconds, his feet going lickety-split in place. Once, when I was with him in his hotel suite, he walked over to a piano that was there and began to pick out the "Tennessee Waltz." Where in the world did that come from? *The "Tennessee Waltz"?*

Yes, there was still some vanity. He'd literally stand on a street corner just to attract a crowd, doing a couple of magic tricks. He performed a sort of personal theater. Along with the sleight of hand, he'd tell the same couple of strained jokes.

"What's the difference between a Jew and a canoe?"

I don't know, Muhammad.

"A canoe tips."

And: "What did Abraham Lincoln say when he woke up after getting drunk?"

I don't know, Muhammad. What did he say?

"I freed the *whaaaat*?"

It was a humorous coincidence, I thought, how he and his old straight man Cosell both regularly employed variations on the same tired routine.

Ali, taking my wife's arm in a crowd, pointing to me, stage-whispering to her: "You could do a lot better than that!"

Howard, taking my wife's arm in a crowd, pointing to me, loudly declaiming: "Oh, I'm so sorry, Mrs. DeFord, that you married beneath yourself."

The one vision I will always retain of Ali, however, came when I was doing that piece about Howard Bingham's great friendship. Neil Leifer, Ali's buddy, was assigned to shoot the story, and for some reason we were in Washington. Nothing to do with the story, but Neil got the idea to shoot Ali at the Vietnam Veterans Memorial. He'd taken pictures of the champ all over the world, so why not at one more signal spot?

I thought the idea was insane. Who, after all, apart, perhaps, from Jane Fonda, was most identified with opposition to Vietnam? But Neil believed it would make a great picture, Howard, as ever, was agreeable, and Muhammad never had, so far as I knew, turned down any opportunity to stand before a camera, anywhere. Off the four of us trooped.

It was a dull, gray morning when we arrived at that long, graceful swoop of a monument, but already there were a lot of people by the wall—women mostly—their hands tracing the names inscribed there, searching for a father, a brother, a son, a husband, maybe just a lover who never got the chance to be a husband.

Neil posed Muhammad and began to click away. I watched warily, as, sure enough, from down the wall, the women and the few men there began to notice us and draw closer. I grew more uneasy as they obviously recognized the man who had refused, so vehemently, to serve in the war that had taken the lives of the men they loved. And then some of the women picked up their pace and began to rush toward Ali. Neil stopped shooting.

I couldn't believe it. They took to Ali. The women gushed. They cooed. They came to Muhammad's side and reached for his hand, or grasped his arm. Some of them handed me their little cameras and asked me to snap pictures of them with the champ. His body shook a little and he smiled, shyly at first, perhaps, then broadly. It was quite a scene. Only then, at last, I knew that, yes, the Vietnam War was truly over. Also, I could see that, if only occasionally, an athlete can grow out of the image of his neon youth and be accepted as the old gray human being he has become.

9

PUSH ON

It is a hoary journalistic custom to certify American antiquity by citing the president in office at the subject's moment of birth. This tradition is exceeded in uselessness only by the one wherein the size of a distant patch of earth is identified as being equivalent to the size of a couple of disparate states. Thus, for example, Yemen is equal to Nebraska and Virginia put together, which they are not.

"I Don't Date Any Woman Under Forty-Eight,"
Sports Illustrated, 1977

Unfortunately, I had a wonderfully happy childhood of little note. If you are to become a writer it helps immensely to have suffered a miserable upbringing, rife with trauma—ideally with a drunken father who beat you and a mother who was a prostitute, albeit a saint when not turning tricks. But, just my luck: nothing of the sort.

Nor, for that matter, have I ever been placed in any real jeopardy, found myself in a perfect storm, or even been afforded the opportunity to display heroics—all the personal experiences writers thrive on. The one and only time I was actually in anything approximating proximity to anything remotely dangerous was at the 1996 Olympics, in Atlanta, when some nut blew up a bomb in Centennial Park, which was right outside my hotel room. As it happened, though, loud bands had been playing nightly in the park; I had complained about this at the bar one evening; and Edwin Pope of the *Miami Herald**

---

*Eddie is distinguished by the fact that he is one of three surviving sportswriters who have attended all forty-five Super Bowls, in person. There but for the grace of God . . .

had given me an extra set of spectacular earplugs that molded to the ear. So I inserted them, and that very night the bomb exploded and sirens wailed and entire battalions of law enforcement troops marched about right outside my window, but I heard not a peep. We often speak of people who are larger than the sum of their parts; I imagine I'm the other way round, that the sum of my parts is larger than me.

Nevertheless, despite an adult journey free of thrills and chills, and despite my own hopelessly happy upbringing, I was raised by parents who had been forced to confront the unexpected. Both of them had enjoyed childhoods of great privilege, even luxury; both of them lost that. I always especially admired my father for accepting such a really extraordinary reversal of circumstance without complaint; and Mother was likewise a good sport about her loss of affluence. People don't much say "good sport" anymore, but both my parents were just that. Mom always said "push on" when anybody either slowed down, complained, or, well, got in her way. My parents both pushed on.

Mother was a McAdams, from aristocratic southern Scots-Irish stock. It seems almost impossible to believe, here in 2011, but Edward McLure, my great-grandfather—only three generations before me—was a major in the Confederate army, Sixth South Carolina Volunteer Infantry. He was one of 357 Harvard graduates (class of 1854) to fight for the Confederacy, raising his own company, the Chester Blues, and he was a Johnny Reb till the bitter end, not laying down his sword until the last, there with Lee at Appomattox.

It just seems that there should've been so many more generations between me now and that long ago, but my great-grandfather's first wife died, so he married again, and my grandmother was a product of that later union. Before she was born, though, Great-Grandfather McLure—who was a lawyer and a newspaper editor—had departed Carolina after the Civil War, taking his younger second wife to a burgeoning little railroad junction in Texas. There he hung out his shingle. Sometimes his cash-poor clients paid him with local real estate deeds. Soon, however, his wife longed for a return home, and so, in 1881, Major McLure hied back east to Chester, South Carolina. He accepted the best price for the Texas land he'd accumulated. Had he not, my family would have owned a nice chunk of downtown Dallas. Take that, Boone Pickens.

Back in South Carolina, Edna McLure, my grandmother, was born in 1884. Alas, by the age of five she was orphaned, and so, as a young woman, she left Chester for the bright lights of Charlotte, North Carolina, where she gave piano lessons. More providentially, there she was successfully courted by my grandfather Thomas McAdams, a young banker, visiting from Richmond. The music line ended decisively with Grandmother. Nobody else on either side of my family can so much as carry a tune. This also applies to the family I married into. I can't dance; don't ask me.

Grandfather McAdams, the banker, was smart as a whip and prospered, so that my own mother, her two sisters, and her brother grew up in a large, fancy house hard by a fine park with a lake in the best part of Richmond. Mom, who was Louise—or LOU-ise as they say down South—attended private schools, and after her debut in 1930, when she was, as they say, "presented to society," she was given a choice: she could either attend college or go, with a chaperone, on the grand tour. Mom chose Europe and had a ball . . . as was her nature all her born days.

Sometimes, though, I had to wonder: what if she'd chosen college, like her quieter, redheaded younger sister, Juliet, who opted to go to Vassar? Mom was smart and curious and would have prospered in college. Indeed, what writing skills were passed on to me (and my two brothers—they're both more intelligent than I am, and both are good writers, too) all came from her side of the family. Mom read all the time. Daddy, on the other hand, never read books. I don't think any of the Defords did.

As I was closest to my mother, I also took after her in looks. In fact, my wife says that the older I get the more I not only look like my mother but also move like her and gesture like her and am generally turning into her. I can only imagine how truly unnerving this is when I grow amorous, and poor Carol feels as if her late mother-in-law is making a move on her.

By contrast, my two brothers, Mac and Gill, don't look like much of anybody—although they both still search valiantly to verify some scant family resemblance. Certainly, none of us looks like my father. Myself, I'm tall, angular and dark-haired; Daddy was about 5 feet 8 inches and auburn-haired. On my desk, I have a picture of him, with Mom, at a football game the year after I was born, and he bears quite a resemblance to Robert Redford. Just as my father and I shared no looks, neither did we share much common interest. We didn't do a whole lot of father-and-son stuff together. But I certainly loved Daddy, and, like everybody else, I really liked him.

Anyway, by the time Mom got back from doing the best of Europe, the Depression wasn't kidding around anymore, and there was belt-tightening in the McAdams household. Still, Mom could not possibly have had any idea that her life was never going to be so luxurious again, ever, as it had been on the grand tour when she was a teenage belle.

Mother's fall from riches was nothing like Daddy's, though. The Defords were really fat cats, among the wealthiest families in Baltimore. Over the fireplace in my house in Connecticut is a grand painting of a great nineteenth-century paddle-wheel steamer, the *Benjamin Deford*. The Defords of that time owned a leather company, which had been started by that original Benjamin Deford (1799–1870). He was obviously most intrepid. Orphaned, he had somehow started the Deford Company "without capital or friends" when he was only twenty-three years old, but by his death, an old history book notes, his company would "stand foremost among its kind in the land." His ship carried the family leather, creating the family wealth, down the Chesapeake, and then out to sea, both north and south, to exotic ports beyond.

Benjamin Deford rose to be among the most prominent of Baltimoreans. He was a philanthropist and an ardent unionist, and during the critical few months after Lincoln's election, when Maryland was passionately split over the subject of secession, Great-Great-Grandfather Deford used his position and voice to help keep Maryland safely in the union. He left the family company to his two sons: Thomas, my great-grandfather, and his bachelor brother, my namesake and great-granduncle, who was the first of four Benjamin *Franklin* Defords.*

The mansion that my father was born into in 1902 was so large that a couple of decades later, when it was sold, it was bought by the Roman Catholic Church and turned into a nunnery. My grandparents also owned an elegant winter residence downtown in Baltimore a couple of blocks from where the future Duchess of Windsor, a family acquaintance, was growing up.

Oh my, what a time my father must've had as a child, with maids and butlers and cooks and all other manner of servants and groundsmen. Daddy was not an especially reflective man, but once, when he was about sixty years old, he told me he had a couple drinks at a business lunch (usually he just dined at his desk on a pack of peanut-butter cheese crackers and a Coke; none of us Defords are gourmets), and, feeling a bit tipsy, he didn't go back to the office but found himself driving out to the old family estate. He parked there, by the side of the road, and, despite himself, began to absolutely bawl. It was, for him, not just idly remembering a fond childhood, but, rather, like looking back on some exotic lost world peopled by strangers from an entirely different epoch.

---

* I being that fourth, but officially: Benjamin Franklin Deford III. Never mind.

What had happened was that, about the time Daddy was getting out of prep school, the Deford Company caved in. I heard various vague reasons for the company's failure, but, really, it doesn't much matter anymore. Like in a lot of families, with family businesses, you reach a generation where the family businessmen aren't as good at it as their predecessors were. So with the Defords in the third generation, when it was my grandfather and his brother in charge.

But here's what my grandfather did then. With what money he had left, he picked up and moved to Richmond. As far as I can tell, the poor man must've been too ashamed to stay in Baltimore, where he'd failed. He and Grandmother moved into a dark, dreary Gothic house in downtown Richmond. It had an upstairs sitting room, where Grandfather did just that—sat, wearing a suit vest and high buttoned shoes, for the next forty years or so of his long life. He was humorless and stingy, and possibly bitter, too. Especially after Grandmother died, God, but that gloomy house was an awful place to stay when I was a boy and we'd drive down Route 301 to visit.

But, Silver Lining Department: because the damn leather company went belly up and because my grandfather fled to Richmond, my father moved down there himself after college, and that made it possible for him to meet my mother. He was ten years older than she was, and he had no money and no prospects, and it was the middle of the Depression.

However, my father was one hell of an attractive man. He was boyish and delightful, freckled, and natty. Somehow, from somewhere, I've ended up with a clipping from the society pages of the *Baltimore Sun* in 1923, when he was twenty-one. "And speaking of the Defords," the writer chirped, "one cannot fail to notice Benjie. Besides being endowed with the family's handsome features, Benjie has the charming manners and poise of a man of the world. . . . Yes indeed, with this combination, do you wonder that the sub-debs go mad over him?" As would my mother, when she got back from the grand tour.

Daddy could dress to beat the band. He had no money for clothes, but, Lord, did he have taste; somehow he managed to dress perfectly, invariably with a boutonniere in his lapel. Every day, he looked as if he had stepped out of *Town and Country*. For some reason, even though I don't believe he ever saw an opera in his life, while ambling about the house, he would whistle the drinking song from *La Traviata*. Likewise, although I never recall him discoursing on the spiritual, every night, without fail, Daddy would get into his pajamas, then go down on his knees by the side of his bed, clasp his hands in the classic worshipful position, close his eyes, and pray for a while. Then, as Mom read a book, he'd cross himself, climb into bed, and immediately go sound asleep without a pillow. Someone had told him, when he was a child, that sleeping without a pillow was better for your back, and so he never tried sleeping otherwise, all his life.

He was peculiar without being an eccentric. He showed me that you could be perfectly normal and yet do some weird stuff. In the event, you'd be hard pressed to find anybody, man or woman, who didn't like Benjie Deford. He was not stodgy, but he was old-fashioned. He talked to me about honor all the time, and, I swear, whenever I do anything wrong, even now, thirty years after he died, I think how I've let Daddy down. *When the One Great Scorer comes . . .*

Unfortunately, Daddy had no great enthusiasm for business. When he was growing up, with all that money, he wanted to be a gentleman farmer, which he would've been great at, since he was accomplished at both those things. But that was not to be. Instead, he brought Mom back to Baltimore, where I was born, and he ended up working in a family manufacturing business. I used some of his circumstances in a novel—my sweetest—that was mostly about polio, entitled *An American Summer*. Daddy was about the number-four or number-five executive in the firm; his title was secretary. He handled things like labor relations.

A few years before he would retire, the family sold the business to Glidden, the paint company. The deal was that the family members in the business would keep their jobs, and the other valued executives would be protected. Yeah, sure. Almost as soon as the ink was dry on the deal, the Glidden people became, as we said in Baltimore, "as common as cat shit," and started to try to run Daddy off. Essentially, then, he spent the last few years of his working life being shunted around and insulted—an old traveling salesman. Mom was furious, and she told me how much he was hurt, but I never once heard him whine, though. Daddy pushed on.

Mother had begun to work by then. She became a school secretary, and was famous for making announcements over the PA in her southern accent, which LOU-ise never really lost. She also drove a car pool. One of the kids she chauffeured for a couple of years was John Waters, who would become the bizarre movie director. She liked him. She got colon cancer and had to wear a colostomy bag for the last twenty-five years of her life, but I never heard her whine either. She pushed on.

So, Mom and Dad managed, mismatched in personality as they seemed to me. Sometimes I'd even have to ask myself what the hell was it that made two such different people fall in love and stay in love (and, in that bargain, give us all such a loving home). The one thing I know they shared was bridge. Even when Daddy began to suffer from dementia, damn if Mom didn't swear that he could still play a good game of bridge. Maybe that's why she tolerated his chickens.

You see, even though we lived within the city limits of Baltimore, my father raised chickens out in the backyard. It was the one thing he could do that connected him to his dream of farming. Really, raising chickens to him was a hobby, just as other men play golf or take on civic chores for Rotary. When I was growing up, the highlight for the children on Mossway, our little street, was when word got out that Mr. DeFord was going to kill a chicken, and all the neighborhood kids would come running to watch the executed chicken flop around with its head cut off. Those were high times in them olden days, before children had video games—and, hey, maybe even better than when the Italian organ grinder came down Mossway with his monkey.

Daddy raised rabbits and guinea pigs, too. He also tended wonderful vegetable and flower gardens. He had a green thumb. So, at least he became a gentleman farmer on a miniature scale, and Mom even had mock stationery made up that said "Mossway Poultry Farm." Still, she thought he was downright nuts to get up at dawn to feed some goddamn fool chickens.

So Mom and Dad accepted their diminished circumstances gracefully. I wrote a story once about Jack Nicklaus, who, although the son of a pharmacist, learned to play golf as a member of the fancy Scioto Country Club in Columbus, and I said that the very best way for any child to grow up was to be the poorest kid in the country club. By that, of course, I meant that you enjoyed a certain privilege, but you were not spoiled, and thus you became more ambitious on account of that nexus. Well, obviously, I was thinking of my own upbringing, even if we weren't members of any country club. Instead, my parents scrimped to put all three of us boys through the best private schools in Baltimore. I know that made me more determined to succeed. Push on.

So even if it wouldn't give me much material as a writer, I do believe I had the best of both worlds, growing up in that bland, uneventful, but ever so contented childhood. I look back upon it fondly, and it helps me still, I think, that I don't believe I've ever measured up to either my mother or my father. They were very special after their own fashion. When Glidden finally ran Daddy off for good, it was the union that he'd dealt with—his adversaries, if you will—who

honored him. At its annual dinner the union surprised him by award-
ing him a plaque.

I keep it in a prominent place in my office. It says simply:

Presented To
Mr. B. F. Deford
A True Gentleman
From
United Steelworkers
Local 6221

I've never earned anything quite so dear myself.

10

THE BEST ADVICE I EVER GOT
IN MY WHOLE LIFE

*The idea then wasn't to clash head on; rather, children were
taught to test the world by bending the rules rather than to defy it
by breaking them. We were the generation of the incremental, the
oblique, and what we lacked in candor, we gained in civility.*
                                        An American Summer, 2002

One time during the 1970s I volunteered to cover an NCAA convention. I did foolish journalistic things like that occasionally. Big-time
college sports is, of course, a complete fraud, a fountain of deceit,
so every now and then—particularly when I was younger and not
entirely jaded on the subject—I would involve myself somehow
and seek to shine a bright light on this great American hypocrisy.
This particular year there was talk of reform in the air concerning
such-and-such, and, although, of course, nothing would come of
it, I arrived at the conference in my Lincoln Steffens mode, still
possessing a ray of hope.

But then, as any hope for honor, truth, and the American spirit of
fair play was, once again, tabled, I took that as a good enough excuse
to have a few drinks of consolation with other reporters, to bemoan
this sad state of affairs in higher athletic education. So it was that I
awoke the next morning feeling somewhat unwell, but the conference
had an early start time, so I made my way to the hotel coffee shop for
some sustenance. I always like a hearty breakfast; unlike lunch, which,

I've always thought, gets in the way of the day, breakfast is important to my diurnal constitution.

The conference was being held at the Palmer House in Chicago, and wouldn't you know it, even though there was a free breakfast buffet for the NCAA pooh-bahs, the coffee shop was jam-packed. I spied only a single stool open at the counter, next to the last seat at the end. I shuffled over to the stool, taking no notice of the proximate company, and plunked myself down. Only as I pulled up my newspaper, intending to bury myself in it, did I happen to notice the gentleman to my left, in the last seat. He was hard on my eyes, being attired all in a dazzling white. I blinked my bloodshot orbs.

Heavens to Betsy! It was none other than Colonel Harland Sanders, he the legendary founder and purveyor of Kentucky Fried Chicken.

Being polite, not wishing to bother a celebrity while he dined, I swallowed my surprise, barely acknowledging him. He was not, at breakfast, eating chicken; he had only some form of gruel, but as he spooned it away, he greeted me and prompted something of a conversation. As the waitress came, and I ordered and the Colonel finished up his plate and asked for his bill, we carried on an amiable if unremarkable chat. Nonetheless, I must've been more engaging than I felt, for when he arose, he told me that he had most enjoyed our tête-à-tête. "So, young man," he declared, "I want to give you an important piece of advice."

I had swiveled around to bid him good-bye, and now I stared into his famous face, offering him my full attention.

"If you want people to listen to you," the Colonel began, holding his cane up some for emphasis.

"Yes, sir?" I replied, in his thrall now. Remember, the Colonel looked like what we imagine God to be—white suit, white shirt, white hair, white mustache, white goatee, kind countenance—and so, as I sat staring up at him, it was the closest I had ever felt to having the

Lord himself address me. I was Abraham upon the mount, I was Noah before the flood.

The Colonel nodded, and for emphasis repeated: "Son, if you want people to listen to you . . ." He paused, and then, with firm finality, intoned, "Wear a white suit."

And then, without another word, he turned away from me and walked out of the coffee shop.

11

SCRIBES FOR THE CRANKS AND THE FANCY

In the modern United States, in the modern world, the promulgation and acceptance of sharp new attitudes—what are called movements or trends—utterly depend on the emergence of a personality to embody the philosophy. When was the last time you saw two minutes of an idea on the six o'clock news?
"Mrs. Billie Jean King," *Sports Illustrated*, 1975

Sportswriting began to develop during that era, after the Civil War, when Americans were leaving the farms for cities, when leisure time was increasing, when the Deford Leather Company was still raking it in, when Great-Grandfather McLure, the former newspaper editor, was struggling as a lawyer in Dallas. Magazines dedicated to horse racing had appeared as early as the 1820s, but it would be baseball and a fop from Belfast that really created the discipline of sportswriting in the United States.

The *National Police Gazette* had started publication in 1845, but by the 1870s it was foundering, so one of its salesmen, Richard Kyle Fox, was able to take it over simply by agreeing to assume its debts. Fox should be in the Sportscasters and Sportswriters Hall of Fame as nothing less than the founding father, but he's largely been forgotten; this is too bad, because he not only is important professionally but, to boot, was quite a character.

I stumbled across Fox in 1988, quite by chance, when I was planning to write a story about "Casey at the Bat" on the centennial of America's quintessential poem. Unfortunately, what I found out, and rather quickly, was that there hadn't been anything new to say about "Casey" for at least seventy-five years, and even before that, there'd been pretty slim pickings.

A Harvard philosophy major named Ernest Thayer, who never wrote anything else of consequence in his life, had dashed the poem off and published it in the *San Francisco Examiner* . . . and that pretty much ended the story. Thayer never volunteered—*and nobody asked!*—if Mudville was based on any town in particular, although it's generally assumed that Stockton, California, was his probable model. Likewise, Thayer never allowed that Casey himself was suggested by any particular player, although it's hard not to believe that the narcissistic Irish hero King Kelly didn't at least influence the poet. But that's that. The rest was but sonorous vaudevillians endlessly reciting "Casey" to beguiled audiences.*

Anyway, after I gave up on writing about the poem "Casey," I had an inspiration. I thought I'd imagine a whole life for the poor guy besides the one game when he went down swinging. So I gave him a complete name, Timothy F. X. Casey, and a beautiful girlfriend, and threw in some nasty villains and adoring cranks (which is what baseball fans were called then), plus a cameo by John L. Sullivan, the boorish heavyweight champion, and wrote a novella that I called *Casey on the Loose.* And while doing that research I chanced upon the

---

*Coincidentally, the other most popular American sports piece, "Take Me Out to the Ball Game," also has no glamorous history attached to it. The lyrics were hastily scratched out on a commuter train by a guy named Jack Norworth, who'd never seen a baseball game in his life, and then, arriving in Manhattan, he handed his scrap of paper to a composer named Albert Von Tilzer, who had likewise never seen a game, and he wrote the music. This was in 1910, and Norworth was so interested in baseball that despite the fact that his baseball anthem became an eternal oldie but goodie and enriched him considerably, he didn't even have the curiosity to take himself out to a ball game for another thirty years, until 1940. Poor sportswriters. All the billions of words we've lovingly written and a couple of guys passing through turn out the classics.

redoubtable Mr. Richard Kyle Fox and made him another featured character in Casey's saga.

In real life, after he took over the *National Police Gazette,* Fox restyled it, printing it on large pink pages with lurid illustrations (most often of damsels in distress, whose disheveled dresses invariably revealed nubile bare calves), thereby turning the moribund journal into a huge success that sold about 150,000 copies a month. It soon earned the sobriquet "The Barbers' Bible," for no red-white-and-blue tonsorial parlor could be without one. (Neither could any saloon.) Fox's editorial formula was a three-legged stool of crime, sex, and sport. In this sense, he inspired tabloid journalism, and, more or less, *Playboy* and (two outta three ain't bad) the *Sports Illustrated* swimsuit issue, as well. Some things not even technology can improve upon. Why, a hundred years on from Fox's inspiration, a *New York Daily News* editor proclaimed that the way to sell papers was "tits, cops, and the Yankees."

Not only was Richard Fox a genius in his line; he was likewise recognized as quite the man about town, for he was regularly turned out in a Prince Albert coat, top hat, ruffled shirts, and outlandish amounts of jewelry—yes, ahead of his time in sports with bling, too. And, so snappily attired, not long after he took over the *Gazette,* Fox created the first editorial sports department. Baseball was generally a bit too tame for the pink sheet, though. It favored boxing; Fox conceived of the idea of the bejeweled championship belt; for a big bout his circulation would leap up to 400,000. He made it a point to "feud" with John L. Sullivan, the Boston Strong Boy, of whom his Irish idolaters sang: "No fighter in the world can beat / Our true American. / The champion of all champions, John L. Sullivan." How dare the *Gazette* oppose our hero, his admirers would snarl through gritted teeth, as they rushed—flies into the spider's web—to buy Fox's latest edition.

When times were slow for "the fancy," as followers of boxing were called, Fox was inclined to feature even more sanguineous blood sports, like cockfighting and ratting. The stuff was not necessarily pretty, but it sure proved that a reading audience for sport existed, and by 1883 Fox and his magazine were ensconced in their own swanky seven-story Manhattan building, his wardrobe had grown even more stylish, and the *Gazette*'s advertising rates were among the highest in the land.

Seeing how successfully Fox used sport, newspapers began to earnestly cover games. Joseph Pulitzer created the first newspaper sports department at the *New York World* in 1883, and William Randolph Hearst upped the ante by publishing the first all-sports section at the *New York Journal* two years later. Baseball was tailor-made for newspapers, of course, because both were daily institutions, and precisely as the popularity of professional baseball ballooned in the last two decades of the nineteenth century, the number of American dailies tripled to more than two thousand. Sports pages became de rigueur. Also, a new weekly, devoted solely to the "national pastime," the *Sporting News*, was launched in 1886 in St. Louis by Alfred H. Spink, a former newspaper reporter.

Whereas football would be of no professional consequence for decades, it had become the favored school game, and even though its best teams were those of the snootiest Ivy League universities (at a time when few enough Americans got through high school), the big college games began to attract national interest beyond the campus.* Besides, now that we had *sports*writers, they had to write about other sports once the baseball season was over. And precisely because football *was* a college game, it sold newspapers and magazines and the advertisements therein to the carriage trade. The fetching "Gibson girl," who emerged from the illustrations of Charles Dana Gibson in the 1890s, was the embodiment of the active new American woman, and there she was, often as not waving a pennant at a football game,

---

*The annual Princeton-Yale Thanksgiving game in New York took on such prominence that the whores in town started wearing orange-and-black or blue-and-white undergarments, the better to please their elite young clientele.

or toting a tennis racket, while tricked out in her most glamorous lawn court attire.

The press began to make such celebrities out of athletes that, in 1896, a hack writer named Gilbert Patten created a fictional star "more in touch with our times," who became the hero of every red-blooded American boy. Writing for the *Tip Top Weekly,* a publication known as a "dime novel," Patten introduced Frank Merriwell, who, first at prep school and then at Yale, improbably won at baseball or some other sport each and every week (usually with two out in the ninth or with the clock ticking down). Before the rise of the nickelodeon would finally outdo even Patten's literary melodramatics, Frank Merriwell sold 500 million copies, and not only was he all-conquering, but his incredibly moral demeanor was such that to call a flesh-and-blood boy "a regular Frank Merriwell" was the highest compliment you could pay any young nephew of Uncle Sam.

Thus, when the wide-eyed Grantland Rice left Vanderbilt and began his career in 1901, the new profession might have been a mere generation old, but it was already thriving. Already, too, it was distinguishing itself, in a negative way, as something apart from the rest of real journalism. "Sportswriters," a promoter snarled at about this time, "you can buy them for a steak." And likewise, sportswriters, well fed or not, had begun to use odd synonyms in their copy that never appeared in any human conversation. Have you ever heard a single sentient person say "frame" or "gardeners" or "knotted" when discussing sport? "Garnered . . . tabbed . . . inked?" Perhaps the idea was to make mere games seem more important or artistic, but for whatever reason the writing grew more florid and rococo than what appeared in the rest of the paper. Jonathan Yardley, the critic, wrote that old-time sportswriting was "like a bad dream by Sir Walter Scott."

But despite itself, the profession began to attract some real talent. Good grief, Heywood Broun came directly out of Harvard to start covering baseball for the *New York Morning Telegraph.* There, of all people, his editor was Bat Masterson, the erstwhile gunslinger, who had laid down his six-shooters and taken up the sports pages in his declining years. Of course, Broun's first newspaper was not exactly at the top of the journalistic tree; rather, it was mostly a horse-racing sheet that was perhaps best known around Broadway as precisely half of what was called "a whore's breakfast." The other half: a cigarette.

Likewise, in Chicago, Ring Lardner had come from South Bend to be the sports columnist at the worst rag in town, the curiously named *Chicago Inter Ocean*. Lardner's precocious talent was so obvious, though, that soon he would move up from the journalistic bushes to the *Tribune*, where the teenage Ernest Hemingway was so impressed by Lardner's sports-page style that he signed his own schoolboy pieces "Ring Lardner, Jr." Later, Lardner's friend F. Scott Fitzgerald would sneer that such a talented humorist had let himself be limited by his déclassé subject matter: "However deeply Ring might cut into it, his cake still has the diameter of Frank Chance's baseball diamond" (Chance being a mere player). However, Lardner's book about a guileless pitcher, *You Know Me, Al*, showed that sports could support literature more realistically and engagingly than Frank Merriwell's simplistic derring-do.

As with the *Tribune* in Chicago, even the finest newspapers had added sports staffs and were not above putting sports on the front page on the occasion of major games. Nor were specialists in this new journalistic realm only an American development. The forerunner of the world's most famous sports daily, *L'Équipe*, was a going concern in France before the turn of the twentieth century, and in England, the vaunted *Times of London* boasted perhaps the most famous sportswriter in the first half of the twentieth century, that side of Grantland Rice.

Starting in 1907, Bernard Darwin gave up the law to cover golf for the *Times*. He was the grandson of Charles Darwin, and although the *Times* certainly did not lower itself by extending bylines to its writers, so that Darwin could sign his pieces only "Our Golf Correspondent," his identity was well known. Esteemed as Darwin was, he remains, surely, the most supercilious snob ever to cover any sport.

Since he was convinced that he knew golf better than anyone else, only very rarely did he bother to actually speak to the ignorant golfers he was covering. If Darwin ever did feel that his own words could possibly be insufficient, rather than turning to another living authority, he would dredge up a quotation from Charles Dickens that he thought best applied to the current situation on the links. Although Dickens knew golf not at all, Darwin made up for this inconvenience because he felt he knew Dickens's mind only slightly less than he knew golf.

And, it can be safely said, the evolution of golf quotes has not much advanced since Darwin held sway. Moreover, every time I hear somebody on CBS tell me again that the Masters doesn't start till the back nine on Sunday, I can't help wondering: what would Dickens say instead?

12

EL TIGRE

Old-money people seldom blow up at small things. If you have money all your life, small things can remain forever small.
"The Line on Jimmy The Greek," *Sports Illustrated*, 1980

The sports pages have flourished for more than a century, and they're not dead yet (anyway, not as I write at this hour), but I suppose that even if in some future come-and-lose-it day there is no longer such a thing as newsprint for a sports fan to hold in his grubby hands, nonetheless it still will be me who will go down in journalistic annals as the man most associated with the greatest sports page—sports literature?—failure, ever, in all of sportsdom.

It's ironic that I would be cast as a grim reaper for newspapers, inasmuch as I had had nothing whatsoever to do with the sports pages since that time long ago, when, as a teenager, I had been Roamer for a day and a copyboy for two summers on the *Baltimore Evening Sun.* Well, I did have a brief dalliance with the *New York Times* in 1977, when the editor, Abe Rosenthal, tried to lure me to the great broadsheet, to be the columnist who, he kept saying, would be "the heir to Red Smith." Even though I was sure by then that I was better at writing longer pieces than short columns, it was seductive. The *New York Times.* The certified, accepted, designated, approved Paper of Record. Plus, the heir business. It could turn a fellow's head.

Looking back, I'm sure it would've been the wrong move for me, but fortunately, Rosenthal was so disagreeable, so arrogant, that every time I might begin to convince myself to come over, he would manage to talk me out of it by talking on. To give the devil his due, the little man was so thoroughly convinced that the *Times* was the be-all and end-all of journalism that it was impossible for him to conceive how someone in the business—and a lowlife sportswriter, to boot—might actually deliberate about accepting his offer, let alone reject it.

I never did have the heart to tell Rosenthal that, at the time, his paper's sports section wasn't all that scintillating, or that, in this respect, I'd be joining the hindquarters of his champion thoroughbred. More personally, it was apparent that Rosenthal was simply dismissive of sports and sportswriting and had to hold his nose and pretend to play up to a person of my vulgar specialty. So, in the end, I stayed at *Sports Illustrated*, and, like that new thing called a free agent in baseball, I got a sweetheart deal with my old franchise.

I remained extremely happy with what I was doing, too, and was perfectly content, but after another decade or so I decided that I needed something to shake me up. Maybe it was just that I was turning fifty. Whatever, I concluded that a year of writing stories abroad would be just the ticket, a sort of working sabbatical. Carol was all for it; the managing editor, Mark Mulvoy, heartily approved; and we chose London. We put our house in Westport up for rent; looked into housing in Saint John's Wood and the right school for our young daughter, Scarlet; and prepared for a wonderful little interim, living the glamorous life of expats.

And, what do you know, but just then, out of the blue one day, at precisely this most vulnerable moment in my life, I got a phone call from the past, from an old college colleague. Peter Price and I had been on both the *Daily Princetonian* and the humor magazine *The Tiger.* I was editorial, he business, and we were in different classes, but I had tremendously admired his abilities. He was one of those people who are natural grown-ups, having jumped over adolescence, and probably childhood, too. Also, I trusted Peter and trusted his judgment.

At this time, he was the publisher of the *New York Post,* but he had a new deal for me. There was, you see, this billionaire with a funny name from Mexico who wanted to start an all-sports daily in the United States. Peter had been chosen as the publisher. He wanted me to be the editor. I hastened to point out to Peter the salient truth that, unfortunately, I was not an editor. In fact, like most writers who possess any talent, I didn't, constitutionally, like editors—not professionally anyhow (and otherwise, see: Rosenthal, Abe). I generally subscribed to the view of a grand old newspaperman named Gene Fowler, who once allowed, "Every editor should have a pimp for a brother so they could have someone in the family to look up to."

Peter explained that this was no problem, inasmuch as my main assignment, initially, would simply be to lend my name to this unusual enterprise, a type of newspaper unknown to provincial Americans, and thereby attract the necessary talent to staff the new daily. As such, more than an editor, I was, at least at first, to be rather like one of those basketball coaches who can't really coach very well, but who pay savvy old assistants to do that, while they themselves employ a snappy wardrobe, an ingratiating manner, and a silver tongue in order to sweet-talk recruits. As Al McGuire once told me about his coaching staff at Marquette, "Only one of us can wear the brassiere, and that's me." What Peter told me gave me total assurance that, for our purposes, baby, I was going out in a D-cup. I would have the most ample pot o' gold in newspaper history to disburse to talent. If I could talk a good game, we could buy ourselves a good team.

Then Peter told me about the man behind the bankroll. His name (of Basque origin) was Emilio Azcarraga. He was a prominent member of the oligarchy that essentially ran Mexico, with a net worth that was generally accepted to be the largest south of the Rio Grande. He was known (and feared) throughout his homeland as El Tigre. Immediately, this sounded better to me than any bad movie with ominous music. Also, this sidebar: whereas Azcarraga was a celebrity of the first order in Mexico, he hated publicity, and even though he was going to start a newspaper, he generally despised newspapers and would not agree to talk to the lowlifes who were employed by them.

So, of course, I was instantly sold. Precipitately. There are moments when the current is flowing so fast that you have to jump in because your mind is already swirling downstream. I, who am not an editor, am going to be the editor of a national daily sports newspaper, of which there had never been one in the United States, working for a mysteriously romantic foreign character named El Tigre, who dislikes newspapers, and who had obtained that name both for his ferocious personality and for a stripe of white hair that cut through the jet black at the top of his crown.

In that respect, he was reminiscent of some character from the old Dick Tracy comic strip. But—trust me—there was no cartoon in Emilio Azcarraga. Carol and I took our house off the rental market, I shook hands with Peter, and after twenty-seven years at *Sports Illustrated*, off I flew to Mexico City to meet my new boss. As befitted associates of the great man of Mexico, Peter and I were whisked through customs without having to bother with customs and soon I stood before El Tigre himself.

He was a formidable sight, climbing out of his massive bulletproof limousine, his bodyguards convoying him. He approached, looking me over. Let me tell you: there are times when being tall is the best thing you can have going for you. This was definitely one of those occasions, for I had already heard the tale of how Emilio had kept a high wooden chair in his office, so that any visitor who sat in it could not touch the floor with his feet and thus felt like a child before him. Now, although El Tigre was certainly a figure of imposing enough size, when he stood there, eyeing me, measuring me, at least he had to look up to me. It's a small thing, to be sure, but, still, my feet touched the ground, and I was able to meet his eyes from my vantage point. He shook my hand, and then, with a bit of a crooked smile, El Tigre spoke these pungent words to me: "Well, what are they saying about the Spic up there?"

Naturally, it took me aback, but it certainly alerted me to his attitude, some mixture of bravado and prickliness, which he presented to the superior sons of bitches who looked down on him from *el Norte*. Emilio had a hole card, too. He had been born in San Antonio. He could've been one of us, but although he owned elegant houses all over the world—Mexico City, of course, Acapulco, Los Angeles, Madrid, London, New York (on Sutton Place), and God only knows where else—he remained proudly, if ruefully, Mexican. He could, with me, sometimes fulminate about his country, irritated that its citizens could not move up in the world, but then, just as quickly, he would sympathize with his impoverished countrypeople in the fashion of an avuncular lord of the manor. And never forget, it was he who gave them their circuses.

Indeed, I wondered whether Emilio ever accepted the fact of what a really considerable part he played in Mexican culture. After all, because his networks were so dominant in Mexico, he determined not only pretty much of what poorer Mexicans saw and what they knew, but even how they saw themselves. It was illustrative of his duality—aristocrat and patriot—that the two projects in New York that were also simultaneously engaging him at the time I met him were: (1) getting a marina on the lower west side expanded so that his gargantuan yacht *Paradiso,* which included a seaplane on the deck, could conveniently berth there: and (2) overseeing a huge historical exhibition at the Metropolitan Museum of Art that celebrated the heritage of indigenous Mexican art.

His father, Don Emilio, had launched the family fortune by selling cars and then had made more in radio. The story was that Don Emilio came up with the idea of putting horns in mariachi bands to make them sound better on the air. Who knew? I just assumed mariachi bands had been born with horns.

Emilio himself was, as a young man, a ne'er-do-well playboy, the despair of his father, who dismissed him as "my son, the idiot." Then he decided to grow up and took command of his own life. "You wanna see my stadium?" he asked me once, in the manner of *You wanna see my club cellar*? The stadium just happened to be the centerpiece of the 1968 Olympics, which was the first great project Emilio directed. Then the former prodigal son proceeded to exceed the father, expanding the family broadcast empire into a television monopoly, creating downscale entertainment that the nation's masses adored. Next, it was Azcarraga who foresaw the potential for satellite programming before almost any one else in the world, pioneering, taking little Mexico's TV programs abroad. His soap operas, *novelas,* were dubbed in various languages and played all over the world. Even the Chinese loved Mexican *novelas.* One night in New York, at a lavish black-tie tribute to Emilio, Julio Iglesias paused in his singing, moved toward Emilio as a troubadour would dare to approach the lord at court, and, before him, all but credited Emilio Azcarraga alone with keeping the Spanish language alive amid the global tsunami of English.

There was a joke in Mexico that El Tigre died, and when he handed Saint Peter his card, heaven's gatekeeper looked up, impressed: "You're *the* Emilio Azcarraga?" Emilio nodded.

"The richest man south of the Rio Grande?" Emilio nodded.

"Head of Televisa, showing stories to the whole world?"

"Uh-huh."

"Owner of magnificent mansions all over the world?"

"Uh-huh."

"And your great, fantastic yacht with a staff of—?"

"Yes, yes."

"The man who's slept with many of the most beautiful women in the world?"

"Yes, of course, that's me," Emilio said.

"Well, look, then," said Saint Peter, "why don't you come in and look the place over and see if you'd like it?"

His Christmas cards would come with the following return address on the back of the envelope:

Paula y Emilio Azcarraga
Mexico

I was going to send ours out next Christmas:

Carol and Frank Deford
United States

But then I thought better of that.

However, notwithstanding El Tigre's extraordinary wealth, his brilliance at business, and all the beautiful women he married, the one after another, he was forever alert to gringos dismissing him—just another dirty Mex'can. How many English-speaking Americans knew that his Mexican *novelas* were a worldwide smash hit, that he was Ted Turner taken to another level? So if Emilio could establish, in the United States, our first national daily sports newspaper—an institution that had been a success for years in many countries, the world over—even snotty Americans would have to credit the Spic.

After meeting Emilio I was even more primed for this new challenge. I probably needed a change, and very frankly I liked the idea of not always working as a single, but for once going inside, belonging, being an intimate part of something. So I took over what I entitled the *National Sports Daily.* That was a very prosaic name, I know, but for once I told myself not to be too slick by half. I wanted to call it the *Spirit,* the name of a forgotten nineteenth-century sports periodical, which also had a nice evocative ring to it—school spirit and all that—but I just knew that if we fell on hard times, every cheap-shot artist in the business was going to start using "spirit" to refer to our possible demise, so I finally figured I wouldn't give anyone the chance. No, just: the *National Sports Daily.*

Meanwhile, I set out to find a staff, to hire, very simply, people who knew what I, the presumed newspaper editor, didn't know: how to be an editor and put out a newspaper. I was very lucky that I found the right guy to be my right-hand man. He was Van McKenzie, the sports editor of the *Atlanta Constitution.* Van was a big, hulking panda of a man, with the most instinctive journalistic talents. Curiously, you see, he didn't read all that much; that is certainly strange for someone in the business of getting other people to read, but maybe, perversely, it worked to his advantage. Van was like those musicians who can't read music, but just naturally pick out the right notes. He was simply a natural-born, great newspaperman. And Van was a leader, too.

In my self-centeredness as a writer, only now did the scales begin to fall from my eyes. For all that we sports*writers* bitch about not being appreciated as literary artists, it is sports *editors* who are really more invested in the institution. Writers *post*–Bernard Darwin do get bylines. We get our egos stroked, because even when people say sportswriting is rubbish, they invariably exempt you, polish the apple, and say that certainly *your* writing is far finer than the whole shabby genre. But it's the editors (and the producers on TV and radio) who are at the core of sports journalism. In an odd way, sportswriters are more attached to one another, to their rival colleagues out there in the field working with (and against) them, than they are to their own publication, with desks and landlines, back in some air-conditioned building somewhere. Writers are like golfers or runners, playing for themselves. Editors are the team players.

One day, a couple of months into our planning, Van came to me and said, "I think we can get Vince Doria."

He was the sports editor of the *Boston Globe,* one of the two or three others in the business who were ranked in McKenzie's class.

Today, Vince is director of news at ESPN, probably the single most influential executive in the front lines of sports journalism. "He'd come here?" I asked. "Doria would accept being like the number-four or -five guy?"

McKenzie nodded. "It's not Boston," he said. "It's the *national* sports paper. He wants to be a part of it."

"Hey, great with me," I said. El Tigre's inexhaustible treasure chest was still chock-full. So Van called Doria. And all I could think was: McKenzie is going out of his way, for the good of the paper, to bring in a rival, because Doria is very good, and he's very well liked, too. And sure enough, when things would go wrong and Van would blow his top or drift into a funk, the other editors would naturally go to Vince for sympathy. But Van had known how valuable he could be on the team, and Vince never did anything but accept his subsidiary role with grace and energy and support for Van.

I was always touched by that. Why, if I didn't watch myself, I was going to start to like editors.

I remember one subeditor in particular. I was interviewing him for a job, and I spelled out, as I always did, what a risky venture the *National* really was, and then I asked him if he was positive that he wanted to leave a secure position, move his family to New York, and sign on. "Look," he answered, "all my life I've been putting out C1. For once, I want to be A1." That is: not just work the front page of the third section, but the front page of the whole damn paper. That mattered. There was such great passion evident when you finally had the chance to be the marquee, to be A1.

We had momentum. We had focus. We were hungrier. We exuded intensity.

So, most of all I'll never forget the camaraderie at the *National*, especially when it became clear that it wasn't working, that we weren't selling enough papers, that we were losing gobs of Emilio's money. Most of the staff drew close. An editor named Lee Gordon ran the agate section. I couldn't think of anything less romantic than putting out a bunch of numbers every day in small type. But Lee and his guys came up with all kinds of new statistics and new ways to present statistics, and he made that damn agate *sing*. He designed typically tacky yellow bowling shirts for the agate team, and made me an honorary member, with the name "Top Gun" written in script across the breast.

I was touched by that, too. If I didn't watch it, I was going to turn into an editor. OMG.

But one day, after only eighteen months of issues, I had to clamber up onto a desk in the newsroom and stand there and tell the men and women clustered around me that we were finished. The last great newspaper experiment in America had failed. I might as well have called it the *Spirit* after all. It had fled the journalism corpus.

I'm the worst person to judge, but I think we put out an excellent editorial product. Why, talk about the alpha and omega of admirers: Pete Rose wrote to me from prison to say how much he enjoyed the paper, and when we folded, the *New York Times* itself was sweet enough to hand us a little editorial eulogy, calling ours "a brave, if brief, expedition." And the *Times* wrote: "The candor and irreverence that marked the paper's coverage, survived even in its own obituary, written by Frank Deford, the editor. 'If it hadn't been a recession, we might have gotten some legs. The one thing we never got was legs. Gee, we're sorry it couldn't have been longer. We wanted to be an institution.'"

Unfortunately, we couldn't deliver the *National* at a reasonable cost. Readers in other countries buy their sports papers at kiosks, next to where they take public transportation. Americans want their paper on their doorstep at six-thirty, before they have breakfast and get into their car. Especially in a land of sprawl, that's a massively expensive delivery problem. Also, it's something of an inconvenience that we just happen to have four time zones and all our teams play night games.

Oh well, it showed me how everybody was watching the wrong targets. Before we started publishing, when I was constantly being interviewed about our prospects, nobody ever asked about circulation. Everybody: Can you get enough readers, Mr. DeFord? Can you sell enough ads, Mr. DeFord? Nobody got it right where we would go wrong. Certainly, we sure as hell didn't.

Mostly, it was Peter, the publisher, who would have to discuss the bad news with Emilio. But El Tigre would call on me every now and then, too. We met on his yacht. Or at his estate in Acapulco, where, for a front yard, he'd had transplanted his own personal oyster beds from the Mediterranean. (Nice touch.) Or in his offices in Los Angeles. Or he'd come into New York, and he'd take me to La Grenouille, and we'd drink martinis long into the afternoon. I don't drink martinis. The only other guy I ever drank martinis with was Johnny Dee, when he was the basketball coach at Notre Dame.* Johnny liked to mix martinis. He called them "martoonis" and was the only person who ever called me "Francis."

But writers are trained to be chameleons, and, hey, if El Tigre drinks martinis, you drink martinis, too. Besides, he did agree that the product wasn't the reason for the paper's failure to thrive. And he put up with me. Like me, too, Emilio had lost a young daughter. The one thing everybody told me before I met him was: Look, please, whatever you do, for Chrissake, whatever, don't ask Emilio Azcarraga about his daughter.

So, shortly after he asked me what people thought of the Spic, I told him I was sorry about his daughter, because I'd lost a daughter too. Everybody held their breath. "Yes," he said softly, "I'd heard that. Thank you." One thing I've learned about interviewing is that

---

*Johnny also had a wonderful old priest, Father Tom Brennan, who traveled with the team, sat on the bench, and then got on the refs. Big-time. When I was with the team at Evansville, the lead ref came over, waggled his finger at Father Brennan, and threatened him with a technical if he didn't shut up. "Hey, Father," he said, "you call the Mass, and I call the game."

most people appreciate talking about what they love, even if it's been lost. No, nobody likes being criticized—don't kid yourself: *nobody,* except possibly Donald Trump or O. J. Simpson, is really thick-skinned—and nobody wants to be accused of anything or called to account, but people really don't mind discussing their sorrow, if it's founded in love.

So, as the *National* lost money because we couldn't deliver it, we'd all talk about the situation and other people would talk and talk, but we never could, for the life of us, figure out how to beat those economics. I mean, I knew we were in trouble when they couldn't even deliver the paper to my house, and I was the editor. Don't tell me about putting a man on the moon. I don't know technology. But I was in awe at how *USA Today* got its papers into all the hills and hollows of America, so you'd wake up in the morning in some Motel 6 on the edge of nowhere and there *USA Today* would be, always so incredibly bland, its editors positively petrified to be lively or daring or even charming; journalism jejune—but so what? It was there where you were, and it even had all the damn West Coast scores.

Emilio had planned on going into the hole up to as much as $50 million, but in the end he lost $150 million before he threw in the towel in June of 1991—and he paid every damn bill down to the penny. When we'd opened, he'd given everybody on the staff a gold Mexican coin (Carol added a chain and wears it as a necklace), and when we closed he threw a huge, expensive going-out-of-business party for us. Staffers asked me for his address. They wrote him thank-you notes. How many people write thank-you notes to the owner when he closes up shop and puts you out of work? But, you see, just for once in the United States, if only for eighteen months, he gave newspaper sports guys A1.

The last time I saw Emilio was a few months after the *National* folded. He asked me to come to Mexico City to talk about an idea he had. As it turned out, on that very day there was a total eclipse of the sun over that whole part of the country. I don't know if it was symbolic, but it sure as hell was eerie. Pitch black at noon. Then, when the midday sun shone on Mexico again, he drove me up to his estate in the hills above the city to have lunch with Paula and him. We wound higher and higher. It was bright and clear up there, Shangri-la, but when you looked down the whole of Mexico City below lay somewhere beneath this ugly pot of smog. No wonder the people sat in front of their TVs and watched El Tigre's singers and dancers and soaps.

What Emilio had in mind for us to do together was a huge project for the millennium, a sort of video encyclopedia. It sounded fascinating, but massive and indistinct. He said we'd talk again, but he never got back to me. He had a lot of fish to fry, and after all, I, on the hoof, reminded him of his $150 million gone *adiós*.

El Tigre never made the millennium himself, either. He died of cancer in 1997. Someone told me he'd known he had cancer all during the whole *National* adventure. So it wasn't just another investment; the *National* was going to be the Spic's last great success—and north of the goddamn border, to stick it to the gringos.

It was late at night when Emilio's New York secretary called me after she'd gotten the word he died, because she said he'd want me to know. A few days before, when Emilio had understood there was no more to be done for him, he went out to sea, like a Viking of yore. In Miami, he got on his great new yacht, one that was even bigger than that behemoth he'd had to fix up a whole new marina for in New York, and they filled him full of morphine, and they just sailed it away into the Atlantic till he passed beyond.

So the last American newspaper was gone, and now the foreigner who dreamed it up, too. Poor Van McKenzie, who made it as good as it was, also died of cancer, much too young, a few years later. At least the *National* itself isn't yet forgotten. At grantland.com, the new sports Web site funded by ESPN (and named for Grantland Rice) I understand that the insiders refer to it as "the National 2.0." The funny thing is, so many people still come up and tell me, nicely, that they read every copy, which I know is a polite lie, since I was the editor, and even I couldn't *get* every copy. That was the whole damn problem. Or, more reasonably, lots of people tell me they saved a copy of the last issue or the first issue. I believe that. People bring copies for me to sign all the time when I'm autographing my novels. There are plenty of first and last editions in attics and basements and nooks and crannies, I know. Artifacts of a dream—and of another time gone.

The other thing a lot of people tell me is that it's just too damn bad the *National* didn't come out a few years later, because all the material it had, all the amazing statistics that Lee Gordon's agate team gave the world—why, it'd be perfect for the Internet.

I just go along and agree, and I don't bother to mention that, never mind sports, the whole trouble with newspapers and the Internet is that the Internet destroys newspapers. The people are right, of course: the *National* would have been perfect for the Internet. It's just that the Internet would have been terrible for the *National.* But at least we beat the rest of the newspaper crowd. We went out of business on our own before the Internet could do it to us.

A lot of the guys who signed on to the *National* dislocated their lives and bought houses they had to sell, and, wherever they came from and whatever better job they went on to, it wounded their pride terribly that the *National* folded. They knew the long odds, but it still hurt them when we went belly up. It's corny, because newspaper guys are supposed to be cynical hard-boiled cases, but there were a lot of hearts that bled there. Not just that they lost a job, but that sports lost its paper.

As for Emilio, well, don't worry, he still had some loose change left over. Only two years later, I read that at a dinner at the Mexican president's house, he'd up and volunteered to donate $50 million to the PRI, the ruling party then. But however wealthy he was, I was always sorry I let the billionaire down, because, at the end of the day, a lot of people in the United States look down their noses at Mexicans, the same as some people look down at sportswriting. So that was the one little thing we had in common, El Tigre and I.

Anyway, after I helped blow $150 million my one time as an editor, I went back to being a writer, and once you've been a sportswriter, it's awfully hard to find anything else in the writing line.

13

IN WHICH I FINALLY DISCOVER THE DIFFERENCE BETWEEN WINNING AND LOSING

Golf has become an utter phenomenon, ubiquitous upon the earth (especially the United States division), a dominant cultural force that has replaced most sensible, traditional American activities, such as reading, the cocktail hour, sunbathing, worship of the Almighty, bridge and matinees.

"Hooked on Golf," *Sports Illustrated*, 1998

I am not, as Gilbert and Sullivan might say, the very model of a modern manly man. This is because I do not play golf, I do not like to barbecue, and I don't know the first thing about wine. But primarily it is the golf, or the lack thereof, that astounds other men. Males of my sort simply *expect* that you play golf. They begin conversations that way and are genuinely taken aback when I reveal that I do not play—all the more so, I'm sure, they're put off their feed because I am a *sports*writer who doesn't play golf. It discombobulates them and leaves them unsure how to respond. It is as if I said that, of my free will, I did not choose to use indoor plumbing.

I try, then, to put them at ease and, if possible, help to seek some other conversational subject where we might find common ground:

the weather or the goddamn airplanes or the stock market. Those few things that men are otherwise comfortable talking about.

Whereas golfers are, of course, terrible bores on the subject, please, I have nothing against the game as such. I caddied summers as a boy. It was good money, toting heavy bags on those skinny shoulders of mine, over hill and vale, dripping wet in the fiery Maryland humidity, and of course it was a lovely setting, for I have always thought that the prettiest golf courses are about the best that man and God can make together. Nonetheless, on Monday, which was traditionally caddies' day, I had no interest in pulling down my father's old sticks from the attic and going back out and assaying a round myself.

I liked playing tennis, but I have a lung condition, alpha-1 antitrypsin deficiency, which is essentially genetic emphysema, so I had to give tennis up as my breathing deteriorated, and it was just too late to get into a cart and start up on golf then. I do suspect I have missed something. Camaraderie, for sure. Certainly, too, as with all golfers, had I only picked up the game, I am assured that my testicles would have grown larger and more metallic. And I think I envy the escape that the links provide for so many men whose dream seems to be to get through the week so as to play a round on the weekend, and then get through their work so as to play rounds forever in retirement. Golf must be wonderfully addictive. There is some part of me that is envious that other men of my time and place have found this pleasure. It is as if something is missing in me.

The better question, though, is whether I have taken good enough advantage of the hours I have had in my life not playing golf. That's an awful lot of time I've been blessed with that other men gave to their game. When I didn't play yet another eighteen, did I think enough, pray enough, read and study enough, do enough good things, help my wife and children enough? Or did I just piss it all away as surely as if I, too, were once again pulling out a six-iron and arcing another one to the green and then striding after my ball, with the sun overhead and my fellow linksmen all about me? I really don't know.

There lies Frank DeFord, RIP. What a waste of a life. The poor sonuvabitch never even played a single five-dollar Nassau.

But it is also the case that because I did not myself play the game, I seldom wrote about it. Sportswriters (and sports announcers) love to cover golf, because then they can get to play golf. It surely colors the way they report on the game, for they adore it so and feel they are part of it, more so than when they write about other sports. When I was playing tennis, for example, I never had any desire to myself play on the courts where I might be doing a story, but part of being a golf writer is to dream of participating. *There.* Oh, to actually get the chance to go round Amen Corner yourself, no less than the brave knights of the tour! And perhaps because golf writers play the game, I suspect that they can't quite ever stand back and view it as objectively as they do other sports.

Golfers almost never seem to choke, as all other professional athletes do. It's a hard game, is all. Unyielding. Unforgiving. Everybody's trying. He didn't *mean* to get a bad lie. Just bum luck that he pushed that easy three-foot putt that could've tied him for the lead. Likewise, the fans never boo anybody in the sport, and every course is a home field for every golfer; I suspect that this inhibits journalistic criticism, too. *You da man.* Never mind all the salacious sex stuff that came out—Tiger Woods always got mulligans for his surly behavior on the links. My favorite euphemism in all of sport is that a drive *finds* a sand trap. Not that some bum actually hit his Titleist there. But in all of baseball history, there's never been a batter whose ball *found* the shortstop's glove with the bases loaded.

Perhaps, then, it was my distance from the game that led Mark Mulvoy, the managing editor (and a manic golfer), to ask me, in 1986, to write about the great duel nine years previously between Jack Nicklaus and Tom Watson at the British Open. That match had been played on the Ailsa course at Turnberry, to which the Open was returning; this accounted for the reprise story. Not being an avid follower of golf, I had to admit that I couldn't even recall who had won. I assumed it had been Nicklaus, of course, because certainly he was the best ever, while Watson was but very, very good.

It is hardly uncommon, though, for upsets of that magnitude to happen in any game. A sporting life is like climate, and any one game the weather, so we should never be surprised when greatness is eclipsed on a particular day,* when somebody gets unusually hot or cold. So I learned that indeed it had been the lesser, Watson, who had won, by a stroke, as the two Americans led the rest of the field by *eleven* strokes, playing straight up against each other in the last two-some for the final thirty-six holes. It was stirring stuff I reread, and I was glad to get the rare opportunity to write a golf story, because the sport provides such great set pieces to chronicle. That is:

The static score. He's exactly four under and will be for the next ten minutes. And stage directions—Wide shot: the beautiful background. Zoom in: The lie. Precisely so many yards. For drama: perhaps a sensual toss of some grass in the air to gauge the wind. A learned discussion with the loyal valet, the caddy. The club choice. The stance (interminable). The shot. See it fly high. And there it lands, just so. And again: The static score. The lie. So many yards . . .

A writer can do so much more with that great stage blocking, whereas reconstructing something like, say, the bang-bang of an ice hockey goal can't ever catch up on the page to the speed of the pre-ceding whirlaway action. Then too, in general, all individual games are more dramatic to write about than team sports, because you can concentrate on the player, a hero, and not be blurred by the team around him. My late friend George Plimpton once allowed that a sport with a smaller ball makes for better writing than one with a larger ball, and for some odd reason that's been quoted as gospel ever since. Actually, I think it's the size of the uniforms rather than the size of the equipment that best informs sportswriting. A basketball player, in glorified underwear, is visible and ours to examine; a football player,

*Or "given" day, as, for some reason, we always are absolutely required to say in sport.

buried underneath armor and visor, is but numbered muscle mass. I suppose that's why football players do all that showing off after a good play: they're entertainers, but they're anonymous at the moment that matters, so they feel the need to take a bow.

Of course, sometimes, no matter how momentous the game—and never mind the particular attire or the size of the ball—there just isn't much to write home about. The first book I ever did was with Don Budge, the tennis player. Now, Don was famous for one thing above all. In 1938, he had won the Grand Slam—the Australian, French, British, and American championships. In fact, Don Budge had personally *invented* the Grand Slam. I could see this as my boffo first chapter, the epic opening to my very first book. Breathlessly, I said: "Tell me about it, Don."

"Well," he replied straightaway, "honestly, not a whole lot happened that year."

This took me aback some. "The whole Grand Slam year—1938? Nothing much happened?"

"Not really," he said. As teachers used to say to us, Don then put on his thinking cap. Finally he spoke again. "Well now, when I was at the French, I was at a dinner party and Pablo Casals was there, and he dedicated a song to me."

"Pablo Casals? The cellist?"

"Yes," Don said, and he smiled warmly at the memory of this one highlight of his fabulous Grand Slam year that would mean so much to tennis and tennis fans and readers of tennis everywhere when I began my inaugural book with Pablo Casals playing the cello.

So, sometimes you just have to take the tide whenever it goes out and ride with it. Luckily for me, though, Turnberry would be a writer's feast.

I adored the place, too, so much so that I took Carol there for an anniversary a few years later. Just to hear the piper play "Scotland, the Brave" at twilight is enough, thank you. But the whole setting is gloriously affecting, and after taking it in, I hooked up with Watson's caddie, one Alfie Fyles, who had caddied *to* (as they say over there) six Open champions. Alfie took me around the course, replaying for me every dueling shot. Therefore, all that was left was for me to get the two competitors to fill in their fond or excrutiating memories, how they had felt and what they might have said. Peace o' cake. But that quest turned out to be even more fascinating and instructive than the showdown itself had been.

I had never met Watson before, but he quickly accommodated my request, and although I would not say he was an easily forthcoming sort, Tom sat down with me, and, smoking Winstons, he began to blithely go through the highlights, embellishing as he went along and got more into it. He grinned when he remembered what he said to Nicklaus Sunday as they stood tied on the sixteenth tee: "This is what it's all about, isn't it?" And, Watson remembered, with relish, how Nicklaus had been astonished at such verbal bravado from the pretender, had no response, and could only force a smile in return.

Meanwhile, Nicklaus. I knew Jack, and had, in fact, done a properly adoring piece on him a few years previously when he had been named *Sports Illustrated*'s Sportsman of the Year. But, although perfectly polite, Jack kept putting me off, indicating, as well, that he really thought it was old history not worth going back over. Slowly it began to dawn on me that for all his many triumphs, it was still painful for such a champion to talk about a defeat—even one from long ago.

You would think I might have already figured out such a thing by then.

At last Nicklaus grew tired of my pestering him and, grudgingly, in that surprisingly high-pitched voice of his, said that if I'd come down to Miami, to the Doral, where he was going to play in a tournament, he'd give me some time on a practice day. But even then, it was a case of dragging it out of him. He couldn't bring himself to sit down with me and speak directly to the event he'd lost; rather, I was obliged to follow him to the putting green, where my conversation could take a subsidiary position to his practice, as I tagged along, scratching out notes.

Please understand, Nicklaus wasn't rude. In fact, I made it a point to remind him how incredibly gracious he had been after that torturous defeat nine years ago. But he didn't remember what he'd said to Watson or how he'd embraced him. He didn't remember that when he'd come in to dinner at Turnberry that night, the entire dining room had risen and cheered him, the loser, as affectionately as, later, the same people would cheer Watson. And then, incredibly, and even, finally, with a little irritation, he said, "Look, Frank, I couldn't even take you around that course."

I was truly taken aback. Maybe the greatest golf match ever, certainly the greatest, longest duel—the best against the best at their best, as I titled it—and he couldn't even remember Turnberry from some run-of-the-mill sunbelt PGA tour stop? I don't know. Either Jack had managed to put it all out of his mind or he was just fibbing because he didn't want to have to recite the agonizing chapter and verse for a pest with a pad and pencil who was bugging him on the practice green. Well, he added, after all, nobody generally went around asking him about the ones he lost. That should've been more obvious to me, too. We don't ask the champions to recall the bad weather; with them, we stick to the climate. We help them to put the inclement days behind them.

I thanked Jack and left him, he grateful for my departure. But, of course, I immediately remembered my interview with Watson a while before. It was still there, resting in the same notepad. When Tom had finished talking about the match itself (and, yes, emphasizing Nicklaus's graciousness), he had taken out another cigarette and, almost as if I weren't there any longer, begun to relive the aftermath. Oh my, you bet he remembered the dining room scene, and the sweet cheers, and then the champagne that had been sent to his room, and drinking it with his wife, and, without my prodding, he told me about looking out the window as the Scottish sun's rays finally went down, with him just taking it all in, holding the vision. His memory was absolutely vivid. Nicklaus couldn't even remember the damn course, but Watson had kept the whole impression in his mind's eye. He had won. Then, he said, he and his wife heard the piper down below, and that was when they both began to cry.

And when he told me that, Watson began to tear up. He let the cigarette lie in the ashtray. He sat there, crying. Foolishly, but because I was so moved, I said, "Tom, you're crying, you know." I thought maybe he would want to brush away the tears. But he didn't. He just smiled and, remembering the happiness, cried some more—"unashamedly," we sportswriters always are quick to add, because, I suppose, any (male) athlete crying is assumed to generally be, ipso facto, "shameful."

Ever since then, ever since I experienced the memories of that Turnberry with Jack Nicklaus and Tom Watson, I've always imagined that, despite what great athletes say, they relish more the victory and hurt more from the defeat than they are wont to let on to you or me.

14

BAWLMER, MERLIN, MY HAMETOWN

The hard part isn't that you can't go home again. The hard part is showing the ones who never left that the best part of you never left either.

"A Player for the Ages," *Sports Illustrated*, 1988

As I grew older I came to believe that my outlook had been affected simply because I came from Baltimore. I'm quite sure I would've been a somewhat different person—and a different sort of writer, as well—had I hailed instead from some swell other northeastern burg such as the one just down the road, our nation's capital, or, say, from up in the Hub. Certainly I would not have been the me I am had I come from the high-and-mighty Big Apple. (I've never been able to make up my mind about Philadelphia—whether it's a small Chicago or just a larger Baltimore.)

But given how and where Baltimore sat, a quick stop-and-go—"All aboard!"—that lay along the rails that connected the two great commercial and political centers of the world, I grew up infected by the defensive spirit of my city, the sense that we were an ugly duckling. At the same time, I was immensely proud of my birthplace, and, my, but Our Town was a wonderful place for a boy to learn to live.

There was, after all, a humility to Baltimore that was sweet and enriching; simply because Baltimore was, altogether, looked down on, we did not tolerate arrogance. I was raised—infused—with a distaste for the smug and high-hat. Indeed, the worst label that a Baltimorean could give you was *common*. Understand, this had no relationship to the ordinary, to the sacred American common man. Rather, to be common was to be rude and insensitive, thoughtless. As we used to say (hilariously), "Call me anything but late for dinner"—but, please, never call me common.

Christopher Morley, a journalist and the author of *Kitty Foyle*, passed a life rather like mine half a century before my own—growing up in Baltimore, then spending most of the rest of it as a writer in New York (well, he was a Rhodes scholar, but unlike me he was not a Lite Beer All-Star, so tit for tat). In the event, I came across this wonderful tribute he wrote to the happy youth that he enjoyed in Baltimore back at the beginning of the twentieth century: "To be deeply rooted in a place that has meaning is perhaps the best gift a child can have. If that place has beauty and a feeling of permanence, it may suggest to that child, unaware, that sense of identity with the physical earth—which is the humblest and happiest of life's institutions."

So it was, for me.

What especially hurt about being from Baltimore was the glory that it had lost. My city was, in that sense, one with my family, for we both had seen such better days. Into the middle of the nineteenth century, Baltimore had been a cosmopolitan jewel, gateway to Dixie, harbor to the world. It was hardly just Deford leather that was shipped out. Only New York City (and Brooklyn, next door) had a greater population. The mighty B&O Railroad steamed over the Alleghenies, carrying goods and civilization to the benighted West. Johns Hopkins Hospital cared, best, for humankind. It was in Baltimore that Samuel Morse took the whole world a step up from Gutenberg, punching out "What hath God wrought?"

Pipsqueak Washington, which merely got the message, was less than a quarter the size of our real metropolis, and, of course, it had been Baltimore that had saved the hide of Washington and the whole damn country when Fort McHenry bravely held off the marauding British after James Madison and his Dolley and the rest of the pusillanimous government had turned tail and fled the li'l burning capital . . . *The rocket's red glare, the bombs bursting in air / Gave proof through the night that our flag was still there.*

Yes! The *there* was flying over Baltimore!

But by the time I grew up, Baltimore was a tentative place, only a stream or two short of a backwater. It had become the quintessential branch town. The brand-new airport was lacking only one thing: airplanes; every respectable airline flew on to the Potomac. The harbor had become a Stygian tributary leading to a humdrum skyline that was dominated by a bizarre faux-Florentine building that was topped by a rendering of an antacid fizz bottle. (And wouldn't you just know: it was Bromo-Seltzer, the runner-up heartburn remedy, not the preeminent Alka-Seltzer.)

There was a void of leadership and imagination. I wrote once, in an article for *Smithsonian* magazine, that Baltimore was so bereft of distinguished citizens that, in the whole first half of the twentieth century, the only truly illustrious Americans to have been born there were two African-Americans who had managed to rise above their segregated confines: Thurgood Marshall and Billie Holiday.

That created a firestorm of local criticism. You idiot, DeFord— what about H. L. Mencken and Babe Ruth? As if I could forget that pair. But, of course, they had been born in the nineteenth century, in those waning moments of the city's belle epoque and its prominence.*

---

*I would have to amend my remarks now to note that Nancy Pelosi, my contemporary, was born in Baltimore in 1940, the daughter of the mayor, Tommy D'Alessandro, and thus she certainly qualifies now to stand with Mr. Justice Marshall and Ms. Holiday— although, as Ed Markey, the Massachusetts congressman, has noted, the former Speaker is a hybrid, "San Francisco on the inside, Baltimore on the outside."

Well, yes, Spiro Agnew grew up in Baltimore, too. And on one occasion I did meet with our esteemed thirty-ninth vice president. I was doing a story on Chick Lang, the man who had restored the Preakness to glory, and because Chick had worked with Agnew on his campaign for governor and idolized the man, I thought a quote from the vice president would be a nice touch. After deep negotiations with Agnew's minions, it was agreed that I would be allowed to visit with the great man for precisely fifteen minutes one morning, mindful that I would restrict my searching inquiries to the singular subject of the said Mr. Chick Lang. Agreed.

I was ushered into the vice president's office in the Executive Office Building. He looked, as ever, like a president—as was, in fact, supposed to be in the cards come 1976. Beware what you would behold: no one since Warren Harding had *looked* so much like a president. Agnew wore a gray tailored suit, white shirt, perfect tie, perfect pocket hankerchief. He grinned, greeting me warmly, then resumed sitting erectly behind a desk that was all but bereft of anything on it except for a bunch of various little elephant statuettes, gifts from grateful Republicans, that lined the back.

Right away, he told me how much he admired Chick Lang and what a fine fellow he was, what a gift to Baltimore and Maryland. Well, that was that, just what the doctor ordered, but I had my fifteen minutes, so I dragged it out with standard queries about any details, anecdotes, what have you. The vice president accommodated me. His PR secretary glanced at his watch. I figured it was time to go, but no, just as I prepared to rise from my seat, Agnew began to question me about myself and my own Baltimore heritage.

I settled back and explained that I had hailed from just inside the city line, and we discussed that familiar territory, where the Number Eleven bus snaked into the county. I knew he had begun his momentous climb up the political ladder by serving in the PTA nearby, only a few blocks from my house, and, feeling more comfortable now, I noted that I had once been thrown out of a sock hop at the Rogers Forge

Junior High for smoking. Might he have been that very chaperone? We tossed that around for a while. Yes, indeed, he might have been the very sock-hop sheriff to have ejected me.

Small world.

The PR man looked at his watch again.

But my new pal, the veep, and I were just getting warmed up. Hey: BFF. We started on who do you know and moved on to favorite Baltimore minutiae and civic characters. It was somewhere in here, half an hour or so since I had been escorted in for my fifteen-minute audience, that it struck me: the vice president of the United States of America had nothing to do. (Later I assumed he was just waiting for the bag man to drive over from Baltimore County with his regular payload of graft.) No, he was delighted to have some company to talk about familiar things. So, we chatted some more, until finally I decided that, although he might be at loose ends, I had better things to do. So I begged that I must take my leave and grab the shuttle back to New York. Only reluctantly did the vice president bid me a fond farewell, rising to shake my hand across the many stylish little elephants on his slate-clean desk.*

Baltimore has also been belittled simply because too many of us talked funny. It was (still is) a horribly grating nasal accent, sort of lispy, somehow produced because it was here where the harsh Bronx

---

*By coincidence, the only president I ever interviewed was Nixon, when he was just starting his public rehabilitation some years after his hurried departure from the White House. The sole, approved subject of our discussion was to be: Washington as a sports town. We met at his suite in the Waldorf Towers, and from the first, Nixon struck me as being as nervous as Agnew was at ease. And for God's sake, I wasn't going to ask him about anything more serious than the Redskins. Nixon played with a pack of matches the whole time, rather like Captain Queeg. There were three points he was determined to make: (1) When he had played college football at Whittier, a teammate had been a young black man and, notwithstanding, everybody got along hunky-dory, sports being a great leveler. OK. (2) He knew from memory the entire lineup of the 1929 Philadelphia Athletics, which he recited for me—this to establish his bona fides as a sports fan. OK. And: (3) Why was it that *Sports Illustrated* and the rest of the sporting press didn't devote more attention to bowling, because millions of Americans bowled? OK, I said I would look into it.

tones from the North crashed head-on into the softer hillbilly lilt moving up from the hollows of the Blue Ridge. All sorts of dictionaries have been written, trying to capture the accent and its spelling. Here's my own sample:

> Bawlmer, air hametown, is in the state of Merlin, which is bounted onna ees by the Lanick Ayshun and onna souf by air Merkin captil, Warshin, Deecee. You better bleeve it, hon.

Funny as that sounds, hon, the Bawlmer accent was a seriously debilitating measure of class, for as I caught on very early, a person's standing in the community could be measured quite accurately by how thick his accent was. It was said in England that an egalitarian society could never be achieved so long as people spoke Cockney; so too in Baltimore. The accent was no better for mobility than was it sweet to the ear.

Moreover, as I discovered, when I grew older and moved abroad in the land, my Baltimore was reknowned for only three other distinctions: (1) crabs, (2) the white marble steps of the city's endless cavalcade of row houses, and (3) the Block—which was actually several blocks of Baltimore Street, that tawdry entrepot of sin: sailors' bars, girlie shows, and associated nether establishments, such as the one where I obtained my tattoo. The most famous denizen of the Block— indeed, of all Baltimore (at least until my good buddy Spiro Agnew came along)—was Blaze Starr, proprietress of the Two O'Clock Club, an intriguing lady whose business acumen equaled the size of her magnificent bosom.*

---

*I am not much for autographs, but I treasure an eclectic quartet from Baltimoreans: Brooks Robinson, on a letter; Johnny Unitas, on a football; Charles Carroll of Carrollton, a signer of the Declaration of Independence, on a £100 note dated 24 January 1772; and Blaze Starr, on a glossy topless photo inscribed to me "With love and lust."

So my Baltimore was provincial and pinched and insecure. And as for sports, it's no wonder we had no good sportswriters, for we had no sports. Sixth-largest city in the nation we may have been, but we had not had a major-league baseball franchise since New York had spirited the Orioles away in 1902. The one national sporting event we did claim was Chick Lang's Preakness, which is always described as "the second jewel in the Triple Crown," but at ratty old Pimlico, it was more like a zircon, glistening but for a moment in the spring sun, for as soon as the race was run, even before night shades fell, the racing aristocracy would clear back out to New York.

In those years, the National Football League was still small beer, but even then, Baltimore didn't have a franchise. It did get a team in a budding pro basketball league in 1947, but that sport was then microscopic, and the Baltimore Bullets played in a filthy little arena which dared to call itself the "Coliseum"; old players told me that they tended to eschew showers there in order to avoid the manifold cat droppings.

Of course, when I was growing up, rail travel limited movement, so that many American cities a far piece from the East didn't have big-league franchises—Los Angeles, to start with—but at least they all had big-time college teams to cheer for. Not Baltimore. The only college games that mattered in Baltimore were those played by plucky little Johns Hopkins University in lacrosse, a game that, except for bits of Long Island and some Indian reservations, barely registered in the forty-eight states.

Now, only forty miles down Route 1 there was this place called Washington, where the Washington Senators played major-league baseball and the Washington Redskins played NFL football, *but nobody in Baltimore ever went to Washington. Nobody in Baltimore cared about Washington.* Occasionally you hear about how Baltimore is to Washington as Oakland is to San Francisco or Brooklyn is to New York, but that simply has never been so. Washington could have been Budapest,

Hungary, for all we cared. Guaranteed, we sure didn't give a rat's ass about Washington's teams.

Barry Levinson, the movie director, is another Baltimorean contemporary. Meeting for the first time a few years ago, discussing our growing up, we discovered many parallel experiences. Then I mentioned to him that a friend of my father's had once taken Daddy and me down to Washington, to see a Senators' major-league game at old Griffith Stadium. Barry looked at me oddly, cocked his head, and expressed utter astonishment. "I *never* heard of *anyone* ever doing that before," he declared.

You just didn't go to Washington. You didn't even go to College Park, where the University of Maryland was located and played big-time college sports. Oh yes, some Baltimoreans might matriculate there, although it was then a dubious citadel of learning—the football coach, whose name was "Curly," had been promoted to president—but the university was in a Washington suburb, and, thus, although we might nominally cheer on the Terps, we kept our distance from the entire capital orbit.

As a consequence of this singular, utter lack of a significant athletic presence in a major American municipality—you will not believe it, but it is so—while I was growing up, the single most renowned sustaining athletic figure in Baltimore was a bowler. And it was a woman. And she wasn't even a real bowler. In Baltimore, we did not bowl tenpins like everybody else in the country. No, just as we almost alone played lacrosse, we almost alone bowled duckpins.

Duckpins are scaled-down versions of the real thing; they fly like ducks when they are hit, thus . . . I sometimes made money as a pin boy, working at a duckpin establishment on York Road, and I can attest that those little buggers could really fly.

But that's what we in Baltimore had to boast about in sport. Duckpins. There was even a television show, *Duckpins for Dollars.* And whereas the championship male bowlers in town were pretty equal, there was only one Queen of Duckpins. No, it was not Ethel Dize or Alva Brown or Min Weisenborn. It was . . .

Toots Barger.

Toots won a dozen world championships ("world" essentially meaning "greater Baltimore" in this context) and was forever setting records. The Triple A Oriole players—Bob Repass, Al Cihocki, and other of our diamond immortals—would come and go. The Preakness was there for but a day, and the Hopkins lacrosse "all-Americans" would graduate and disappear. Only the Queen of Duckpins was there, triumphant, year after year.

Toots Barger was sports in Baltimore.

And then we became a Big-League City, and it was transforming. Oh, there was still a small-town intimacy to it. Not far from where I lived, on York Road, there was Moses's Sunoco station, and it was nothing to go by and see a couple of the Colts hanging out there, kicking tires. Even when he was a star on the Orioles, MVP-to-be, Boog Powell lived in a row house, just beyond center field. He'd hit a home run, knock in a few more, then amble home from the game, sit on his stoop, and have crabs and beers with his working-class neighbors.*

Things were so genuinely casual back then that I personally worked on the grounds crew at Memorial Stadium. My cousin Will Browne and I were going to the game one night, and a guy came up and said, "Hey, wanna work on the grounds crew?" Just like that. He ran the grounds crew. We'd sit in a little extra dugout right next to the Orioles dugout. You'd get paid a dollar at the end of the game—and another dollar every time Jupiter Pluvius arrived and obliged us to actually spread the tarp. Somehow, I thought it was probably organized differently at Yankee Stadium.

But the larger point is that, by getting the Colts and Orioles, we were the first new city to step up to the majors, and what I saw then as a boy with air own Balmer Colts first and then air Birds, I have seen

---

*I've always found it symbolic of the city's modest pretense, too, that the greatest two Oriole heroes were Brooks Robinson and Cal Ripken. One was best known for his glove—fielding!—and the other just for showing up to work every day.

again and again—how it has affected so many American towns that longed to be lumped in some way with New York and Chicago and Los Angeles. Towns that wanted to be *big league*. Baltimore was the first, going into the NFL. Then Milwaukee into the National League and then Kansas City and the Twin Cities and on and on down through Jacksonville and Nashville. Oklahoma City is the most recent, moving into the NBA, into that holy metropolitan pantheon. It is the signal triumph for an American municipality to be a big-league town.

Still, I saw Toots Barger in her heyday, and you didn't.

15

GEE WHIZ

Never is ignorance bliss more than when it involves bliss.
Love and Infamy, 1993

While the prolonged athletic torpor of my Baltimore was unusual, it was also the case that in the country at whole sport remained incredibly static. Certainly, no other twentieth-century American institution changed so little over so prolonged a period. Oh, sport became larger and more prominent as the decades passed, and when the Depression blunted its economics, radio helped make up for that as its new evangelist, but the big picture barely wobbled on the wall. A sportswriter, such as Grantland Rice, entering the profession as a young man at the turn of the twentieth century, might just as well have been given a card that said: Steady As She Goes, Hold the Course.

While, say, show business went from music halls to vaudeville to nickelodeons to the follies to movies to radio to sound movies to Technicolor and to television, in sports there was no real difference between what mattered in 1900 and 1950. Everything was played in all the exact same places, and there was a distinct pecking order. Baseball ruled absolutely supreme, then came championship boxing fights and the big horse races. College football came next down the ladder and, apart from baseball, was the only team sport that merited serious attention.

In fact, in terms of coverage, the sport that came right after college football was baseball in its winter hibernation. The "hot stove league," it was called, and the columns of possible trades and can't-miss prospects and retold tales of loving lore far exceeded any coverage of sporting events that might actually be *played* in the wintertime. The major winter sporting event in many cities was the town's stop on the Rubber Chicken Circuit, its own baseball banquet, where awards would be handed out and hearty stories shared, before, assuredly, "a galaxy of stars." Back then, instead of working out with a personal trainer at their in-home gymnasium all winter, baseball players hunted and fished, drank and smoked, picked up walking-around money at some mundane sales job, and, if lucky enough, received invitations to banquets.

For many frosty weeks, in the manner of little children looking forward to Santa's arrival, sportswriters counted down to spring training, when pitchers and catchers would report. In every culture, there are the religious and cultural prologues to the winter's end. In the American sports pages, spring training entered such spiritual company. It was not uncommon for sports editors to send a photographer over to the frozen stadium to take pictures of the team's equipment trunks, just sitting there, when they were packed and ready to be sent south along with (honestly) "the advance guard," which would be heading off (for sure) on the Orange Blossom Special. At a time before plane travel for the lowly multitudes, when all major-league franchises were located in the North, the coming of the Grapefruit League was proof that God would indeed warm the earth again, as surely as the selfish holdouts would ink their pacts and join the fold.

In 1974, I wrote:

Hollywood died when the denizens of the silver screen stopped taking milk baths and started professing to be just folks. Tinker Bell could be sustained only if we expressed a loud belief in her species. And baseball, like the ocean liner, could hold its place only as long as people accepted the proposition that getting there was half the fun. All those stock reasons to explain why baseball lost its iron grip on the public—too slow, not enough

action, not good for televising—just add up to so much bunk.
The explainers simply have forgotten how vital spring training was to the illusion. When American turned to hockey and
basketball instead of re-pledging allegiance to the fantasies of
the Grapefruit League, the Tinker Bell went out of baseball.

But for so long sportswriters did prefer the dream of spring to
the reality of basketball and hockey. When, in 1938, Paul Gallico was
asked why he was giving up sportswriting to flee across the Atlantic
to the solitude of the Devonshire countryside, there to try to write
novels, he famously replied only: "February." There was just nothin'
cookin' from the bowl games on New Year's Day till the Grapefruit
League opened, and neither, surely, would there ever be anything
new to fill those athletic doldrums of winter.

So let us recap the ranking of the way it forever was ordained:

Baseball
Boxing and horse racing
College football
Hot Stove League

In the next tier came golf and tennis, then track and field and
perhaps a soupçon of swimming in Olympic years. While some of
those runners and swimmers were female women's sports were so
far down the certified list that only segregated games played by black
athletes merited less press attention. College basketball did begin
to fill up some space, but without arousing much enthusiasm. Paul
Gallico opined that "there was something vaguely sexual" about the
ball dropping through the net. Word of the National Hockey League
'twas barely a whisper except in a handful of scattered northeastern
precincts.

There was a brief enthusiasm for six-day bicycle racing. It passed.
There was no soccer. None.

Certainly it never occurred to any sportswriter to feel guilty that only America had no taste for the "beautiful (*sic*) game" that so many strange foreigners played with the wrong limbs.

NASCAR did not exist, although auto racing was thrown the bone of Memorial Day, when the Indianapolis 500 was contested.

That was it, year after year.

All else was, well . . . bush—that word, then profligately employed by grizzled sportswriters to describe just about everything in sports except that which had forever been inscribed on the approved athletic ecclesiastical calendar/atlas. There were bush towns, of course, and bush events and bush promoters and bush leagues. If any American sportswriter had ever bothered to go to the World Cup, it would surely have been labeled as bush. So too the countries where it was played. Bush countries.

Not surprisingly, the men who rose to the top of the profession may or may not have been good writers, but they were, first and foremost, the high priests who had grown up in this becalmed cosmos and their natural bent was to be suspicious of change, to defend the status quo and to display their journalistic superiority by taking a wide berth of all that was bush.

There were, though, two competing attitudinal schools that grew up. By far the larger was the Gee Whiz Academy, where, of course, Grantland Rice was the paterfamilias. Reporters of this stripe were disposed to treat sport tenderly, turning a blind eye to even some of its most obvious flaws. The name was not facetious. It was actually given by a sports editor at the *San Francisco Examiner,* who advised his underlings that he wanted readers to gleefully cry out "gee whiz" whenever they read the *Examiner's* breathtaking game stories.

The other camp, much smaller, was the Aw Nuts Gang. These cynical fellows tended to take sports a great deal more skeptically. The most illustrious representatives were W. O. McGeehan, Ring Lardner, and Westbrook Pegler, who once even dared refer to Rice's upbeat offerings as "pantywaist stuff."

It confounded almost everyone that Rice and Lardner were bosom buddies. The sunny king and the sourpuss and their wives even had vacation houses next door to each other in East Hampton, where the four of them constantly spent their evenings together enjoying cocktails and dinner and then playing bridge. If that wasn't enough, the two couples traveled all over together, mixing business and pleasure. Mardi Gras was on the schedule every year, for sure, even in the years when it came late and interrupted spring training.

The notorious episode that must have vexed the relationship, and that, in fact, sorely tested the whole profession, was the "Black Sox" scandal of 1919, when Chicago players fixed the World Series. It was such a botched, haphazard job that it was almost an open secret that the favored American League champions were in the tank. After all, gee whiz, fixed regular-season major-league games had long been a common, if guarded, secret among the cognoscenti. So with the World Series, too: mum's the word. However, from the start, Hugh Fullerton, a most respected writer from the *New York Evening World,* enrolled the great, beloved pitcher Christy Mathewson to sit next to him in the press box, and mark, in red, all those plays that appeared suspicious. The honorable Mathewson, a victim of gassing the previous year in France, dutifully bloodied Fullerton's scorecard.

Moreover, when the Series shifted from Cincinnati to Chicago, Lardner, in his cups, staggered through the White Sox railroad car, and to the tune of the popular "I'm Forever Blowing Bubbles" sang, "I'm forever blowing ball games." Worse, the embarrassed players, the crooked and straight ones alike, didn't try to silence him. Everybody knew what was up.* But Rice, like virtually all his colleagues, never wrote a doubtful word to enlighten his faithful millions. Throughout the Series, only Fullerton dared voice veiled suspicions in his copy. Then, two months later he wrote a long expository article, and although it did not specifically claim that Chicago had thrown the Series,

*Or, as we say now, "going down." When and why did up become down?

it did maintain that baseball was ridden with corruption. The piece was such a rare and shocking denouncement of the national pastime that the *World* forced him to tone down his charges, and no Chicago newspaper would even dare print such blasphemy. The *Sporting News,* aghast, jumped in and said that it was all just one big misunderstanding, that the fault was with Jewish gamblers, who had simply planted rumors of a fix in order to get better odds.

In due time, of course, the truth did out, but if the reputation of the sporting press was damaged by its failure to dig out the truth, that quickly passed, for soon the so-called Golden Age of Sports arrived, as the good times afield rolled in with flappers and speakeasies. It was incumbent to cheer—to, after all, *roar* in the twenties—and America could not get enough of its athletic heroes. Sportswriters obliged, venerating the stars: Ruth and Grange and Dempsey and Jones and Tilden. Clearly, veneration sold newspapers. Nobody wanted to know that the Babe overindulged or that Dempsey was ducking a black fighter or that Big Bill was so sad and repressed that he would someday be imprisoned as a pedophile.

However, by gushing over its idols and employing its affected sportswriterese, the profession eventually paid a price. It became too well known as a home for hacks. That wasn't the all of it, either. As I came into the business, I learned that in some cities, it was the local custom for my brethren to be on the take. If you had, say, like a 'rasslin bill or a donkey baseball game coming to town, and you wanted publicity for this enterprise, then it was expected that you would grease the sports editor's palm, as well perhaps as the tobacco-browned same of the assigned reporter. One time, in Florida, when Al Capone was somehow connected to the promotion of a fight, he held a press party and scattered $100 bills about for the boxing writers to scoop up at their leisure. (They obliged.) When Red Smith was first assigned to the sports section on a St. Louis newspaper, the only two questions that the managing editor asked him were if he knew much about football (it was autumn) and whether or not he'd take $10 from a boxing promoter. When I became a real sportswriter myself and ventured into the hinterlands for a story, it was still not altogether unusual for a promoter or PR man to offer to provide me with the town's finest available distaff companionship in my motel room. On the cuff, of course.

Sportswriting was still in something of a netherworld. I got in just before the sun came up.

Years later, I remember standing at the bar talking to Pat Putnam, who had become a much-respected boxing writer for *Sports Illustrated*. I don't remember what prompted it, but all of a sudden Pat started talking, in a melancholy way, about, years before, covering boxing for the *Miami Herald*. There had been a big bout coming to town, and, Pat told me, the promoter approached him about ladling out more ink, laying it on thick in the *Herald* about what a fabulous match this was going to be.

"I was dead broke, Frank. We owed a lot of bills. I can't tell you how tempting it was."

It was obvious Pat wanted me to ask him what happened, so I did. "Well, did you take it?"

"No, I didn't."

"Then maybe that's why you're here now."

"I'd like to think so," he said.

So, yes, virtue could be its own reward.

And yes, if sportswriting could receive, as a whole genre, few accolades, it did include, at least for a while, writers who would subsequently gain considerable reputations away from the arena. Lardner was the first, but men like Gallico, Pegler, Damon Runyon, Heywood Broun, and James Reston would all start out in journalism writing sports. So the field was certainly not without its gentlemen and scholars. In one movie, Spencer Tracy was cast as a sportswriter opposite Katharine Hepburn, and we couldn't ask for anything much better than that.

In fact, there developed quite a respectable parish of sportswriting. In many towns, the sports editor/columnist of the dominant newspaper was by far the best-known local journalist, a revered, even benevolent figure, who was sort of the de facto head of the chamber of commerce for sports in the community. San Diego even named a stadium after such a fellow—Jack Murphy. Can you imagine that today? In Boston, say, Dan Shaughnessy Park or Bob Ryan Stadium?

So sportswriters grew into a very discrete journalistic breed. It wasn't just that we covered the fun stuff. Institutionally there was probably more real camaraderie to be found among sportswriters, because more than our more serious colleagues, we traveled together and then regularly gathered to write en masse in the press box. As if to signify our oneness, we are the only journalists whose subject is part of our title: *sportswriters*. All the others are separated from their subject: editorial writers; movie critics; war correspondents; even, yes, sports *editors*. But sportswriters: one word.

The assumption, I suppose, is that we do not stand apart and clinically observe so well as our more respected brethren who better keep their distance from their subjects and are properly, clinically *objective*, and whose titles are therefore worthy of a space bar.

I came in after airplanes became the accepted mode of travel, but the tales of writers—especially the baseball reporters—caravanning on trains with the players they covered were still fresh and legion. It's hard to expect that a reporter could remain distant and objective from the subjects he was covering if he joked with them, ate with them, drank with them, and played cards with them on trains crisscrossing the Northeast, day in and day out, for months each year. Upon alighting, writers and players even visited whorehouses together. Talk about *embedded*. So every sportswriter had to pretty much put away his notebook when the sleeper pulled out of the depot.

There is a famous story, which really does sound more accurate than apocryphal, of two Yankee writers, playing bridge with two ballplayers, when the door to the car opened, and a giggling blonde, in dishabille, appeared, dashing by, as Babe Ruth, in considerable disarray himself, brandishing a Scotch bottle, stumbled after her.

"See anything?" said one writer.

"Two no trump," replied the other, playing a card.

It was a long, hot, and humid trip, New York to St. Louis. Fellowship ruled.

Meanwhile, the leading men of the sports page, the columnists, would often drive south together to the Grapefruit League, reassembling thereafter for the regular progression of prime events that began with the Masters, which, indeed, had been scheduled purposely to catch the writers coming north. It was a well-ordered universe, invariably ending in Pasadena or Miami or New Orleans for a New Year's bowl game—a pure routine, laid out the same, year after year, neatly scheduled, unlike other news, which can take place at inconvenient times in unexpected places. Really, only the World Series site was not booked in advance (and, what the hell, you could figure on New York most Octobers). Las Vegas hadn't been conjured up, so almost all the big fights were in New York, *the* Garden or *the* Stadium. Maybe Chicago in extreme circumstances. Everything else was pretty much set in stone. And there were certainly no playoffs.

Indeed, it was obligatory for sportswriters to lampoon playoffs when they began to pop up. Playoffs were hokey, tainted, not of the ordained way of life. They were bush. The NBA, it was harrumphed, "played seventy-two games to eliminate the Knicks." Like so, sportswriters had previously thought night baseball was Satan's work when it was introduced, and they were chary of anyone, like Bill Veeck, who, sacrilegiously, dared try to marry sports with showbiz. That was bush.

Late in September 1964, when the Phillies appeared to have the pennant locked up, they suddenly went into a death spiral, and, as Maynard Parker, who would be my editor when I worked for *Newsweek* many years later, used to say, it was time to "scramble the jets." As the third-string baseball writer at *Sports Illustrated*, I was hastily dispatched from Cleveland, where I had been covering the Davis Cup, to go directly to Cincinnati, where the Phillies were desperately trying to right the ship.

I had barely covered the sport since spring training and knew no one, so, there in the ancient press box at old Crosley Field, I sat alone. An early autumn cold snap had descended upon the Ohio valley, and the place was freezing. Because the Phillies had apparently run away with the pennant, nobody in Cincinnati had been prepared for games that meant anything, so, given the nasty weather as well, almost no one showed up.

But like me, all sorts of other reporters had been parachuted in at the eleventh hour, including three or four young hotshots, who were being celebrated (or despised) in the business for taking the old Aw Nuts Gang to new, modern heights (or depths). These fellows were hip and snide and full of themselves, the new wave sportswriters. I didn't know any of them at the time, but I wished I did. I was like a high school freshman trying not to let the cool seniors know that I was listening in on them, hanging on to their every bitchin' word.

They had been tabbed the "Chipmunks" by censorious elders, because one of them had prominent teeth and all of them chattered like a bunch of the cute rodents on a humorous record by Stan Freberg. The sportswriter Chipmunks were trying to top each other in putting down the choking Phillies, and the boring ball game, when not complaining about the goddamn cold.

Also just arrived at the Crosley Field icebox was the one and only Jimmy Cannon, star sports columnist for the Hearst chain, out of the *New York Journal-American*. Cannon, a lifelong bachelor, lived alone in a hotel, ate out all the time, and was, it seemed, bereft of much life beyond his column, which consumed him. In 1964 he was fifty-five, but his Irish puckishness was faded, his shortness had gone to squat, and—in the kind of language that he would employ—he looked scuffed up and worn, like a pair of wingtips that hadn't seen a buffing for a while. In fact, he'd be dead at sixty-three, and then pretty much forgotten, which is a damn shame, because he was absolutely the one columnist around then whom you could mention in the same breath as Red Smith. Jimmy Cannon was an original.

Like so many other of us writers I admired his stuff immensely. He knew sports, but he prided himself on his writing. In fact, it was he who named the sports department the "toy shop." Statistics were also just then coming into vogue, starting to overwhelm the written word on sports pages. When Cannon saw Leonard Shapiro of the *New York Post* arrive in the press box one day with a briefcase, he snapped, "Whatdya got in there, Leonard: decimal points?" Looking back, that was absolutely prescient, the leitmotif for what would happen to the craft.

In Cincinnati, in 1964, though, words still reigned and Jimmy was still at the top of his game; he still sold newspapers, too, earning something like $1,000 to $1,500 a week, by far the best pay in the business, for doing it. Cannon had been a war correspondent and he wrote very masculine prose; he liked, in fact, to be associated with Ernest Hemingway, although he was more usually deemed an heir to Damon Runyon. "Joe Louis is a credit to his race," he inscribed once, most famously. The pregnant pause was there, clearly, on the page, so he needed no ellipses. "The human race."

Cannon also had created an inspired irregular column called "Nobody Asked Me, But . . . ," which allowed him to express wonderfully colorful and bizarre opinions about sports and the associated life he encountered. He had a fabulous eye and his juxtapositions were priceless.

OK, a few of his typical Nobody Asked Me, Buts:

"I can't ever remember staying for the end of a movie where the actors wore togas."

"Guys who use other people's coffee saucers for ashtrays should be banned from public places."

"Women aren't embarrassed when they buy men's pajamas, but a man buying a nightgown acts as though he were dealing with a dope peddler."

"Fishing, with me has always been an excuse to drink."

"It's almost impossible for a girl to be homely if she wears a
    gardenia in her hair."

And, obviously, in a moment of personal conflict:

"A sportswriter is entombed in a prolonged boyhood."

But, physician heal thyself: back to Crosley Field, where the all-
important Phillies-Reds game passed before us, even as the clash of
generational sportswriter cultures cut the frigid air in the press box.
As Cannon stewed, the Chipmunks kept cracking wise. Sitting alone,
at the end of a row, I kept my counsel, staring ahead at the action on
the field, pretending not to hear (let alone to break a smile at) what
these humorists were hooting about. But then, it was easy for me to
appear to be concentrating, because I had just met the girl I would
marry, and I realized I was falling headfirst into love, and I could think
about Carol to take my mind off the cold.

Mr. Cannon took this heartsick woolgathering of mine for pure
devotion to the game and our profession. He was sitting by himself
in the row above me, looking down upon the field over my shoulder,
as he sipped cup after cup of coffee. He had been off booze for years
and drank so much coffee he could fit comfortably into one of those
Swedish detective stories. At first, I only heard him mutter at the
profane Chipmunks. "Watch the fucking game," he half-whispered
to himself.

I stared ahead, trying to remain inconspicuous, figuring he might
already be jotting down a note on me for next week's "Nobody Asked
Me." Maybe: "A quiet kid who sits alone in a press box ought to look
for a new dodge." Something like that. But at last, when another inning
ended, and I rose to get a cuppa hot java for myself, he engaged me,
as a worthy colleague of the same right temperament. "You'd think
some guys would pay more attention to the game," he said.

I nodded in agreement.

"It's a big fucking game."

"It sure is," I replied.

That prompted Mr. Cannon to look out over the stands and raise his hands in wonder. "So where the hell is everybody? Look at this crowd."

"Well, you know, it's cold and nobody—"

"You'd think they'd know how big a game it is." It was clear to me, from his tone, that the failure of Cincinnatians to show up this evening was a personal affront to Jimmy Cannon. Goddamn it, he had come all this way.

A few seats over, the Chipmunks cackled again, prompting Mr. Cannon to shake his head in utter dismay. In consolation, I asked him if he could use another coffee, and he certainly could.

When I returned and handed him his cup, he put a wry smile on his face. "Lemme tell you something," he said, and when I nodded and waited expectantly, he spoke as if he were typing the words out on copy paper: "When I woke up at my hotel this morning, I realized I had a hard-on."

I don't know how I responded to that. I mean, talk about "Nobody Asked Me, But. . . ." Then his expression grew more thoughtful.

"But after a moment, I just tucked it away." And I dutifully watched as he pantomined this action. "And then I said, Jimmy, you're just a big-league guy in a bush-league town."

16

BEAUTY AND THE BEASTS

Most street fighters are little guys. Big guys grow up figuring nobody will challenge them, so they don't learn how to fight. Big guys break up fights. Little guys are the ones who learn to fight because they figure they better.
　　　　"The Boxer and the Blonde," *Sports Illustrated*, 1985

Being something of a frustrated ham, I was especially delighted, in the summer of 1980, when I got a call asking me if I'd be interested in doing a commercial for Miller Lite Beer. The campaign, which had been steamrollering along for seven years, was fantastically popular, featuring, for the most part, out-to-pasture athletes of my vintage, who argued about the product's greater attribute, screaming in counterpoint, "Tastes great!" or "Less filling!"

The commercials were original and funny, and they not only had made Miller Lite the second-best-selling beer in the land, after mighty Budweiser itself, but had virtually invented the low-calorie beer category. As numerous as beer drinkers might be, it is one hearty cohort of males who dominate the market. Specifically, 80 percent of all beer in the United States is consumed by 20 percent of the drinkers. If you don't reach that crowd of beer bellies, you don't sell beer, and before Lite's ad agency had hit upon the idea of having broken-down old athletes—who were called the Lite Beer All-Stars—push the product, beer drinkers had dismissed light beer as sissy stuff. "Everything you ever wanted in a beer . . . and less" changed all that forever.

Part of the charm of the commercials was that the athletes—many of whom had been genuine champions—made fun of themselves. It absolutely astonished me, then, when I made the commercial, that a couple of distinguished colleagues asked me if, by appearing in such a vulgar divertissement, I wasn't denigrating our noble sportswriting profession, rolling poor Granny Rice over in his grave. Excuse me, you had every bad stereotype being flaunted: big, black guys acting tough; stupid jocks acting stupid; a blonde with big boobs playing dumb; even an umpire acting blind. And sportswriting's reputation is going to be tarnished?

Besides, it was a money grab.

On the appointed day when I was to shoot the commercial, I went into New York and met one of my costars, "Marvelous" Marv Throneberry. He had obtained that nickname, facetiously, when he'd become the face of the woebegone 1962 Mets. Likewise, it was Marv's role on the All-Stars to portray himself as an incompetent. In his debut commercial, Madison Avenue had been appalled that the script actually dared to suggest potential harm for the product, having Marv opine: "If I do for Lite what I did for baseball, I'm afraid that sales may go down."

Marv had no compunction about playing the oaf. He was a sweet guy, not dumb, but guileless. One of the first stories he volunteered to tell me, with great delight, was about the time, at the Waldorf-Astoria, when he got up to go to the bathroom in the middle of the night, sleepily opened the door, and then, as it closed behind him, realized he was standing not in the bathroom, but in the corridor. Naked. "What did you do?" I asked, breathless.

"I just waited for someone," he replied, shaking his head.

"God, it must've been awful."

Marv shook his head. "Well, it was. Remember, I really had to take a piss."

When we met at our hotel to head over to the bar where we were going to tape the spot, Marv asked me why I was carrying a garment bag. I explained that somebody from the agency had told me to bring several sports jackets, so the wardrobe people could pick the best one for the screen. "No, no," Marv said. "If they don't like what you have on, they'll give you a jacket, and after you've been under the hot lights they have to let you keep it. I got one musta cost $75."

So, I ran back to my room, selected the jacket I thought was least likely to fill the bill, and left the others in the closet. Sure enough, when I got to the bar, the wardrobe lady clucked disapproval at my jacket and put me into a lovely brown Harris tweed number, which became a prominent part of my fashion statement. Marv literally stage-winked.

The commercial itself was easy: Me standing at the bar next to the third member of the ensemble, who was Billy Martin. This particular year, he was managing the Oakland A's—Billy Ball: remember? You never quite knew what you were going to get with Martin, but it was well before cocktail hour when we shot the commercial, and he arrived on time and was most genial, perfectly happy to be the conceited fall guy in the script.

I Barrymored the opening line: "I've had to write some tough things about some tough guys. But there's one guy I can't write anything tough about." And then I went on, explaining how I'd brought a Lite Beer for a "renowned, yet humble man," as Billy gave a proud thumbs-up for himself. Aha! But then the drama heightened, the camera view widened, and there, revealed, was Marv, the surprise hero, whom I saluted by studiously reaching right past Billy to toast Marvelous with my brewski.

It's a take—not the best of the Lite Beer oeuvre, not the worst.

But, even better, Miller soon invited me to be an accredited member of the All-Star team. I inked my pact and joined the fold. I'd give a few speeches, on those rare occasions when someone wanted a more serious, *literary* All-Star, and make other eclectic appearances. Carol and I went on a Lite Beer cruise to the Caribbean where we had to run in three-legged races; I judged a chili contest. Every couple of years or so the entire All-Star troupe would assemble in Milwaukee for a beer seminar, learning how it was brewed, what exactly hops is, how to pour a pilsner correctly—that kind of heavy inside-baseball beer stuff. Best of all, though, now I qualified to be in the annual alumni commercial, when the entire ensemble gathered to shoot a minute-long extravaganza.

I was a little worried when we first mustered, unsure how the old jocks might take it, having a sportswriter smack in their midst. I quickly found I had nothing to fear, especially since I had known some of the guys back when they were active, and they had let on that I wasn't subversive. Actually, the All-Stars didn't care if the devil himself was in their midst, as long as you didn't blow your lines and drag the shooting on. Since I was strictly a spear-carrier in the alumni commercial, my lines were restricted to either "Tastes great!" or "Less filling!" I was not a problem in this regard.

The one guy who had the most difficulty with his lines was Bubba Smith. One time—honest to God—the line that Bubba blew was his own name. The All-Stars were supposed to be voting for the most popular of their cast, and when Bubba reached into Mickey Spillane's fedora and pulled out the victor's name, he said: "Says here the winner is . . ." And then he stalled, unable to remember that it was he. It broke up all assembled.

Another time, Dick Butkus told me, when Bubba and Butkus were shooting a commercial on a golf course, the conceit being that golf was a more difficult game than football, the line Bubba was supposed to deliver, as they strolled down the fairway, was: "Yeah, it's a lot easier hittin' a quarterback than a little white ball." Only time and time again, what came out of Bubba's mouth was: "Yeah, it's a lot easier hittin' a little white quarterback."

But then, when I thought about it, it wasn't surprising that the All-Stars accepted me so courteously. They were, by definition, nice guys. If you were looking to make appealing commercials, well then, find appealing has-beens. The big, rough football players, like Matt Snell and Ben Davidson and Buck Buchanan, were often the nicest.

If you're big and tough, you don't have to act big and tough. A lot of the All-Stars didn't even drink much beer. As a group, they could get a little loud, but, all things considered, they were pretty well behaved. Martin got drunk one night and was hysterical about some woman or other and melodramatically threatened to kill himself, but that was about the height of the histrionics, and big, soothing Boog Powell—the nicest guy on any team he was ever on—got Billy to settle down, and we all had another beer, and life went on.

The All-Stars really were like a team, too. They grouped just as you would expect, with the guys from the premier team sports—football, basketball, baseball—tending to hang out together, like the cool guys in high school, while the more exotics (like me, a pool shark, a surfer, a bowler, and assorted wild-life types) plied the fringes of the dynamic.

When we would board the bus to head to location, it was downright anthropological, because the guys would choose the precise seats on the bus exactly as I knew they must've taken them when they were riding their old real team buses. On team charters—any team, any sport—the coach or manager takes the first seat on the right next to the door, and sure enough, that's where Red Auerbach always plunked himself down on the All-Star bus. Then, at the other extreme, the back of the bus: that's where the rowdy wisenheimers sat, talking loud, cackling, trying to top each other. Bob Uecker, always in character as a wise guy, would take the central seat, back row, and be the loudest naughty boy.

The quieter guys filled up the rows in the middle of the bus. Lee Meredith, the Doll, would always sit with Mickey Spillane, who was her leading man in the commercials she was featured in. John Madden was the one All-Star who invariably sat quietly, by himself, reading a book; this was, of course, in complete contrast to how he was cast, as a frantic, arm-swinging, out-of-control nutcase coach. Even in the midst of shooting, when there was a lull, I'd look over, and there John would be, hunkered down, reading.

This is not to say that all of us wouldn't regress to the puerility normally associated with men in teams. One time I caught Madden surreptitiously pinching Lee Meredith's bottom, and then neatly turning away, so that when Lee pivoted around to catch the randy culprit, Madden was a choirboy, looking away, while she thought she had nabbed Tommy Heinsohn, red-handed.

Lee was a great sport and a great lady, and despite her va-va-vroom figure—she was best known for playing Ulla, the Swedish knockout in the movie of *The Producers*—she was invariably treated with dignity, more like everybody's kid sister than a sexpot. All the guys knew that, when not performing as a bombshell, she was a refined, happily married Jersey housewife. Besides, as Lee clinically explained to me, she was fully shaped by the time she was twelve, and therefore treated her endowments casually, as just a naturally developed part of her game, rather as Heinsohn might view his jumper from the corner or Boom-Boom Geoffrion his slap shot. When Lee stood at the plate in the All-Star softball game alumni commercial, Boog Powell eyed her carefully. "I'd pitch her under the tits," he advised me. But, understand, now, he was speaking only strategically, as a student of the game, not lasciviously.

One time I did a convention gig with the Doll in Puerto Rico, and when we were finished with our spot, the two of us went for a swim on the beach. Let me tell you, walking down a crowded resort beach with Lee Meredith in a bikini must be like walking onto the green with Tiger Woods. Everybody's looking at you, but nobody sees you.

So, we were a pretty happy gang and everybody got along. Well, except for Rodney Dangerfield. He was a total horse's ass. His trademark line—"I don't get no respect"—was well deserved, and he was as insecure in person as he portrayed himself in his act. Rodney was, I think, utterly intimidated by the All-Stars and dealt with this fear by setting himself far apart from them. Plus, he was generally disagreeable.

A former Japanese ballplayer named Koichi Numazawa had starred in a couple of commercials, and since the script had him call Dangerfield "Lodney," so did a lot of the All-Stars. Dangerfield's bug eyes would widen in anger every time he heard the name mispronounced. His worst social gaffe, however, was not to travel on the team bus. Hey, you can do a certain amount of prima-donnaing when you're one of the stars of a team, but everybody rides the same bus.

So, for the softball shoot, when the other guys had been on location for hours and Dangerfield finally only bothered to show up at the end of the day when everyone was assembled for the team picture, Billy Martin began the chant as soon as Rodney stepped out of his limo. "Big fucking deal!" Martin cried, and all the others picked up on it. "Big fucking deal! Big fucking deal!" The chorus rolled across the diamond, and Dangerfield's face turned as red as his signature tie. He just silently, sullenly took his place in the photo, though. Hecklers in a nightclub he could deal with. These burly athletes scared him into silence.

Two years later, though, when we were shooting another alumni commercial, the haunted camping trip, Rodney suddenly stormed into the makeup room when Lee Meredith was in the chair, and lit into her, because he'd read some rather mildly critical comment she'd made about him in a newspaper article. The Doll was a woman. He could bully her.

Suddenly, Mickey Spillane appeared. In the commercials, Spillane more or less played himself playing his tough-guy private eye, Mike Hammer, the star of *I, the Jury* and others of his stupendous sex-and-gore best sellers. Now, though, Mickey was all Mike, and he was Lee's protector, and he was judge and jury *and* executioner. "You never go near her again," Mickey roared, holding up a menacing fist.

Dangerfield, like any bully who's been called out, shrank away, only to seek out another target of his anger. That would also not be an athlete. It would, in fact, be me. I'd written a silly little picture paperback about the All-Star campaign entitled "Lite Reading," and in it I'd mentioned how unpopular he was. Actually, for the sake of All-Star camaraderie, I'd pulled my punches and what I wrote about Rodney made for much milder criticism than he deserved, but still, he was enflamed by my words—all the more so, now that Spillane had just ripped into him.

He caught up to me on the set of the campsite when we were actually taping, and there, between takes, muttering, jabbing a finger into my face, over and over he threatened to sue. Sue? Because he'd been criticized? It was unbelievable, but then, Dangerfield was famous for suing. I tried to ignore him, but, to my embarrassment, he kept up the invective. Damn, I was a chorus boy in this production. I didn't want to make any fuss. I just wanted this awful, crazy old man to go away. Finally, Ben Davidson, famous in the bowling commercial for growling, "One pin, Rodney, just one pin," stepped up out of nowhere. Ben is around 6 foot 7 inches. In his low, gravelly voice, he just stood over Dangerfield and announced, "That's enough, Rodney."

And for Rodney: Curses! Foiled again! He wasn't going to mess with Big Ben. Muttering still, he backed away, mercifully, never to go near either me or the Doll again.

Still, as distasteful a human being as Rodney was, he remains only first runner-up in my "Commonest Bigwig I've Ever Met in My Entire Life" category. The champion thereof is Vince McMahon, the wrestling impresario, he who has grown filthy rich over the twisted bodies and broken minds of the muscular drugged drones of his WWE—World Wrestling Entertainment.

Talk about common. In the summer of 1991, Carol and I attended the fortieth birthday party of John Filippelli—"Flip" to the world—my former producer on the NBC NFL pregame show, who had taken charge of McMahon's TV operation. Flip's party was at a country club in Greenwich, which happened to house a couple of bowling lanes down in the basement, and so after dinner we all went down there to hoot it up, bowl a few frames.

McMahon was accompanied not by his wife, Linda, the wannabe politician, but by one of his bobos, a former wrestler named Pat Patterson, whose shtick in the ring was to play a queen. This was typecasting, as Patterson is, in fact, openly gay . . . also, personally obnoxious. Well, I'm sorry, but you just can't expect everybody in the LGBT world to be sensitive and caring.

McMahon had, like his ring underlings, bulked up substantially, and as the bowling soiree went on, he seemed increasingly manic, his actions forced and vaguely menacing. He has wide, wild eyes that hint that, at any moment, he's going to lose it and explode for real, as he so often does in his manufactured wrestling bits. Still, Carol and I were not so much threatened by him as we were simply aghast. He was rude, loud, and abrupt, almost childish, especially when encouraged by his good buddy, the irrepressible Pat.

One of the other guests was named Dick. Whenever his turn to bowl came, McMahon and Patterson would snicker and giggle like eight-year-olds, repeating the word "Dick" again and again, letting us all know how hilarious it was that a man had a name that they, clever little devils, knew could also be used as a slang reference to the male sex organ. Every time poor Dick got up to bowl, the two WWE stalwarts regressed some more. "Dick! It's Dick!" they would shriek.

Carol and I were so embarrassed for poor Flip and his wife, Geena. So finally, mercifully, we decided that it was all right to leave. We took off the fashionably lovely multihued bowling shoes that we'd borrowed from the club, and went to put on our own shoes. But from each of our pairs, one shoe was missing. McMahon and Patterson smiled maniacally, and then, as we began to search around for the missing shoes, they broke out laughing.

OK, hiding our shoes was of a piece with the other childishness, but now the big joke was surely over. No. "Where's Frank's shoe?" McMahon would cry out, beside himself. "Has Carol lost her shoe?" Patterson cooed, almost gagging on the hilarity of this situation.

So I asked politely, and then, perhaps, cajoled. But the two men only repeated their performances until it occurred to me that we were supposed to beg, to plead—and for how much longer? I could see Flip and Geena growing more and more humiliated.

"Let's just go," I said to Carol, but even as we departed, I still believed that McMahon would surely, at last, run after us with our shoes. He didn't. We never got them back. We wouldn't play the game, so McMahon just kept the two shoes—pretty nice ones, too.

Incredibly, that wasn't the end of it either. First, McMahon sent us a Christmas card with some snide notation, wondering if we'd ever found our shoes, and then, a few years later, he actually, proudly brought up the episode himself in an interrogation—get this now— before staff investigators for the House Committee on Oversight and Government Reform, who were inquiring into his wrestling operation. During the interview, McMahon was asked about a critical piece that Dave Meltzer, my wrestling columnist at the *National,* had written about the uncommon number of WWE deaths.

To defend himself against Meltzer's numbingly sad statistics, this is how McMahon responded, on the record: "[The editor, Deford,] has no sense of humor, and he doesn't like me. We were bowling one night and I borrowed one of his shoes and he never found it. And so he had to walk home in a bowling shoe and one of his others, and he was upset about that, I understand."

One of the staffers, rather taken aback at this confession, felt obliged to comment: "I'm going to have to note that would be upsetting, too."

Even McMahon's own lawyer, one Jerry McDevitt, was stunned at how blithe his honorable client was about stealing shoes. "I never heard that one," he blurted out in disbelief.

But like one of those homicidal nuts who cry out, "Stop me before I kill again," that only prompted McMahon to baldly volunteer: "Well, actually I borrowed one of his wife's shoes too."

"That's a whole different story," the stunned lawyer observed.

"I left that part out," McMahon sheepishly admitted.

Vince McMahon: what a dick.

17

THIS JUST IN:
WRITING CAN BE FUN

That is the natural part of being a natural athlete: not that you are capable of performing naturally, but that you are natural in accepting the fact.

Everybody's All-American, 1981

I found out I could write when, I believe it was in the third grade, we had learned our alphabet, and the teacher said it was time for us to take it up a notch and write sentences, possibly even paragraphs. So I did. I could write. Some other kids were whizzes with numbers, and others could draw pictures or play the piano. I found out I could write.

In time, I would also find out that I couldn't do much else. One of my first books was a light cultural history of Miss America, *There She Is*, so I got invited to lots of book functions for women, in order that I might regale them and thus have them rush out to purchase my tome.* At one of these sessions, a book-and-author luncheon in Hartford, another of the speakers was Isaac Asimov, who wrote something like eight thousand books—sometimes I think it was a dozen

---

*Everybody wanted to review *There She Is*, too. It was published by Viking. Saul Bellow was a Viking author, and I was told that Viking collected far more clips about my book than Mr. Bellow did about all of his. Unfortunately, nobody wanted to read a whole book about Miss America. The reviews were terrific, though, and everybody loved reading the reviews.

or so a week. He titilated the little old ladies by saying, "All I can do with my hands is type and sex."

I thought: you are my brother.

Indeed, members of my family are loath to let me do anything around the house. The lightbulb joke for me is: zero. That's because they wouldn't let me change one, for fear I would break the lightbulb and God knows what all else, ancillary, in the process.

So, anyway, I'm eight years old, and I realize I'm different. I'm a natural writer. Please understand, that is not necesssarily braggadocio. "Natural" can be very close to "facile." I've seen too many natural athletes who didn't accomplish nearly as much as those with lesser gifts who managed to work harder, get better, and accomplish more.

Sure, I know that precocity is fine and dandy, and we have Mozart and Alexander the Great to prove that, yet I suspect that most of our largest talents are not so immediately evident, but must be developed and honed. Otherwise, you are just pretty at something but never get to grow to beauty. I suspect that the full measure of proficiency flows only at the confluence of what God gave and what the benefactor nurtured himself.

Probably there's not as much skill around as there used to be. A modern society doesn't lend itself to craftsmanship. Rather, people are more businesslike. Yes, of course, I know you can be a skillful business-man, but, really, it's not the same as being a skillful artisan, is it? Maybe we reached the acme of sustained skillfulness with *The Ed Sullivan Show*, where everybody—one after another—put some special talent on dis-play for the world to see. It's wise to go to a circus now and then, if for no other reason than to watch people doing amazing things—even very small, unusual things—better than anybody else in the world.

But we are a society today that is, like sport, entirely too hung up on numbers, figures, rankings, and statistics, so in this corporately technological world we do not so easily appreciate the odd, singular achievement anymore. Subtlety cannot be quantified, so what may be glorious can get lost nowadays if it can't be measured.

In any event, as I've said, my writing genes obviously all come from my mother's side. The ace writer in the family tree is James Branch Cabell, who was an esoteric novelist in the early twentieth century. He was my grandfather McAdams's first cousin, making me James Branch Cabell's first cousin twice removed. Mencken was nuts about him, and, indeed, his work was influential. Mark Twain was reading Cabell when he died. Cousin James's most celebrated novel was *Jurgen*. I made an effort to read it once. It must've been brilliant, if Mencken said so, but I found it impossibly turgid and gave up only a few pages in. That's the kind of writing I'm simply not capable of reading, let alone of writing. So, please understand: natural is really only a starting point.

And, of course, as I am not a manly man, neither am I a writerly writer. Certainly I appreciate that writing is creating and therefore it doesn't necessarily come easily, but, notwithstanding, I have simply never understood why writers *revel* so in the pain of writing. Actors don't bitch about how hard playing a part is. They love the challenge. Football players are crazy about playing football, even though it hurts. Musicians adore making music. Did you ever once hear Renoir complaining that he had to fill up another goddamn canvas? No. Just gimme another tube of blue paint and Katie bar the door. Hell, politicians like it even when they lose. But writers are whiners. Bitching about the angst of writing is our menstruation. Get over it.

It particularly amazes people when I tell them about writing the memoir of my daughter, *Alex: The Life of a Child*.

It must've been so difficult for you.

No. It was very easy, actually.

First of all, you write best when you like your subject matter, and I adored the person I was writing about, even if her illness and death saddened me. What is hard about revealing a little angel? But it was more than a chance to sing praises to Alex, for I also was seeking to make her short life mean something. I hoped that by writing about this one extraordinary little person, I would give a face to her disease—cystic fibrosis—which was then struggling to achieve the recognition that it needed to secure research funds. As a father who was a writer, I would've felt simply irresponsible had I not written the story about what was the most important thing that had happened in my life —never mind how tragic that was—especially since writing that story might help others.

And it did. The book (and the subsequent ABC network movie based on it) succeeded exactly as I hoped, by bringing great attention to the Cystic Fibrosis Foundation through Alex.

So, no, it was not hard to write. After all, strictly on the subject of craft, it was a simple narrative of love that did not require any tricks of literature or storytelling. The pages just rolled through the typewriter. This is not to say that I did not have to type through my tears, or that the work never left me limp. Indeed, when I finished the first draft I was so emotionally drained that I had to lay the whole manuscript aside for about six months before I could return to it and type up the final draft.

But if ever I learned anything about writing when writing about my daughter, it is that the subject, above all, determines the degree of difficulty. And I loved my subject.

In a somewhat similar vein, even shortly after Alex died, when the pain was deepest, I was still able to stand up before a crowd and speak about her with emotion but without breaking up. I could will myself to do that because I knew that Alex's story touched people, and thus it helped the cause. I decided that in some sense I became, before an audience, an actor playing Alex's father.

Yet, in private, when I was me again, alone, the slightest sudden memory could sometimes trigger an emotional collapse. One time, at a book-and-author luncheon in Cleveland, I got up when it was my turn, called upon the actor to play me, and spoke tenderly about Alex. But when I returned to my seat, I found that the next speaker, Gloria Steinem, had left a note there for me. She had just dashed it off on the back of an envelope:

Dear Frank,
Thank you for telling us that even a little eight-year-old girl can be
a hero.
Gloria

It completely dissolved me. I had to bow my head, trying to hide the fact, all the while Gloria spoke, that I, who had appeared so under control, was now crying like a baby.

While I am a pretty versatile writer, one thing I've never really been able to accomplish well is working with another writer. I just can't grasp how two people could write something well together—collaboration, they call it, which always makes me think of weasels *collaborating* with the Nazis. I guess you have to have the right personality to be collaborative. I imagine I'm either too vain or too stubborn to make it work, but I have tried to do it a few times.

The only occasion when it worked at all wasn't really collaboration. It was with a movie producer named Gerry Abrams, who is very low-key, very much a gentleman. He'd just call me up and say, well, I think we need this, or why don't you try this, and then I'd write it, and we got a movie made about Roger Bannister breaking the four-minute mile, entitled, of course, *Four Minutes.*

Because Bannister's wife didn't come along in his real life until after he'd retired from running, I thought we ought to give the kid a girlfriend, a little love interest amid all the cinders, and Gerry agreed that this was a good idea. Then, when Gerry hired an English director, he decided that young Roger and the girlfriend ought to have a steamy sex scene. I explained that I was taking enough liberties with Bannister's life just giving him an imaginary girlfriend who breaks his heart, but the director answered, rather archly: "Well, I know it's hard for you Americans to believe this, but we British had intercourse just like everybody else in the 1950s."

I said I really did understood that, but even though British people, in the aggregate, copulated in the 1950s, viewers would just have to use their own imagination on that score vis-à-vis the youthful Roger and his fictional girlfriend. Gerry backed me up. It's a small point, but that's why I don't think I ever could've been very good at writing movies, because everybody gets to put his two cents in. In fact, it's amazing to me that any movies are ever well written—especially when directors write them. Very few people can do two things well, but directors think they can write better than writers. It's like the new owner of a football team who went to his general manager and asked what else he could do for the team. The general manager replied, "You're an owner, Ed. Own." You're a director. Direct.

When I did collaborate, it never worked, but, of course, that never bothers anybody much in Hollywood, because then people will all tell you stories about screenwriters who have been at it for literally decades and made absolutely *millions* of dollars writing scripts that are never made. It comforts everybody to believe this, even if I'm sure it's mostly a Beverly Hills urban legend. Anyway, then they remind you about how F. Scott Fitzgerald couldn't cut it out there either.

But I had a lot fun *trying* to collaborate. Dan Curtis hired me to write a movie for HBO about the West Point football cheating scandal in the 1950s. Dan had been around Hollywood forever. He was best known for making *Dark Shadows* and *The Winds of War,* during which, I understood, he and Robert Mitchum came to blows. Dan was a tough kid from Bridgeport who didn't take any crap. In his office, where I worked with him, he would curse and throw tantrums every day, but we got along famously. He would just save most of his venom for the HBO producer, whom he was trying to get to, as they say, green-light my script, but the guy was English and didn't give a rat's ass for American football, so we probably never had a prayer. Myself, I never understood why HBO commissioned the script in the first place. F. Scott Fitzgerald probably felt the same way sometimes.

Then ESPN came to me and wanted to use the script HBO had rejected, but the people at ESPN didn't want Dan to direct, because they thought he was too much of a handful. Or they thought he was over the hill. Either way, that was stupid on their part, and I told them it had to be Dan and me, together. We were a package deal—collaborators. The old man appreciated that. He never made another film, either. He died a couple of years later still looking for that one last shot.

Edgar Scherick was another old producer who ended up the same way. Even until shortly before he died, Edgar would call me up every now and then and ask if I had any ideas for him. The even sadder part was that by the time he was old and ignored in Hollywood, almost everybody had completely forgotten how Edgar Scherick had practically invented sports television. Probably, in fact, nobody *in* sports television knows that anymore either. Nothing before ESPN really counts now.

The script I worked on with Edgar was about a college coach, only we had disputes all along because I thought he should be a tyrant and a crook and Edgar saw him more as a molder of fine young men. One time when we were arguing about this he suddenly cried out to me, "I beseech you, in the bowels of Christ, think it possible you may be mistaken."

I said: "What did you say, Edgar?"

"Didn't you go to Princeton?"

"Well, yeah."

"So, didn't they teach you that Oliver Cromwell said that? What kind of fucking university is that?"

"Edgar, they couldn't teach me *every*thing. Even Harvard couldn't teach *you every*thing."

He accepted that, if grudgingly. "Well, anyway, that's what I usually write back to studios when they turn my ideas down."

"When you do, do they know Oliver Cromwell said that?"

"Of course they don't."

"Well then, why should I?"

"Because you're a writer. Because you're not a studio. Because you're supposed to be literate, for Chrissake."

I took that as a backhanded compliment. You know, if you're a sportswriter, being told that you're *supposed* to be literate is at least getting thrown a bone.

When Edgar and I were not haggling over our coach, he would tell me the forgotten old stories about the late 1950s, when he left the ad business and got into producing sports. Basically, the company he started, Sports Programs, Inc., developed or purchased everything of any consequence that grew into ABC Sports, which in turn became a juggernaut under Roone Arledge, whom Edgar had hired. Roone took over after Edgar just up and sold his company one day, leaving sports behind to go west and make movies. Edgar was a man who kept re-creating himself; this was true right up to the end of his life, when he gave up Judaism and converted to Roman Catholicism. *In the bowels of Christ* . . .

But back when ABC was still, essentially, outsourcing its sports department to Edgar, he created *Wide World of Sports* for Jim McKay and the bowling show for Chris Schenkel, and he brought Gillette's *Friday Night Fights* ("Look sharp, feel sharp, be sharp"), a major-league baseball playoff, and college football all to ABC. The last was my favorite adventure of his, and this is how Edgar told me he pulled it off.

In 1960, ABC was still rinky-dink, a distant third to NBC and CBS. NBC owned the television rights to college football, which then consisted of the one lousy game a week that the NCAA permitted America to watch on television. Because CBS had the NFL locked up, it was unlikely to bid on the NCAA contract, so when the college rights were coming up for sealed bids, NBC figured it was a shoo-in.

NBC Sports was run at that time by a man named Tom Gallery, who had previously been a silent movie actor and then a boxing promoter. Edgar was sure that Gallery would show up personally to grandly deliver his network's bid to the NCAA. He also decided that Gallery would bring two envelopes, each containing a different bid.

MERCHANTS & MINERS TRANSPORTATION C⁰ IRON STEAMER.
BENJ. DEFORD.
RUNNING BETWEEN BOSTON, NORFOLK AND BALTIMORE.
CAPT W™ A. HALLETT.

The good ship *Benjamin Deford*, which was named for my great-great grandfather (1799–1870), an orphan whose brilliant business acumen brought the family distinction and great wealth in the nineteenth century. Alas, I was born in the twentieth.

Mom and Dad at a football game, the fall of '39. She was Louise McAdams. Daddy called her Weezie. I take after her.

The little dude is my father, Benjie, posed with his parents and sister—about 1906 when the Defords were still in high cotton.

Grantland Rice's famous aphorism (slightly incorrect), on display as our ideal at Camp Virginia, out in the Blue Ridge. I'm the scrawny little guy standing second from the end on the right. I grew real late.

Reunion with coach Nemo Robinson. The gentleman on Nemo's left is Alan Yarbro, the point guard who nicely passed me the ball.

In the backyard of our house in Baltimore, where I lived virtually my whole childhood, about 1952: Mom, Mac, me, Gill, Dad.

Number 6 in your program, number 1 in your hearts. This is me as a high school senior at the very height of my athletic powers before I was so astutely advised that I wrote basketball better than I played it.

Jimmy Stewart visited Princeton my junior year, the spring of 1960, when he was a member of the Board of Trustees, and I interviewed him as chairman of *The Daily Princetonian*.

A *Life* magazine photographer came down right before I graduated in '62, gave us beers and posed us in hideous nightshirts in front of the Ivy Club. Ours is not to reason why.

Bernard Darwin, Charles' grandson, golf writer extraordinaire of *The Times of London,* playing golf (as all golf writers have ever since).

President Warren Harding was privileged to meet the one and only Grantland Rice and his odd-couple buddy, Ring Lardner.

If it wasn't for me Kingsley Amis would have had no idea that Red Smith was the best newspaper columnist, ever. Did I set him straight.

Nobody asked me but this is Jimmy Cannon, a terrifically original sports columnist. I met him one cold night in a bush-league town.

Andre Laguerre was the Frenchman who saved *Sports Illustrated* for Americans. He had been de Gaulle's press secretary and gave me my chance. Giants walked the earth in those days of lore.

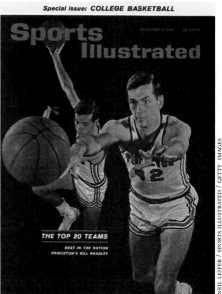

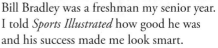

Bill Bradley was a freshman my senior year. I told *Sports Illustrated* how good he was and his success made me look smart.

Carol was a top runway model when I started taking her out. We met at the beach in Delaware and were married a year later in 1965.

I covered very little boxing, but did a piece on Sugar Ray Leonard when he was selected as Sportsman of the Year in 1981.

Carol and me, when I was covering a tennis tournament in Newport, where, coincidentally, we were married a few weeks later.

I think I'm supposed to say that I'm the one on the right. His name was Victor and he pinned me in about eight seconds. Flat.

SI still did some style stuff in the sixties. Laguerre was horrified to learn I'd never been to Paris, so he sent me over on a boondoggle to write captions about the beautiful people at Longchamps.

If, when he got to the hotel suite where the NCAA was holding the sale, he saw someone from CBS there, Gallery would then put down the envelope with the higher bid. If he didn't see a competitor, then he would plunk down the low ball. Edgar calculated that this would be $3 million, maybe a little higher.

Now began his machinations. "I got a guy from the ABC accounting office," he told me. "I picked him because you figure an accountant is dependable, and also because nobody knew him from Adam. I gave him an envelope and told him to go over to the suite and just try and remain unnoticed, which was easy for him to do because nobody had ever noticed him before."

The figure Scherick wrote in his envelope was $3.125 million.

As it was, predictably, nobody did notice the accountant. Tom Gallery looked around and saw that there was no one there from CBS. Full of confidence, he stepped up and slapped down the envelope containing the lower bid on the desk. Only then did Edgar's accountant emerge from the shadows, slink forward, and lay down his envelope. As a stunned Gallery waited, the NCAA man opened the two envelopes. ABC's contained the higher bid. ABC Sports had college football. Never again was it just a two-network sports competition. In fact, a few years later, using much of the money Scherick had gotten from Gillette to air boxing, Arledge won the rights to the 1968 Mexico City Olympics, giving ABC Sports even more eminence. (And here came Howard Cosell and *Monday Night Football* just over the horizon.)

Edgar mentioned to me a couple of times that he was still annoyed that Arledge gave him so little credit for pretty much creating ABC Sports out of whole cloth. But then, he was not a man to hold grudges. He was a man to move on. And so, in full-blooded collaboration, we would struggle with the script about the coach. It did not go well. One day, in frustration, I got up and started walking fitfully around the room. Suddenly, in a loud voice, Edgar screamed at me: "Sit down, you sonuvabitch!"

Surprised, and even a little bit frightened, I pussyfooted back and took my seat. "What is it, Edgar?"

He rose and, in dead seriousness, loudly declared: "I pace, you sit." And then, purposefully, he began to walk about the room. Unfortunately, even these perambulatory ruminations still did not help us come up with a successful script about our coach, whom we fashioned as a tyrant and crook who, nonetheless, molded fine young men.

So, no, writing certainly does not always go smoothly. But, as a child, when I discovered I could write—not knowing that most people thought writing was supposed to be a disease that I had been afflicted with—I started writing. Longer compositions than all the other kids. Little stories. In the sixth grade, I mimeographed a class newspaper, complete with news, gossip, sports, and a serial entitled "Tanganika," which involved intrepid American explorers and dastardly Soviet spies. A year or so later, I wrote my first really successful short story, about two buddies—"Pat and Me"—one of whom falls for his first girlfriend. It won some prize. Sometime after that I wrote my first sports fiction, and it really was ahead of its time. It was about a little college that brought over a giant from Africa to star on the basketball team. Years later, there would be all sorts of collaborative bad novels and bad movies on that very theme. Art Buchwald sued and won a pot of money for having his idea along this line stolen—which was my idea originally, when I was a child.

But I was moving on in the writing line. Naturally, I wrote for the school newspaper and the literary society. What the hell, I wrote. It was the one thing this boy could do a little—and sans excrutiating pain.

18

IN WHICH I HAPPEN UPON
AN EYE-OPENER

*History shows us the most successful ages in sport are not
distinguished by events but by individuals. The '20s were
memorable because of Ruth, Dempsey, Tilden and Bobby Jones, not
because of the events they won.*
                    "What Price Heroes?" *Sports Illustrated*, 1969

During these prepubescent times, while I was discovering writing as
I waited impatiently to grow, I stumbled upon a journalistic light to
guide me. By dumb luck, my father was an avowed Eisenhower Republican, and he started subscribing to the *New York Herald-Tribune*, a
journal that espoused his own sensible views. The paper would come
in the mail a couple of days late, but I began to peruse the more time-
less bits. After the stale and hackneyed local Baltimore offerings, I was
stunned to find such fine writing in lowly newsprint.

The *Trib*, I would later discover, was known as a "writer's paper"
(so it was all the more depressing, but predictable, that it wouldn't be
long before it went out of existence, after the fashion of all writer's
papers). Walter Lippmann anchored the editorial page, and although
I doubt that I often bothered to linger on his Olympian offerings, I
certainly read a guy named John Crosby who wrote clever things
about television, and Walter Kerr, who sagely critiqued the theater.

And I found the sports section, which was, for a time, printed on
bilious sea-green paper. Although I certainly didn't know it, the *Trib*

was widely recognized as having the best sports section in the land. "Holy smokes," a competitor is supposed to have cried after another brilliant reporter was brought on board, "these guys will hire Thomas Edison to turn out the lights."

TRIB INKS STAR SCRIBE!

This team of titans had been largely assembled by Stanley Woodward, who is forever recognized as the finest newspaper sports editor of all time. I never met Mr. Woodward, but he was a Massachusetts Yankee, a tall, hulking, myopic fellow, who had come down from Boston to the *Trib* in 1930. He described it in his memoirs as a "lively place and a really good newspaper, even though much of its business was carried on in a gin mill." Despite being an independent cuss, Woodward ascended to the sports editor's job in 1938, and by the time he was fired for insubordination in 1948, he had built up that legendary department.

In my experience, editors fall into two distinct categories. The first—and I'd bet anything Mr. Woodward was of this stripe—is a fellow who may have deep abiding personal interests, but who has a natural curiosity for almost anything he *doesn't* know. *You've got an idea for a story on medieval kitchen architecture? Wow, that's fascinating—go do it.* The other type may be just as good an editor, but he wants to play only with his own toys, run stories about subjects he already knows well and loves.

After the *National* folded and I worked on novels, I bounced around as a contract writer, for *Newsweek* and *Vanity Fair.* Maynard Parker at *Newsweek* was a classic of the tell-me-what-I-don't-know type, while Graydon Carter at *Vanity Fair* only felt comfortable playing to his strength. He hired me because he thought sports would bring in more male readers, but he had so little interest in sport that I very quickly learned that, for both of us, it was a marriage of inconvenience. When my contract was finally, mercifully, up, Graydon actually apologized. "I'm sorry," he told me, "but I just don't care enough."

Actually, he's also the only editor (or producer) I ever worked for, wherever, who didn't have even the slightest interest in *me*. Now understand, it didn't bother me. Graydon was a nice enough guy, and he did make the effort to occasionally invite me to little lunches in chichi hotels where a bunch of fey Europeans always joined him and everybody still smoked cigarettes and bitched that it was just like the goddamn Americans to get snippy about people smoking. Still, it was obvious that because Graydon didn't like sports, I had no more to engage him as a person than I did as a writer. I wasn't hurt, you understand, because I do have a number of people who do like me, but the rejection did sort of intrigue me. It proved to me, though, that if, like Graydon, you really, really, *really* are interested in just a few things, and you concentrate on them, you can put out a good magazine—assuming there are enough other people who want to read about what you care about. Which is to say, Graydon is perfect for the *Vanity Fair* crowd, and if I were him I wouldn't have given a hoot about me, either.

But, on the other hand, even if he was just editing sports, Stanley Woodward was, like Maynard Parker, obviously an editor with a wide range of interests. Red Smith, of course, was his prize catch. Woodward had found Smith hidden in plain daylight on the lowly *Philadelphia Record*, spiriting him to the big time only a few years before the *Record* went to its demise.

Nevertheless, while Smith was the most celebrated of the *Trib*'s sportswriters, several other of Woodward's men had distinct, engaging styles. I was especially charmed by Al Laney, who covered tennis and golf. Just as Arthur Daley, a rather pedestrian columnist, won a Pulitzer years before Red Smith, simply because Daley worked for the *Times*, Laney never received as much recognition as Allison Danzig, a nice, thorough gentleman who covered golf and tennis for the *Times* little more than nicely and thoroughly. Laney, though, was a far more accomplished writer than Danzig. He despised artifice in writing, and went about his work in an offhand, leisurely way. In fact, he'd been influenced by Bernard Darwin, Charles's sportswriting grandson.

Not surprisingly, Laney, so admiring of Darwin, owned a special dislike for reporters who depended on quotes, especially as he saw American sportswriting headed in that baleful direction. Laney had fought in World War I and was wounded in the fighting in the Argonne forest. The brutality in football disturbed him; maybe if you'd been in those trenches it took away some of your appetite for the stipulated violence on the gridiron. Anyway, a few years after the armistice, Laney returned to Paris, where, of all things, he became something of a secretary to James Joyce. The great novelist had several eye operations and was even blind for periods during these years, so it was Laney who would read novels to him, both in French and in English.

I met Mr. Laney later in his life; he had a bushy salt-and-pepper mustache and always wore a fedora, rather resembling the fellow who adorns Moretti beer bottles. The last time I spoke with him, I was researching my book on Big Bill Tilden, and Al was in a nursing home. Still, though, he talked lucidly about the glamorous events and heroes of the 1920s. Like a lot of old people, he welcomed the opportunity to speak to some young person who wanted to hear tell about the days of his youth. History being of no interest in America, because it's, by definition, old, this is a rare occurrence, especially nowadays. I can't, for the life of me, for example, imagine that any run-of-the-mill young person will want to read the old stuff I'm writing about now.

Still, I wish I'd kept my notes, but, unfortunately, it never occurred to me when I was young that I might want to remember more when I was old. I threw away all sorts of notes and barely saved anything important. I'm always amazed when I hear about so-and-so leaving his papers to some university. The University of Texas wants mine, and I promised I'd look up in the attic for them, but papers were mostly precisely the things I threw out. The only good stuff I saved was the eye-catching flotsam of a travelin' man's life—press passes, decals, snapshots, funny headlines, bumper stickers—which, for EZ viewing purposes, I've tacked up willy-nilly in our garage. Among the prize thumbtacked keepsakes I have not one but two certificates designating me a Kentucky Colonel and another certifying that I am an Arkansas Traveler (signed by the unknown governor at the time, one Bill Clinton).

But I do recall how much Al Laney enjoyed having me, a young person, listen to him talk about the past. He knew his stuff. Once, he wrote a short, single line that probably sums up the whole business of playing a sport as well as any of the long, philosophical treatises. Simply: "An athlete leaves only statistics and memories."

Generously, Red Smith himself thought the best writer on the *Trib* staff was an actual professor of literature named Joe Palmer, who wrote, of all things, strictly about horse racing. Understand, though, Palmer was not a handicapper, but, rather, a chronicler of the very human characters, the dandies and rapscallions and broken-hearts, who populated that crazy quilt of the backstretch; Palmer said of one such fellow that he "has a great respect for the truth and uses it sparingly."

Nowadays sportswriting is too much about predicting games; then, it was more about revealing human nature, and the *Trib* in general and Palmer in particular were exemplars of that. In a way, he was something of a Damon Runyon; it was just that one worked Broadway and Seventh Avenue by night, the other Belmont and Saratoga when the sun came up. Palmer once profiled a wooden-legged stable cat, explaining that he "could catch mice with one hand and blackjack them with another." Not one of the guys or dolls was ever painted so well.

Palmer had been working on his PhD thesis at the University of Michigan when he was offered the chance to write about racing. He had taught English there in Ann Arbor and also at the University of Kentucky. In 1946 Woodward brought him to New York, where Palmer soon distinguished himself by sprinkling classical references amid the more prosaic equine chatter. Somehow, for example, he managed to cogently compare, in great detail, the jockey Eddie Arcaro, who was known to railbirds as "Banana Nose," to the sixteenth-century Italian goldsmith and sculptor Benvenuto Cellini. You got me. In describing how a groom mourned the death of Man o' War, Palmer likened it to "Tennyson on the passing of Arthur." He himself wrote this when the greatest steed died: "Man o' War was, if not more than a horse, then more than a horse had ever been before."

Alas, Palmer had only a short time to make his mark. He died in 1952, when he was only forty-eight, and especially since horse racing has lost so much popularity, his distinctively fine work has largely been forgotten as well. The irony is, too, that the racetrack is such a lode of good writing, as proved by Laura Hillenbrand with her grand tale of Seabiscuit, and the many wonderful pieces by Bill Nack, whose touching story on the death of Ruffian probably exceeds, in beauty and pathos, anything any sportswriter has ever done about the passing of a great human athlete.*

Smith's column, as is typical in sports sections, always appeared, with his mug shot, above the fold on the two left-hand columns of the lead page, but any dunce could tell he wrote a better column than anybody else, in any part of the writer's paper—or, eventually, any paper. Just those same little columns, only a few hundred words, several times a week. Just those, just so. I always thought that discovering Red Smith must have been like being in Delft around 1660 and happening upon some Vermeers, and saying: Hey, Jan, you know, you do those li'l bitty paintings real good, so, why don't you get serious and try something on a larger canvas? But Red Smith had his space down exactly right. Even as that boy in Baltimore, I figured this guy must be a very secure person.

---

*Bill also holds the distinction of being able to recite, in order, rat-a-tat-tat, the names of all 137 Kentucky Derby winners.

19

KINGSLEY

It was sometime, yet, before I perceived everyday truths. The larger ones, about mankind, were much easier to come by.
                                        Everybody's All-American, 1983

In college, at Princeton, I continued apace with my writing. I had a couple of plays produced. On the newspaper, I wrote everything: stories, editorials, humor, columns, movie reviews. I covered the basketball coach, who had told me I was no good, and the dean of students, who threw me out once (on incredibly trumped-up charges, if I must say so myself). Eventually, I became the editor of the daily newspaper, or "the chairman" as we so grandly called it.

Unfortunately, as regards actually going to college and learning something, I wasn't very accomplished at that. I spent all my time writing and screwing around; besides, the 1950s were still an age when professors were not afraid of students, so a professor would give low grades if students deserved them. And I deserved them.

I was immature and ambitious; this is a bad, flammable combination. People who don't think college football and basketball players should be paid, even though they are in "revenue sports" and their coaches make a king's ransom, always argue that the boys are getting a college scholarship, and, for goodness sake, that should be reward enough. But this presupposes that the athlete-student actually wants a college education, and if you are like most college football or basketball players, who only want to play ball, or if you are like me, who wanted only to write, then you are immature and ambitious, so the alleged gift of book learning is wasted.

Besides, a gentleman's C was just fine then. I believe F. Scott Fitzgerald had been in that ballpark, too.

During my sophomore year I got accepted into my dream course. It was pass-fail, and, even better, the understanding was that no one would fail. The professor was Kingsley Amis, visiting from England, where he was celebrated as one of the "angry young men" of postwar literature. He had come to Princeton ostensibly to teach this writing course to the wide-eyed Tiger literati, such as myself. Personally, I believe that once you get past where to put commas and how to go easy on the similes, writing cannot much be taught. I'm quite sure Kingsley agreed with this, although he went along with the presumption so he could come spend a cushy year abroad with the Yankee dollar when times were still tough in Merry Olde. He never did seem the least bit angry to me.

As a getting-to-know-you exercise, he had us list three writers who had "influenced" us. I'm sure that most of my fellow scholars listed the likes of Dostoyevsky and Melville, Henry James, Proust, Flaubert—that crowd—and probably either Chaucer or Keats to suck up to Kingsley's nationality. I, on the other hand, actually tried to think of real writers who had honestly influenced me. Big mistake.

First, I put down J. D. Salinger, because *The Catcher in the Rye* had been an absolute revelation to me. Then Shakespeare—not to show off, but because that was so. I mean, on any exercise like this, Shakespeare should be like the freebie you get in the middle of the Bingo game. The third author I was going to put down was whoever had written the novel *Johnny Tremain*. It was about a young lad in Boston during the Revolution, and it had so enthralled me when I read it as a child that it *influenced* me to start reading other books. However, I couldn't remember who the author was, and there was no Google then, so I momentarily thought I might put down my dear first cousin (twice removed) James Branch Cabell. This would allow

me to flaunt my genealogy. But suppose Kingsley had actually read
Jurgen and gotten through it and wanted to discuss whatever it meant?
No. Luckily, I then had an inspiration, and the name I wrote down
instead was Red Smith.

So, a week or so later, when I had my introductory private session with Kingsley, he could hardly wait to inquire who exactly this
Red Smith chap might be. When I told him Smith was a newspaper
columnist, he nearly gagged, holding in a snicker. His eyes rolled
when I added that Smith's subject matter was fun and games. All the
great writers of great books since antiquity, and this cocky American dimwit had actually named some lowlife sportswriter! In the top
three! Literature! All-time! In behalf of my celebration of Mr. Smith's
talent, I hadn't yet worked up that brilliant analogy to Vermeer, so
even though I explained how the columnist had so impressed me—
influenced me!—as an exemplar of good newspaper writing, it remained
in Kingsley's mind that I was the prime example of the worst kind of
provincial, hopelessly dopey thinking that pervaded even the supposed best campuses on the nether side of the Atlantic.

In point of fact, I *know* he thought precisely that, because that's
what he wrote in a long, arch disquisition about his impressions abroad
for a Sunday British newspaper. But, aha! As luck would have it, my
brother Mac was attending school in England that year, at Rugby,
and he read the article and mailed it to me, circling the part about
the incredible naïf who had listed a sports columnist in the company
of the Bard. "Could this be you?" Mac wrote. It obviously was, even
if Kingsley hadn't used my real name. However, he had, if I recall,
described me as "gangly" (well, better than "pimply") and also hopelessly unfazed, which was, together with "gangly," a dead giveaway.

So, at my next appointment with Kingsley, I just ever so sweetly
told him how much I'd enjoyed his article.

"What article?" he asked, swallowing the bait.

"Why, you know, sir, the one in the London paper where you
made such fun of me."

Well, Kingsley had bad, discolored teeth, and his whole pasty English face turned that off color now. He was mortified—not to also say impressed that I had such a wide-ranging network of global sources. Actually, it probably really didn't matter that now I had Kingsley over a barrel, because, as it turned out, he was even less interested in us, his academic stooges, than I had imagined, inasmuch as it seems he spent the whole year having a torrid affair with a professor's wife. I could've passed the pass-fail course merely by handing in "Three Blind Mice" every week. Nevertheless, once he had stopped chortling at me about Red Smith, I think he kind of secretly liked me better than the other supercilious bastards who'd told him that they'd been most influenced by Dante, Milton, and James Joyce.

In any event, the last assignment I handed in that semester was a one-act play, which he said was much the best thing any of his charges had written all year, so good that he gave it to his agent, and she tried to get it produced off-Broadway. The production fell through, but never mind; now I was plugged into the big time, I had an introduction to a hotshot New York agent, and I was not only immature and ambitious, but also smug. In no small part, you see, thanks to Red Smith.

Kingsley would go back to England and, I believe, write a bad novel about his year in America.

20

MY DAMN NAME

As a rule of thumb, whenever a doctor introduces himself as Doctor,
but calls you by your first name, as if you were a child, be wary.
                                    Alex: The Life of a Child, 1983

When I was starting, back then, to write things with a byline for
the college paper, the first thing that I should've done was to change
my name. Instead of Frank Deford, I would've become either Frank
DeFord or Frank Dufour.

Just look at them side by side:

Deford   DeFord   Dufour

You can plainly see, namewise, that I have had the worst of it with
Deford. It's been a cross to bear all my life.

I will explain in excruciating detail.

First of all, I am not a member of any sanctioned minority—not
even a woman. For a writer, this is another drawback, like having to
suffer a sweet childhood, because, as a minority, you can be put upon
(which, as I said, is part of the writer's job description) and therefore
elicit greater sympathy. Unfortunately for me, altogether, I am the
least minority person extant. In fact, a Hollywood agent once told
me, "DeFord, you are the last of the tall, white, male, WASP, Episco-
palian, heterosexual, Ivy League writers."

Well, I am a Huguenot. However, inasmuch as the last time we
were burned at the stake by the Catholics was about four hundred

years ago, it is hard to gin up much serious sympathy for me for suffering a put-upon heritage. I myself have met only three famous Huguenots in my life: Frank Perdue, the chicken man; Pete Rozelle, the NFL commissioner; and Tom Brokaw, the NBC anchorman. It's hard to sniff us out; people do not go around identifying themselves as Huguenot-Americans.

This is a first, right here.

We Huguenots ought to have more pride, though, because we were a very industrious folk; and because we got persecuted and dispersed, we share a certain emotional connection to Jews—we're sort of the Christian diaspora. Some historians even suggest that France was never so strong again after it drove out its Protestants (and likewise, England became all the stronger for being the catch basin for so many talented refugees).

Back when Huguenots were still celebrated (or even remembered), a history of Baltimore largely attributed the success of my great-great-grandfather Benjamin Deford to his heritage, to wit that he was "reared under those influences that have fashioned into the highest types of manhood that many of the descendents of the Huguenots, who, wherever located in exile, have stamped their individuality upon their contemporaries." But, of course, unlike the Jews, once we got the hell out of France, we were pretty much like all the other everyday Christians, and so we were accepted and intermarried and our particular highest type of manhood disappeared into the ribbons of the human race.

There are various renditions about how my family came to the New World. Well, for sure, we had been Dufours back in France. Our shield was gray and gold, with crossed battle-axes and a gold star; I can show you: nice stuff. Some have us Dufours arriving in Virginia as early as 1621, from Gravesend, in England. Another version has us taking refuge in Geneva, a liberal homestead for its time, before we sailed from La Rochelle, in France. When I flew into Geneva once, on my way to Lausanne to interview Juan Antonio Samaranch, that dreadful old fascist who ran the International Olympic Committee forever, I picked up a phone book and, sure enough, it was rife with Dufours.

But, for whatever reason, as soon as the Dufours alighted over here—eventually settling in Kent County, on the Eastern Shore of Maryland—right away they ditched Dufour. I have no idea why. It's a terrific name, with class and style. If I'd had any sense, I woulda changed my name back.

by Frank Dufour

But, I guess, insecure and anxious to blend in, my Huguenot forebears decided they'd rather anglicize it. Read it and weep: Deford. And here is the upshot: everybody just naturally wants to spell Deford with a capital F. I don't blame people. It simply looks as if it should be that way. Lifelong friends write my name DeFord. People are simply determined that it should be that way, and they follow the line of least resistance.

Apparently, it's always been so. When my great-great-grandfather Thomas Deford, a pretty prominent fellow, the boss of the Deford Company (and a "clubman," a term which left no doubt in those days that you were prominent), died in 1901, even the *New York Times* sent him off as De Ford.* Press passes for me are made out to Frank DeFord. Contracts. I have those corrected. It's the principle of the thing. Checks: *Pay to the order of Frank DeFord.* I just cash 'em. It's the principal of the thing.

Back in the 1980s, for three years, I was on the NBC NFL pre-game football show. One season, it appeared that the Buffalo Bills were going to qualify to host the American Conference championship game in January. Football experts became apoplectic, because they knew for sure that it snowed a lot in Buffalo and that was going

---

*That's right, they twisted Deford into two words with two capital letters: De Ford. My name must be a record for the *Times:* one six-letter word wrong twice.

to louse up a good football game. Worst of all, Will McDonough, he hailing from tropical Boston, was a stalwart on CBS's pregame show, our competitor, and on Thanksgiving Day Will rudely lambasted Buffalo's weather right in the face of the Bills' owner.

So, I went on the air the following Sunday, playing a weatherman, standing before a map of the United States, and as soon as they saw me in this setup all the people in Buffalo groaned. Here we go again, another rip job at poor old Buffalo's weather. But guess what. I then proceeded to point out that, really, Buffalo in January wasn't a whole lot different from Cleveland or Detroit or, yes, even Will McDonough's Boston. Moreover, I explained to pigskin America, the notorious lake-effect snow usually went just south of Buffalo, so, do not despair, football fans, there was actually a good chance that the weather for the AFC game would not be a disaster.

The good people in Buffalo couldn't believe it. Someone on actual national television had actually defended the weather in Buffalo. My picture in the *Buffalo News* was placed at the top of page one, above the name of the newspaper itself. The Erie County executive called me up and personally invited me to come to Buffalo for the Bills' next home game, and—here my legs went limp—he and the mayor of Buffalo wanted to *give me a Day*.

Never before (or since) had I ever been awarded a Day.

Of course, I got to Buffalo, and the banner said

WELCOME FRANK DeFORD

and I was handed a proclamation declaring December 11, 1988,

FRANK DeFORD DAY

Even on my own Day, they misspell my name.

Look, I don't want to drag this out, but before we leave the subject, the other problem with my name being Deford is that, on those rare occasions when it *is* spelled correctly, people pronounce it wrong. They say: "Deaf-ird." Deford looks as if it should be said "Deaf-ird." Often, when I am a speaker, unless, luckily, my name is misspelled DeFord on the program, I am introduced as Frank Deafird. Name your poison, Frankie.

Occasionally people ask me what it's like to be a quote, celebrity, unquote. Well, to start with, now that there are reality-show celebrities, it's a pretty diminished distinction. But, even so, if I am indeed a celebrity, it is of the fringe variety. If celebrities were planets, I would be Pluto, which, of course, isn't even an official planet anymore. I am, in fact, of just the right magnitude: recognized occasionally just enough to be flattered, but never so much as to be bothered by the attention. Still, the point is, I know in my heart that you can't pretend to be a real celebrity if most people either (*a*) don't know how to spell your name or (*b*) don't know how to pronounce it or (*c*) both of the above.

Nevertheless, I soldier on, humbly, and only occasionally do I let myself dream that I really am Frank Dufour. Woulda, coulda, shoulda.

But wait.

There was another Frank Deford.

He was a horse, a thoroughbred, foaled in 1973. He was named for me by Nathan Cohen, who was a co-owner of Pimlico at the time. I was very taken by this honor and gave the Jockey Club permission to use my name for a horse. You can't just go around naming horses after real people without asking. But I could be proud to be associated with the equine Frank Deford. He was as well bred as any human Dufour. For example, his maternal grandfather, Jet Pilot, won the Kentucky Derby.

Unfortunately, although Frank Deford was an absolutely beautiful little horse in repose, he had no interest whatsoever in being a *race*horse. Even as a yearling, he never bucked and was used as a companion for more excitable—that is to say: competitive—horses. In fact, Frank Deford liked to follow other horses, and follow is not exactly the quality you want in your steed at a racetrack.

I went down to Laurel to watch Frank Deford run his thirteenth race. I thought that this might be lucky, inasmuch as he had lost his first twelve. These were some of the notations in the *Racing Form* about Frank Deford's efforts:

No factor.
Weakened.
Far back.
Outrun.
Fell back.
Evenly.

I especially liked the "Evenly." In that race, Frank Deford was beaten by seventeen lengths. But then, I suppose everything is relative. If a guy had met Job along about Chapter Eleven of his travails and said, "Hey, pal, how's tricks?" Job could have answered "Evenly" quite accurately.

Frank Deford didn't fare any better in that thirteenth race, the one I saw him run at Laurel. He finished eleventh in a field of twelve, beaten a short length for tenth.

But here's the thing. That day in the racing papers and on the racing pages of the local papers, not once was Frank Deford's name spelled Frank DeFord. In fact, I never saw it misspelled, ever.

And when the race was run, on those few occasions when the track announcer mentioned Frank Deford's name, he pronounced it Di-FORD and not Deaf-ird.

I shoulda been a horse.

However, in that regard, and not to put too fine a point on it, about a year later, I got a phone call from Chick Lang, Spiro Agnew's buddy, who was the general manager at Pimlico. "Frank," he said, "I've got some bad news for your wife."

"For my wife?"

"Well, I don't know her," Chick said, "but I think it'll be bad news for her."

"OK, what is it?"

Chick said: "I'm sorry, but we had to geld Frank Deford."

21

IT HAPPENS TO
THE BEST OF US

We always say that the ideal is to be color blind. Well, not always.
Sometimes when we are color blind, we are simply, foolishly brain
blind.

NPR, 1999

Trivia time.

Who replaced me on the NBC NFL halftime show?

Answer: O. J. Simpson.

Who was the first musician who performed on the radio in
Nashville when the show was originally dubbed "Grand Ole Opry"
in 1927?

Answer: DeFord Bailey

You had no idea, did you?

Very few people alive have even heard of DeFord Bailey, but
in his heyday he was the most popular musician on the Grand Ole
Opry, appearing twice as often as any other star. DeFord was, in fact,
probably the best harmonica player in the world—although he called
it a "harp." He was so tiny a fellow, his growth stunted by childhood
polio, that he often stood on a Coca-Cola crate to get close enough to
the microphone, but he was so beloved he was known as "The World's
Pet." DeFord was, however, virtually illiterate—save for the fact that
he could write his name, which, as you can see, is one of those DeFords
spelled the right way, with a capital F.

There is another thing you would never guess in a blue moon about DeFord Bailey. Not only was he country when country was cool, but he was an African-American; he was Charley Pride before there was a Charley Pride. His biographer David C. Morton wrote that DeFord "was the only African-American in his day to perform regularly on an equal basis with white performers before white audiences in Dixie and elsewhere."

When I first heard about DeFord Bailey, I guessed that he had gotten his name from some white DeFords—perhaps distant relatives of mine—who had owned his slave ancestors. I had the right idea, too, but I was only half right. When DeFord's paternal grandfather, Lewis, was freed from bondage in 1863, he took the last name of his owner—Jonathan Bailey. But the DeFord? Turns out that when he was born in the backwoods of Tennessee on December 14, 1899, his young mother simply took the names of her two favorite teachers, a Mr. DeBerry and a Mrs. Ford, and combined them to make DeFord.*

DeFord Bailey was a regular on the Grand Ole Opry for fourteen years, until 1941, but thereafter he seldom played his harp in public. In 1974, though, when the Opry left its old building, Ryman Auditorium, and moved out to Opryland, DeFord made some sentimental appearances, especially with his old buddy Roy Acuff, and that helped people remember the little black gentleman with his harp.

Several months after DeFord died in 1982, DeFord Bailey Day was declared in Nashville, just as there would be a Frank DeFord Day in Buffalo. A large ceremony was held at his graveside. A beautiful tombstone had been erected, engraved with the likeness of a harmonica, and the words HARMONICA WIZARD. Beneath it was:

---

*A novel, simply titled *DeFord*, was written by an author named David Shetzline and published in 1968. I contacted Mr. Shetzline, and he explained that he had chosen the title character's name as a reference point for the dehumanizing effect of mass production—that is: out of Henry Ford. This only fictional DeFord is a carpenter who is never given a first name.

DEFORD BAILEY
1899–1982

That's right. They misspelled his name. Of course, it should have been:

DeFORD BAILEY

Even when you're the right DeFord, the most talented DeFord, they'll still get it wrong.

Anyway, unless you're a horse.

22

THE WAY IT WAS. REALLY

*It was the last of the good old days, although we did not know that
at the time.*

Everybody's All-American, 1981

Coming up from Princeton, I made my debut at *Sports Illustrated* on a
Thursday, because the magazine worked a Thursday–Monday week.
This was not advantageous from a social point of view, and I soon
found that I would spend a lot of Wednesdays going to matinees and
racetracks by myself. But then, I was living in New York, it was my
first real grown-up job—a career, for goodness sake—and even better: I had my two *bêtes noires,* academia and the military, both behind
me. Never mind having Wednesdays alone, I was very pleased with
myself. As we used to say in Baltimore: you never know how you look
till you get your picture took.

That first Thursday I had appeared for duty on the twentieth
floor, I was shown my very own cubicle and introduced to the other
baseball reporter, whose name was Herman Weiskopf. Herm was what
my father would call "a honey of a guy"—so impossibly downright
nice. He loved wrestling—not Vince McMahon's make-believe drug-
gie wrestling, but amateur wrestling, armpit wrestling—and he spent
hours and days trying to get wrestling stories into the magazine. Unfortunately for Herm, even today, it's only in Iowa and Oklahoma in
the United States and in Bulgaria, I believe, elsewhere, that anybody
cares about real wrestling. Well, those few people and John Irving,
the novelist, who celebrated wrestling in *The World According to Garp.*

He called me up once and bent my ear for about half an hour telling me what a raw deal wrestling got. John was more exercised about wrestling than Richard Nixon about bowling. But the truth is that wrestling is deadly to watch and you can't bet on it. Herm gave it his best, but futilely.

Herm generously showed me the ropes. He also showed me his one sort of fetish. It was a folder wherein he kept all the clippings he could find that included the phrase "up for grabs." I found that neat, because at that time "up for grabs" was a favored journalistic expression. The tournament was up for grabs. The primary election was up for grabs. The Academy Awards were up for grabs. In retrospect, an incredible amount of stuff was always up for grabs—and more often than not in headlines. So Herm had a bulging "Up for Grabs" folder, and I would always give him an "up for grabs" clipping when I encountered one, which was often. I believe the term is pretty much gone out now, as I wish "perfect storm," "emotional roller coaster," "wake-up call," and "level playing field" would also disappear. I kept telling Herm he ought to write a story about "up for grabs," but he never did. Frankly, it had a better chance of running than a wrestling piece, but I never told him that.

Although Herm was my instructor, my boss, who was in charge of what was known as the "bullpen," was a lady named Honor Fitzpatrick. She was the highest-ranking female on the *Sports Illustrated* manifest. When I met with her that first day, she outlined what my immediate duties would entail—essentially: checking facts, checking spelling, checking dates, and getting them right as rain. Technically I was a "reporter," but in fact, we called each other "checkers," which was a more accurate description.

The preliminaries aside, Honor told me that it was time for me to take an official guided tour of the Timeink facilities. She then paused, took out a cigarette, and, with the greatest of courtesy, almost apologetically, asked me, "Would you mind if a couple of new girls came with you?"

I was momentarily taken aback. I don't think, to this point in my life, anybody senior to me had ever asked if I *minded* anything. Beyond that, it certainly didn't bother me that, should I be so gracious not to mind, I was going to have some distaff company with me on my excursion. Could be a hot chick or two, and I'm getting lucky my first day? Who knew? But what I didn't understand was that Honor was being so solicitous because I was automatically of a higher station than these other two rank newcomers.

I, being a man, had been hired as a reporter. No *girl* could possibly expect to start off in such an exalted position. Rather, women had to begin as serfs, mostly as "clip girls"—which meant that they took the AP wire as it rolled in, clickety-clack, cut it up, and distributed its multitude of carbons to the proper higher-ups. Like, for instance, me. As the baseball researcher I would be personally handed the baseball stories, hot off the wire. By a girl. But please understand. Girls then would absolutely kill for these jobs at Timeink, because at almost every other place of business, the most a girl could expect was to start off as a secretary. Clip girl at Timeink was the Head Start program, female college graduate division, of its day.

I met the girls. Alas, neither was a hot chick, but they were very nice and appreciative, for, having been alerted by Honor Fitzpatrick of my grand benevolence, they thanked me profusely that I'd allowed them to accompany me with my private escort. And here were their CVs. One of the girls was from England and had just finished a master's degree in the United States. The other was from Vassar, where she had been Phi Beta Kappa. Unfortunately, though, tough titty: even being a Depression baby got you only so far in the 1960s if you had happened to've been born as just a girl.

However, because I was a man, those two lucky devils got the premier tour. We visited all the editorial departments on the twentieth floor, me being personally introduced at each stop by the staffer who guided us about. Much was made of my old-boy Princeton heritage. There was, you see, still a certain self-consciousness at *Sports Illustrated* because, well, we were the people at Timeink who covered such a dubious thing as, well, *games,* so the fact that an actual Ivy Leaguer had deigned to throw in his lot with *SI* was something of a plum for the whole team. I had not known, till now, that I threw off so much light merely by virtue of my prior academic address.

Having negotiated all of the twentieth floor, we migrated to others. There was the Timeink library, to which a girl from the clip desk might just get herself promoted if she exhibited promise clipping. Here, she could file and even aspire to answering telephone queries from checkers like me. We visited the company exchequer, where I might someday withdraw expense advances, should I be dispatched to help a full-blooded writer on some story, that first baby step out of the bullpen.

Soon, in fact, I would indeed be given my first credit card. That was a wonderful new convenience in 1962. The card I was presented with was, however, good only for air travel. I think it was called just Airline Travel Card. But it was a plastic marvel of its age. You handed it in, and someone wrote up a ticket for you. No money changed hands. Timeink would get the bill.

There was an old writer with the magazine, Gerry. Lovely guy— been there since the first issue, in 1954. Wrote long, interesting pieces, mostly about obscure sports history—the sort of stuff I longed to do. But Gerry occasionally had something of a problem with Demon Rum. One day, shortly after he got his first Airline Travel Card, he was at Idlewild Airport going to, let's say, Houston. But in the bar, he heard a flight being called for, oh, Seattle. Hmmm. Sounds interesting. Gerry took his EZ-to-use new plastic card and booked a first-class chair to Seattle instead. Arriving there, he heard a flight called for St. Louis. And on and on, crisscrossing the republic. Took 'em days to finally catch up with Gerry. (Of course, that was, as we are all wont to say now, "before nine-eleven.")

The girls and I were escorted next to the infirmary. Timeink had its own doctors and nurses, its own mini hospital. Naturally, the company provided full medical benefits. Dental too, you ask? Of course, dental. Hey, as we say, is the pope a slam dunk? In fact, if you didn't regularly avail yourself sufficiently of these free health services, the company would berate you, they would write you inter-office memos and then call you up and demand that you make time for your complete, free physical. Come on down!

And, of course, the clock started immediately on my pension benefits and my profit-sharing plan, and if you wanted to start a little nest egg for yourself in the stock market, the company would also match it, dollar for dollar. That's just the way it was then. I don't remember being especially impressed at that benevolent way of the world. Certainly, Timeinkers weren't. You see, there actually was a good reason to settle for being a Phi Beta Kappa clip girl—namely, that you could look around the building for a stupider husband, albeit a chump with a lifetime sinecure and great benefits.

So, the grand tour was over, and I bid good-bye to the girls, as they headed off to their respective dungeons, while I hied to the glamorous bullpen. I was presented with my own desk and my Royal typewriter and a double-decker in-and-out box. Timeink even gave everybody in editorial his own dictionary. It seemed to me rather like being presented with a missal when you entered a seminary. I put it on my own personal shelf. And then, of course, we got all the other Timeink magazines and all the many New York newspapers personally delivered to us. Mornings started late and lunches lasted long. After the day's labor, there would be many impromptu parties, delicately called "pourings," to celebrate this and that. Whatever. Yes, I was now officially ensconced on the twentieth floor, and my future was very definitely not up for grabs.

23

THE KID

Over the long haul, the best way to mature is to catch on early, but grow up late.

"The Team of '64," *Sports Illustrated*, 1979

There are many roles a man finds himself in throughout life. Son, Student, Husband, Father, Breadwinner, and so forth. If he is successful: Star, Hunk, Boss, Man About Town, Grand Old Man. But nothing, do I believe—nothing in this world is ever quite so thrilling if just once you get to be The Kid. That is, you, as a novice, are accepted by your elders into their privileged company. You are not quite a peer. You are tolerated more than embraced, on trial, but you are at least allowed to step into the penumbra of the inner circle, permitted there to sniff the aroma of wisdom and humor and institutional savoir faire that belongs to those old hands who have already *made it.*

You can be The Kid when you are the freshman on the varsity, the pledge in the fraternity, the second looey in the officers' club, the junior account executive who's invited to play in the right member-guest—wherever, you are the rare younger aspirant who is admitted to that higher aristocracy. It is a heady sensation. It was at *Sports Illustrated* that I was, for the one and only time in my life, The Kid.

Now, in those halcyon days, there was still a lot of booze in journalism. Writers—perhaps especially sportswriters—were understood to be two-fisted drinkers. You wrote a story, or you finished a chapter, then, first thing, you went out and bellied up to the bar. (Of course, all too often, some of us bellied up to the bar before we wrote a story.)

When I was The Kid, I was regaled with the tales of the sportswriter who covered for his tosspot buddy by filing a story for him after he wrote his own piece, and the punch line was that the sober writer's editor called him up the next day and asked him why he hadn't written as good a story as his rival had—when, of course, he *had* written that story himself.

It was not all just jolly cocktails, of course. Journalists could be just as vulnerable to John Barleycorn as everybody else. As a leprechaun of a guy named Bill Riordan, a recovered alcoholic, who was Jimmy Connors's wink-and-a-nod manager, explained it to me: "Frank, as my dear mother told me: there's only three kinds of people who can be drunks: Irish, Indians, and everybody else."

Nevertheless, drinking was something of a merit badge for writers. Most newspapers had a designated bar in the neighborhood where reporters gathered. That was the tradition. *Sports Illustrated* had one, too. When I arrived it was a humble joint called the Three G's. When it was closed down, the managing editor, Andre Laguerre, took one writer, Bud Shrake, off the mere sportswriting detail and gave Bud the really important assignment of reconnoitering the neighborhood to choose the next appointed vocational gin mill. It immediately became, however undistinguished, the office away from the office.

To be in these watering holes was something like taking up residence in a smudge pot, too, for, of course, back in that day almost everybody smoked—cigars and pipes adding to the mundane cigarette smog. The contents of the glasses were invariably brown-hued: mostly Scotch, a few Canadians, or the odd bourbon, which I, with my southern background, favored. In the summer, some of the crowd would switch to gin, but for the life of me I can't recall anybody drinking vodka then. The goddamn Russians drank vodka, and Russians were commie red rats. Nobody ordered anything neat either. That's the one thing they've got wrong on *Mad Men,* where all the 1960s ad guys throw down straight shots. Perhaps it's all very manly to be a two-fisted drinker, but the hallmark of drinking was camaraderie.

If you just tossed a whiskey back, then you were left standing there without a drink in your hand. Correctly, you imbibed midway between a sip and a gulp.

So it was that one day I was given to understand that I was The Kid who could go down to the saloon where the managing editor and his apostles drank, there to take up a position on the fringes, listen and learn, and dare to speak only when spoken to. The youngest writer above me in this coterie was Bill Leggett, and Bill was almost a decade older than I, but he was so callow compared with the others that he was called simply Young. Just that: "Hey, Young," "What's up, Young?" And here I was, far younger than Young himself. What were they going to call me: Real Young? Too Young? Instead, it became the only time in my life when I was called by my diminutive—"Frankie."

Well, there would be one occasion each evening when I was addressed as "Mr. DeFord." That's when we played the "match game," a traditional divertissement long enjoyed by journalists in saloons—which required (I do not know why) the players to address one another formally, i.e., Mr. Maule, Mr. Werner, Mr. Fimrite, Mr. Laguerre, and, yes, even Mr. DeFord. I sometimes wonder if anybody still plays the match game anywhere. Among other things: who has matches anymore?* Sometimes I even think: is it possible that I am the last living person on the face of the earth to have played the match game—that perhaps I'm like one of those Eskimos who is the last to speak his language? So, I'd better explain, for posterity.

The match game is simplicity itself, and that is probably why it enjoyed such sustained popularity, for it could be played nearly as well drunk as sober. It wasn't like poker or sex; you really couldn't *take advantage* of anybody playing the match game. Each player was given three matches—ideally wooden, although that requirement could be waived. Usually, with us, the matches were distributed by an old

---

*I also wonder occasionally: where did all the ashtrays go? Ashtrays used to be everywhere in people's houses, and now you never see one. For God's sake, where are they?

writer named Morrie Werner, who was the closest friend of Laguerre. Morrie had been a biographer of some note in his youth—notably, in 1925, for his no-holds-barred life of Brigham Young—but now he was on the staff simply in the position of Laguerre's boon companion.

Morrie would gamble on anything. On one occasion, in the Canadian Football League, there were two teams nicknamed the Rough Riders. Well, one of them (I forget which) was the Roughriders and the other was the Rough Riders, but, orally, that was a distinction without a difference (or the other way round; I can never remember). So at the bar, somebody says to Morrie, "There's a big game in the Canadian Football League, and it's pick 'em. You wanna bet me five bucks? I like the Rough Riders."

"OK," Morrie said. On another occasion there was a Morrie Werner Death pool. Everybody chose a year when Morrie would die. Morrie got in on that, too.

Morrie would spend the morning in his office cubicle studying the *Racing Form,* recommending what bets Andre and he should make with their bookie. At lunch hour, and then after work, it was Morrie's job to drink with Andre and entertain him and the others in their company. Morrie was risible (a favored word Laguerre used fondly, in appreciation).

Almost everybody in the office adored Morrie, though, and it seemed only an idiocyncratic detail that he picked up a paycheck even though he really didn't do anything in the nature of actual work. In those days, it took a heap of gothic misbehaving for anyone to get let go at Timeink. Anyway, it wasn't as if Morrie was taking somebody else's job. He was just a pleasant extra, like a stylish gay guy at a dinner party. And after all, truth to be told, not everyone then at Timeink was exactly, shall we say, pulling his weight.

Laguerre was not one to share confidences with me, but one late night at the bar, after I had been The Kid for several years and thus had fully entered the inner sanctum, he told me why Alice, the horse-show writer, was still on the staff. In 1954, when the magazine was created, Alice had been hired to be a regular bylined authority on that sport. Remember, the original assumption by both the sales staff and the editorial staff was that *Sports Illustrated* needed to write about all the swishy, chic sports in order to attract upscale advertisers. One time, smack in the middle of the football season, the cover they picked was "Autumn Leaves." Let's see if that flies at the Tiffany's ad agency. So, likewise, in the same manner of thinking, they had hired Alice as a horse-show writer, although, say, they hadn't thought to have a full-time basketball writer.

It had been Laguerre, who took over in 1960, when the magazine was still bleeding money, who changed all this. He simply thought that if the magazine was so radical as to be called *Sports Illustrated,* it should either sink or swim by covering popular *sports*. Even if they were sweaty. If advertisers didn't want to buy into this, fuck 'em. At least we'd go down swinging at pitches over the plate. So it was that soon there was nary a story about horse shows. But Alice had a fine office, and I'd see her about now and again, and she kept her editor, Roger Hewlett, *abreast* of what was going on in the horse-show world. Roger was basically the guy in charge of all the sports we *used* to cover.

Anyway, Alice was a nice lady, and I'm sure she had the horse-show beat down pat, even if we were no longer choosing to share her knowledge with subscribers, but sharing it only with Roger Hewlett. So this is how Laguerre explained her continuing presence to me: "I'll never let Alice go, Frankie. It's not her fault that the magazine changed around her."

In many respects, Timeink really was the last of the old world.

But OK, now The Kid has had three Old Grandads and it's time for his free drink and the match game. You see, the way it worked at the bars where Laguerre brought in a crowd was that you got the fourth drink on the house. Understand, I don't mean if four guys came in and ordered a round, they only charged you for three. No, it was only *your* personal, individual fourth drink that was free. Well, figure it out. Everybody with any economic horse sense had four. (Or eight.) You come in, you buy a drink, and for Chrissake, you can't fly on one wing, so you have another. Now, you've put away two, so who in his right mind isn't going to order one more when you know that now you've reached the tipping point where it means two for one? The old two for the road.

Guaranteed, too, nobody cheated the barkeep by, say, having three Dewars and water himself and giving the fourth one to a buddy who also drank Scotch. Never. That would've been common.

Sometimes there was the ABF.

That was Laguerre's expression. It meant the Absolute Bloody Final. (Although often the ABF wasn't the ABF.)

So, anyway, here we all are at the bar, and Morrie starts on his fourth, or maybe his ABF, and suddenly becomes Mr. Werner, as the rest of us are also suddenly deemed messieurs. He declares that we will have a trilogy—the absolute minimum, three games. Mr. Werner takes out a matchbox, and although he was usually the official dispenser of the matches, his hands shake as he distributes them. "Watchmaker's hands," someone would always say, guaranteed. Guffaws all around in honor of the brilliant repartee. Dutifully, playing his part, Morrie grumbles.

Mr. Werner then presents three matches apiece to everyone, and we each clutch them in the hand that we choose to thrust into our coat pocket. Now the game begins. Everybody decides how many of the three matches he will drop into his pocket and how many he will retain in his closed fist when he places it upon the bar.

Let's say five gentlemen are playing. That means there can be, total, zero to fifteen matches held in the assembled fists. Each gentleman guesses. Let's say I, Mr. DeFord, have the honor and go first. I'd probably say seven or eight—the chalk, somewhere in the middle. Then, in turn—"And now, to you, Mr. Tower . . ."—each player picks another number, usually first moaning that the winning number has obviously already been taken. (Uttered agreement all around.) Then, when all five players have assayed their guesses, we all open our hands and the total is revealed. The player who picked the right number is excused, thereupon to return to his drink and to critique the further action at will. And the second round in the first game of the trilogy begins with a possible high of twelve matches. When only two players are left, the final competition becomes best of three. Finally, there is a loser, and he pays everyone. It was a dollar a man in those days.

"I'm sorry, Mr. Kram, but it was a noble effort," Mr. Werner says, consoling the loser. There was never any mocking the poor fellow who lost. That would be common.

The match game is still the only contest I've ever been involved with (or even heard about) where there is no winner, just one loser. There was never any sense of triumph, just relief.

It was so very genteel. We played it endlessly. When it was finally time to go home, there would be the Penultimate Game, and then the Ultimate Game, and then perhaps the Ultimate Ultimate Game, and maybe finally the Post-Ultimate Game.

In 1966, when the regular bar was a place called Le Steak de Paris, which had a name fancier than its cuisine, somehow it was decided that to celebrate the Christmas break, at lunchtime on December 12, we would have a monster match game, open to each and everyone on the staff. Mr. Werner drew up the rules. They began with a proclamation:

> As this game, which the NMA [National Match Association] does not sponsor but which as commissioner I have agreed to supervise, is in every respect unusual it cannot go into the record books of the NMA as an official game.

And there were other stipulations, such as:

> Each player will hold regulation matches supplied by the NMA. Any attempt to clown the game by using pretzels, swizzle sticks, or other objects than the official matches will cause the player

to be fined twenty-five cents to each player and to be excluded at once from the game.

Unplayable guesses will also entail fines. . . . Such guesses are usually designed purposefully to deceive unfairly an opponent or opponents. In the case of an unplayable guess the man making it will be automatically declared the loser and will pay everyone else a dollar.

Side bets are permissible. . . .

Players are urged to make their guesses as rapidly as consonant with due consideration so that the game does not take too long. Such remarks during the games as "I don't like it," "You've got me," "That's the number," common in games with less people, can only be aggravating in this one, and players are urged to refrain from them.

Players are also cautioned against making any critical remarks or abusive remarks of other players' guesses. Such remarks are always ill-mannered and in the interests of decorum should be repressed.

Players are especially cautioned to keep their hands closed until all the players have called . . . before opening their hands. Otherwise the game will have to be played over and over and such a process could become interminable.

—M. R. Werner

I can't recall who the poor sap was who lost. I only know it wasn't The Kid.

But Lord knows I lost my fair share. I just looked upon it as if it were a tax on admission to society—or as a ticket to ride on a conveyance into the past, for all the other players were older than I and told tales, firsthand, of things that seemed to me to have happened in history. Not that the conversation was especially high-toned, you understand. It was, however, part of the liturgy that many great magazine story ideas came out of the colloquies at the bar. Truth to tell, though, the ratio of story ideas to blather was about a million to one. It was an article of faith, though, which excused all the time spent at the bar, that a plethora of brilliant story ideas had, through the years, flowed out of the conversation.

Well, all right, I do remember one time, when Volkswagen had a commercial claiming that the Bug could float, and someone said, Why don't we find out?—and that led to a pseudoscientific story in which someone actually drove a Volkswagen Bug into a river. I don't recall how long the Bug actually stayed afloat, but the important thing was that, then, for years, whenever anybody wanted to certify that many unforgettable stories were naturally produced at the bar despite doubts from captious outsiders, someone would say, "Well, remember the time the Volkswagen . . ." and there would follow much affirmative mumbling.

And just for the record: how many stories are dreamed up nowadays by modern healthy journalists hanging out at gymnasiums and vegan restaurants?

Well, would it surprise you that there was, however, almost no talk of women? Certainly none of sex. That would have been common, big-time. Indeed, given that it was a classic men-in-groups, there was only a modest amount of vulgarity. (Werner, when pretending to be exercised, would use the expression "shit sandwich"; that was the apogee of crude dialogue.)

Laguerre would not countenance talk of politics, so there went that generally popular topic. No one even cared to bring up religion. But, talk of writing, of books, did flourish. Both Laguerre and Werner knew who the hell James Branch Cabell was, although I don't believe they gave me any credit for the relationship when I finally dared, discreetly, to mention it. There was a lot of teasing. I didn't understand it then, but just as I wanted to grow up, men who are older seek to hark back to when they were The Kid themselves. Trophy wives aren't the only regressive display in big boys' lives.

It was a wonderful time back then, even better because it was indeed me who was The Kid amid such company—and all the best because I don't suppose that sort of thing goes on anymore in a cost-efficient, globally competitive world. It was also the case, though, that all during this time the magazine got better and better and started making money, too.

So there was some smugness amongst us, too. But then: we god-damn well deserved it.

24

ANDRE

To my surprise, a "Journalist" is a popular drink in some environs.
It is made up of gin, both sweet and dry vermouth, cointreau, lemon
juice, with a touch of bitters. So, I asked the bartender if there is
any drink named "Sports Journalist"? No, he says. So, I have made
it up:"Cheap Scotch and Gatorade, Slivorice for hard-nose-ness,
sherry for sentimentality, and a dash of steak sauce."

NPR, 2005

Andre Laguerre, my first managing editor—always at Timeink: the
ME*—was a singular, almost mythic character, who had personally
refashioned our magazine, saving it from going out of business. He had
a French father and a British mother (she was the daughter of a lord)
and spent his misspent youth just like I had, going to the racetrack and
serving as a copyboy—in his case, in San Francisco, where his father,
a diplomat, was posted for a few years as a consul. Laguerre was an
incredible paradox: on the one hand he was almost constitutionally
withdrawn, a member of the press who wouldn't be interviewed by
the press ("That's intramural, Frankie"), but who, amongst the friends
he chose, was absolutely magnetic.

Andre had not been an especially stylish writer, distinguishing
himself most as a sports columnist in Paris, writing under the rakishly

---

*Or, for the Timeinkers who had been in the war, where commanding officers were called
"the old man," the ME also enjoyed that veterans' appellation.

Yank name of "Eddie Snow," but he adored good writing and seemed to have had drinks with every famous writer extant. He wore the same uniform every day: dark suit, white shirt with the sleeves rolled up to his forearms, solid dark tie loosened at the throat. He was a bit pudgy, was balding, peered through dark-rimmed glasses, and, as he stalked the halls, brandished a taped stick fashioned from the shaft of some golf club. I do not know where it came from or why he wielded it. If he ever played golf (or any sport), I never heard tell. He smoked cigars and drank Scotch and made the sun move across the heavens. Spencer Tracy would have been damn lucky to have been cast as Andre Laguerre.

Laguerre's mysterious past seemed to come out only in dribs and drabs. Born in England (in 1915), he had an early wandering up-bringing in both Europe and the Mideast before his father settled the family in California. Then schooling back in England, but no college, thank you—he turned down Oxford. Instead: freelance writer, in both English and French. International correspondent. At age twenty-three, covered Chamberlain in Munich. Joined the French army as an en-listed man and was on the Maginot Line when the panzers overran it. At Dunkirk, stranded for days on the beach, finally got aboard a French destroyer. Ship hit a mine, sank. Laguerre wounded, treading water, dodging German machine-gun bullets. Plucked out of Channel by British ship. Hospitalized. Joins Free French. Becomes de Gaulle's press secretary. Marries a daughter of Russian royalty. Almost killed by grenades in Saigon covering the Indochina war. Has a racing stable, with silks of white with a black cross of Lorraine, back and front.* You just never knew.

---

*In America, one of his writers, Virginia Kraft, who married into big money and a rac-ing stable, named a horse after him: A Laguerre. He ran no better than Frank Deford.

One rare moment of revelation came of an evening at the bar when the subject of a recent plane crash came up. To my surprise, Laguerre spoke up: "I was in a plane crash once."

We all turned to look to him, shocked that he had actually ventured some personal revelation, never mind that it was so spectacular as well. "It was a flight from Paris to London," he went on. "We crashed just short of Heathrow." But having teased us enough, he then merely reached for his Scotch, perfectly leaving us all in suspense. Well, The Kid couldn't stand it. "So, sir, what did you do next?" I blurted out.

He took a swallow, allowing the drama to build, and only then simply said, "Why, I took a cab, Frankie."

Another time, Jack Olsen, one of his writers whom he was particularly close to, told me that Laguerre had volunteered to him that once he had been sent through the most dangerous waters, dodging Nazi surveillance, traveling in a submarine from England to Norway, carrying some secret message.

While Andre was a considerable influence on me, it is odd now, for as I look back I can only recall two occasions when he directly offered advice. I imagine he mostly somehow guided me by osmosis, for his genius as an editor was that he made you want to please him, but he wanted you to do that by writing in your own distinct way. In any event, when it came to advice, first, to assuage my doubt, when I wondered whether writing about sports was really substantial, he simply said: "Frankie, it doesn't matter *what* you write about. All that matters is how *well* you write." Simple as it is, I suppose that has helped sustain me all these years as a sportswriter.

Then, upon that other occasion when Laguerre tendered advice, I was standing with him and another writer, Ron Fimrite—who had managed, with his wise eye and wry whimsy, first to be a terrific newspaper columnist in San Francisco and then a superb long-form writer for the magazine. The subject of a gentleman's leisure arose. Laguerre withdrew his cigar and portentously declared: "Every man must make a decision: either to drink with the boys or to chase women."

Ron, who was twice divorced at the time, moaned: "Now you tell me."

Actually, while at the bar there was so little talk about women, occasionally a real female would actually join Laguerre's coterie there. Whenever Martha Duffy, a writer at *Time,* would come by, she was accepted genially, and no special notice was made of her gender. Pat Ryan edited more of my stories than anyone else; she understood me, as both a writer and a person, better then than any male editor. Andre was very fond of Pat, too, so on those rare times when she dropped in, she was immediately welcomed into our midst. But people like Martha and Pat weren't, in the context, female persons, you understand. They were like the Asians who were called "honorary whites" in South Africa during apartheid. But women being women—that is, wives or girlfriends—never appeared. It was then, very simply, still a man's world.

It wasn't as if Andre himself didn't like women, either, but there was a certain drawing-room-comedy aspect to him: the idea was to toy with women and escape their clutches until they finally caught you in Act III; he'd courted his wife, Natalie, for almost a decade before she finally gave him the ultimatum.

So it was one evening at the Three G's when I informed Laguerre that I was going to marry Carol. Upon hearing that revelation, he literally put his drink down on the bar and clasped a hand to his brow. "Oh my God, Frankie, that's the worse news I've heard in weeks."

Tex Maule, the pro football writer, was standing beside Laguerre. He had been a catcher in a trapeze act before he obliged into sportswriting. Tex had also been married a number of times. He shook his head in dismay, too, as Laguerre further pondered my shocking news. "Tell you what, Frankie," Andre finally said. "If you don't marry her, I'll give you a $3,000 raise."

I was making about $10,000 at the time. Thirty percent is a hell of a raise. Then Maule piped up: "I'll throw in another thousand myself."

They were both serious, too. There was honor at the bar.

But: love or money? I married the girl.

The first day I came back into the office after my wedding, I was called down to see Laguerre. He told me he wanted me to go to Miami Beach to see Muhammad Ali and ask if the champ would agree to open up for a story about becoming a Muslim. I'd never covered boxing and thought it was an odd assignment for me, but as I left his office, as if it were an afterthought, Andre casually called after me: "Oh, uh, Frankie, you can take your bride."

Ali had already told the magazine he didn't want to do that story. It took me five minutes at the gym in Miami Beach to find out that he was sticking by his decision. A long-distance phone call would have sufficed. It was just that Andre wanted to give me a little extra honeymoon, but it wouldn't have been in keeping with his image, so he couldn't bring himself to come right out and say that.

In fact, away from the bar and his pals, in the office, Laguerre was something of a bifurcated character. On the one hand, he much respected Henry Luce and felt great loyalty to the mother company. He bled for *Sports Illustrated*. In 1974, when the concept of *People* magazine was being auditioned with trial issues, I was shanghaied from *Sports Illustrated* to work for a few weeks on two makeups. They were hugely successful, and so the new magazine was commissioned. The managing editor, Dick Stolley, asked me to be his assistant managing editor. I was, frankly, horrified at the idea.

Years before, Laguerre had himself asked me if I wanted to try editing. I told him, rather condescendingly, that, well, I wouldn't mind having his job, but I didn't want to spend my time doing all the drudgery leading up to that.

"No, Frankie," he said, "it doesn't work that way."

"I know that, sir."

Smiling, he shooed me away from his desk.

When Stolley offered me the post at *People* it was rather understood that a Timeinker was a good soldier who accepted assignments as orders. The proposition happened to come just before I was leaving to cover Wimbledon and, coincidentally, shortly after Laguerre had been relieved of his job and been shuffled off to London to examine the remote possibility that *Sports Illustrated* might start up a European edition. As soon as I got to London I went to his office and told him of the job offer at this new *People* rag.

"You have any interest in it?" he asked me.

"None at all."

"Then turn it down."

"Well, that's what I was planning to do, but I just wanted to talk to you about it first."

He nodded at me, and then, very pointedly, said, "Of course, you understand now, Frankie, if you do turn this job down, you will never be able to take any other position in the company."

"No problem," I replied. My vocational intentions hadn't changed any from the day I'd first arrived at the employment office as not very bright; the only job that interested me at Timeink was being a writer at *Sports Illustrated*.

But the larger point was the one that Laguerre was making *for* the company, that if you were taking Timeink's money and perks, you owed it what it asked of you. I suppose this wasn't a hell of a lot different from committing yourself to de Gaulle.

Yet as much as Laguerre was a drop-dead loyalist, he was also an iconoclast. On the magazine, it was then strictly church and state—editorial and business—but technically, on the masthead, the publisher outranked the managing editor. Laguerre, though, was barely civil to anybody on the business side. There being a proliferation of salesmen named Sandy, he referred to all business types as "the Sandys." They, in turn, were terrified when they actually had to schedule an appointment and trek to his office to petition him about an ad placement or some such thing. And, as for us, writers and editors, we always were proud that our noble ME defended us artistes from the crass sons of bitches who made their grubby living in commerce. He was our Mr. Roberts.

But it was also true that Laguerre could be just as cavalier to his editorial equals at the other magazines. They knew he thought they were bores and bootlickers, too. Laguerre would often blow off the weekly Monday luncheon that all Timeink managing editors were supposed to attend—the meeting of the joint chiefs of staff. When he did show up, he would sulk and not participate in the conversation. Now this is a man who, once, when asked to say a couple of words at a Christmas party, stood up and said: "Merry Christmas." This is a man who once, famously, at a conference, when Luce made a statement, then turned to Laguerre and said, "Wouldn't you agree, Andre?" replied, "No, Harry, I wouldn't." But when Laguerre played the tar baby at the managing editor's lunches and didn't *participate*, it was infuriating to the others—perhaps especially to those comrades of his who might some day be his superiors.

So long as Luce lived and ruled, Andre could be imperious. He had made *Sports Illustrated* work, made it profitable, so that Luce went to his grave batting a thousand on magazines he'd started. But after Luce died in 1967, Laguerre had nobody watching his back. It's revealing that during this period, *Life*, once the wonder of the magazine world, began to founder. Laguerre was not averse to letting us know that he'd love a crack at trying to save it. He was, too, the obvious choice on the Timeink roster. The company was going through a bad patch at the time, and there was even a celebratory article in *New York* magazine about Laguerre entitled "And Now for the Good News at Time Inc." If anything, though, that only made the new higher-ups angrier and more jealous of him. He never was given the chance to save *Life*, and when they finally pulled the plug on Laguerre in 1974, he wasn't offered the kind of cushy make-work job that other top dogs invariably got at Timeink when they were replaced.

He was dead in only another five years, age sixty-three. The *New York Times,* which, as I wanted to tell Abe Rosenthal, didn't know jack about sports, ran a brief wire-service obituary, buried deep, two paragraphs long. But, really, there have been only three sports editors who've been, in the parlance of their trade, superstars: Richard Fox of the *Police Gazette,* Stanley Woodward of the *Herald-Tribune,* and Andre.

The only time in my life when I was an editor, at the *National,* I put one photograph on the wall right behind my desk and above my old typewriter where I couldn't miss it. It was of Andre.

25

MR. KING WILL SEE YOU NOW

*For most of the Republic's existence we had reveled in the folk
wisdom that country bumpkins were the true brains, certain to get
the best of city slickers. Almost overnight, though, the reverse became
true; a new myth held that "street smarts" was the best kind.*
                     "A Player for the Ages," *Sports Illustrated*, 1988

Don King* stood me up twice when I had appointments to interview
him.

Now, understand, there were many occasions when an athlete
was late for his interview with me. You can almost expect that. Constitutionally, a great many athletes don't think they have to be on time
for journalists. Or many other people.

But Donking stood me up twice, and nobody else in sports ever
did that to me even once.

Fool me once, shame on you. Fool me twice . . .

Years later, in an effort to apologize (though why, years later, he
bothered wasn't clear to me), Donking invited me over for an afternoon
barbecue at his brownstone on the Upper East Side.

Mike Tyson was there, out on the stoop. When a pretty lady
walked by, he chased after her down the sidewalk and tried to get a date
with her. She would have nothing to do with him whatsoever. Finally,

---

*More than any other person in sports, he is always referred to by both his names to-
gether: Donking.

in that squeaky little voice of his, Mike said: "Isn't there anything about me you like?"

She said: "Well, I like your tie."

So he took it off and gave it to her, and she resumed walking, without looking back.

I have no recollection of why Mike Tyson would have a tie on at a barbecue in the middle of the afternoon.

Donking never did apologize to me, but he worked the grill himself and made a good barbecue, all the while laughing uproariously at his own many ordinary observations and declarations.

26

HOBEY AND DANNY AND BILL

Perhaps no man is so haunted as the one who was once stunned
by instant success, for he lives thereafter with the illusion that
tomorrow is bound to bring one more bolt of good fortune.
"Tender Cheers for the Prospect," *Sports Illustrated*, 1977

The edge that I had, coming to *Sports Illustrated*, was that I had Bill Bradley in my hip pocket.

Now, let me set the scene first. The magazine in 1962, while changing under Laguerre—putting the NFL on the cover and horse shows on the back burner—was, however, still evolving. Amongst the popular sports, basketball was still viewed as the most downscale. In the 299 issues before Laguerre assumed command, America's prime winter sport had merited exactly nine covers. For purposes of comparison, there had been a dozen covers featuring dogs and nine starring birds (not to mention one seal cover and one monkey cover). During the same period, there had been seven yacht-racing covers. You get the picture. Basketball was bush.

The only person of consequence on the magazine who cared about basketball was a feisty little fellow with a brush cut named Jerry Tax—the last person I knew who smoked unfiltered Camel cigarettes (and he would live a good, long life, so there). Jerry had been the basketball writer, and he was the basketball editor when I arrived. Nobody else really gave a tinker's dam about basketball.

The fact that I had actually played the vulgar game, and at least sorta maybe at least knew the difference between a zone and man-to-man defense, made me both a curiosity and a more valuable asset. Jerry Tax was delighted to find someone of like mind and made sure that I would be designated the basketball researcher. So it was that one day when there was something roughly called a "basketball planning meeting" I advised America's sportsweekly that the best sophomore player in the nation was, believe it or not, hidden away in the Ivy League, at, of all places, Princeton.

Yeah, right.

The general attitude was, naturally, that I was just a loony Tiger fanatic who was blowing smoke about my beloved alma mater. But when I had come back to Princeton after being the guide-on, as a senior in the fall of 1961, Bill Bradley arrived at the same time, as a freshman, out of the blue.

I lived at my club that year. The clubs, notoriously, dominated Princeton then. Nobody since back before Fitzgerald had been able to write a word about Princeton without going on, censorially, about its infamous club system. The clubs were displayed for Princeton's local color as the opium dens were to Shanghai.

They had been created back in the nineteenth century when fraternities were outlawed, and, essentially, that's all the clubs were: fraternities without Greek letters. What distinguished Princeton, though, was that virtually *all* upperclassmen joined one of the seventeen clubs. They were invariably referred to in the press as Princeton's "exclusive" clubs, but, of course, they weren't as a whole because virtually everybody was in one. In fact, they were actually known as "eating clubs," because the university itself stupidly didn't provide anyplace else to eat. A few real individualists (Ralph Nader, for example) simply opted to dine at hamburger joints and take other potluck around town, but that took a strong, idealistic constitution.

The problem was that every February when the clubs selected members in the middle of their sophomore year in what was called by the awful, revealing name of "Bicker," a few guys wouldn't get a bid anywhere. Most of them, invariably, were Jews, so the New York papers would make a big fuss about it, and Princeton was labeled as anti-Semitic, which it could be, and certainly during Bicker. (African-Americans weren't an issue, because, essentially, there weren't any of them.) The handful of guys who didn't get a bid to a club were known as "hundred percenters," because their abject failure to appeal to *any* of the seventeen clubs denied the university the goal of total inclusion and gave Princeton a black eye. Sometimes, then, the handful of hundred percenters were parceled out to the clubs. It was a scarring enough experience if you didn't get a bid to one of the clubs you aimed for and your friends all left you in the lurch; just imagine how wounding it was not to have anyone at all bid you, so that you had to be foisted on someone just to be able to eat. You might as well have had to wear a % sign on you, à la Ms. Prynne.

One night, late, I was with a couple of guys in my club's library. One of them was a hundred percenter we had accepted as our noble part of the bargain to get the *New York Post* off Princeton's ass. He was actually a pretty good guy—different, yes, but really quite entertaining. Let me tell you, he was better company than some of the boring tweedbags who had come through the front door.

The three of us were just shooting the bull, but somehow the subject came around to a point where the hundred percenter started talking about how sickening it'd been to have been rejected by all seventeen clubs. The other two of us just sat there, mute, stunned. He didn't go on for all that long, just long enough to say how it had almost destroyed him, so he had gone into the army and tried to forget it, but then he made himself come back to Princeton because otherwise he would've always been running away. Then he told us that he had come to appreciate how a lot of people in the club treated him nicely even though they knew he was just a bird with a damaged wing whom we'd taken in as our collegiate form of noblesse oblige.

The other two of us never said a word. Then the hundred percenter simply got up, and, really quite formally, said, "Thank you,

Jamie. Thank you, Frank. Thank you for listening. I have to do this every now and then just to let people know."

And he left. And Jamie and I looked at each other, and we were touched and ashamed, both.

My club was Ivy. It was the oldest, founded in 1879. It had a bad reputation and a good reputation, both of which were fair enough. The bad reputation was that it was hoity-toity. We were the Ivy fairies, and fucking-A exclusive. La-di-da. One year at Bicker, Ivy took in only eleven sophomores, and the *Daily Princetonian* noted that "even Jesus chose twelve." The good reputation was that Ivy really could be more of a salon, that snooty though it might be in some respects, it also had this screw loose whereby the club selected a cadre of oddballs every year—like me, for example—who could make the place a little edgy.

The class before me at Ivy—we called classes "sections"—proved all of this in spades. Out of the thirty-four members of the section, three of them were named Rhodes scholars—surely the most ever from such a small sample, anywhere. The three Rhodes scholars were all quite different people, too. Eddie Pell was the president of the club that year. He had gone to prep school at Exeter and was a blue chip all the way, cowinner of the most prestigious award given to a Princeton undergraduate. During my junior year, for the Yale game, which was always the most important party weekend of the fall, I came down to the club for Sunday brunch, and there was a harpist playing in the common room. Typical Ivy Club fairies. But I thought it was really neat, because I knew Eddie had done it without any affectation.

The second Rhodes scholar was Pell's total opposite. His name was Jack Horton, and he was a scholarship kid from Wyoming, from the HF Bar Ranch, wherever the hell that was. He majored in geology. I had no inkling we even had geology at Princeton, let alone that anyone could *major* in it. Jack learned lacrosse from scratch and made all-American. He had a big laugh and sometimes wore cowboy clothes.

Then there was the third Rhodes scholar, whose name was Dan Sachs. He was from Emmaus, a little town in the Lehigh Valley of Pennsylvania. His father, a pilot, had been killed *after* the war, coming home from fighting in the Pacific, when his plane was lost over the Rockies. I know that life is unfair and all that, but life should never be so ironically unfair—especially for a small boy, as Danny had been at the time his father crashed.

But Sachs grew up smart and agile and ambitious. Over time, he decided that he would like to try to become president of the United States. Danny had singled that particular job out because he believed in shooting for the stars. "I fear mediocrity more than I fear anything else," he said. Although he was often uneasy in idle company and was without much humor—"my phlegmatic, essentially German soul"— Danny had the rare ability—characteristic of the best leaders—to make someone whom he got to know believe that whatever quality this friend valued most in himself also thrived in Sachs.

Yet he was not at all facile. He could not even quite appreciate spontaneity, marveling once, "How can people just live for the moment?" Al McGuire's advice, which I loved, was: "Congratulate the temporary." But Danny Sachs just couldn't do that. He was most definitely in it for the long haul. His intensity and scrutiny would have been intimidating except for the fact that he was so gracious.

The fall of 1957, when I arrived at Princeton, he was number forty-six, the sophomore star of the football team—and that was still a time, if in its waning days, when the best Ivy League teams were competitive in the land. It had, after all, only been six years since Princeton had been undefeated, ranked sixth in the nation, with Dick Kazmaier winning the Heisman Trophy. Sachs played Kazmaier's position, tailback in the old single wing, which had gone out of fashion almost everywhere but at Princeton. The tailback would take a direct snap from center and run or pass. Sometimes tailbacks kicked, too, and were called triple threats. There is no one quite like that left in the specialized game of football anymore—not Michael Vick or

Tim Tebow, nobody. There was a different sort of romantic glory attached to a single-wing tailback, especially a wispy wonder like Dick Kazmaier or Danny Sachs.

Great handsome crowds showed up at Palmer Stadium, for football at Princeton was still taken seriously then, and the cheers were as meaningful as ever they had been. We would chant "Go, Tiger, go!"—the singular, you understand, because when Princeton started playing football there were no Clemson Tigers or Auburn Tigers or Detroit Tigers or any other Tigers but us. *Tiger, tiger, sis boom bah.* The girls wore corsages and much plaid, and camel hair overcoats were in profusion. After every game, all the students and alumni—and the players on the field, too—would stand and place their right hand above their heart and then let it drift out and back, in sweet salute, raising our voices in our anthem, "Old Nassau," which was sung to the tune of "Auld Lang Syne."

> *Our hearts will give, while we shall live,*
> *Three cheers for Old Nassau.*

The Princeton uniforms still had orange tiger stripes down the black sleeves. Like the single wing, the uniforms were unique because they were out of fashion. Sachs himself was a marvel. Number forty-six was All-Ivy. He would never be so good again after his sophomore year, though, for he was too brittle, and in every game he got beaten up. "He ran too hard for his body," one of his coaches explained.

Why in the world do you play? his faculty adviser, Charles Gillispie, asked him after Sachs was hurt again. Danny replied only, "But, sir, I must." A few years later, after he saw his first bullfight, he wrote, "Something of the medieval remains in my soul, I guess. Man against beast, the imminent threat of death with his skill and courage—this appeals to my sense of heroism."

The fact was that for all his becoming shyness and his retreat into scholarly solitude—he was Phi Beta Kappa—he privately adored acclaim and, in fact, needed it. When he left Princeton for Oxford, he wrote an admission: "This is a difficult time for me. The successes of my Princeton career are behind me and for the next ten years or so I pass into the shadows of the unknown. I feel the beginning of obscurity, and it has shaken my confidence. I've played before the crowds too long."

At least in this one regard, Sachs was kin to the most legendary of all Ivy Club members and all Princeton athletes, Hobey Baker. He was a football star and, for his era and even more, for long after, he was also the undisputed greatest American ice hockey player. The Heisman Trophy of college hockey is named for him. After Baker graduated from Princeton in 1914, he went to work on Wall Street, but shortly after World War I began he enlisted in the Lafayette Escadrille. Flying in battle against the Hun gave him the thrill he had missed after his *foudroyant* playing days at Princeton had concluded. *I pass into the shadows of the unknown.* As the war came to a close, Baker despaired that he would have to return to the humdrum life of a broker, and so, a month after Armistice Day, he took his plane up, unnecessarily, for a last spin. The plane crashed and Hobey Baker was killed—lyrically: the last man to die in the Great War.

It was page-one news, and the myth grew that Baker had crashed the plane on purpose rather than go back to a sere life that could never be so thrilling as it had been in the arena of players or fliers. That's probably just morbid romanticism, but the very fact that the idea took hold speaks to the glamour of Hobey Baker and his love of his gladiator's life.*

When I first personally encountered Sachs, I was astonished at how small he seemed. He was listed as 6 feet, 175 pounds, but he didn't appear either so tall or so heavy. Several years later, when I wrote the novel *Everybody's All-American,* which is much about the hero worship

---

*Ron Fimrite wrote a wonderful story about him for *Sports Illustrated.* Dan Curtis spent years trying to get a film script good enough to make a movie of Hobey Baker's life. He told me it was his greatest failed quest.

of sports stars, I remembered how I, as a freshman, had stood so in awe of Danny Sachs—even though he was just another student about my age—watching him dance and dodge between the sideline stripes.

Yet when I finally did meet him, he seemed so utterly normal. There was no aura, no immediate sense of his athletic brilliance. These first encounters with him took place on the junior varsity basketball team, when I was a sophomore. Danny was such a good athlete—he also starred at lacrosse—that he was encouraged to try out for the basketball team, too. So, if you will, I was Danny Sachs's *teammate.* But that's a stretch. It was only the next year, when we were in the same club, that I got to know him at all.

Princeton was then a very contained place. You could not call it "isolated," for goodness sake, because it was only a hop, skip, and a jump from both New York and Philadelphia, but, still, it certainly had a sense of insulation. It was a relatively small walking campus; there were fewer than three thousand students, all of them male; and cars were prohibited, so getting away was something of an effort. Girls were hard to come by. Simply by default, then, we were thrown together—often, perforce, with people who were outside your own circle. After all, the whole thing was only a somewhat larger circle, enclosed. So sometimes at Ivy I would end up at the dinner table with Danny, where we were served long, full hot meals by Hispanics from Trenton, who wore ties and cotton waiters' jackets and took our orders, catering to the young elite. We must've seemed insufferable to our servants. I never lived so sumptuously any other time in my life as I did at Ivy Club. You get used to it, though, and accept it, and rather quickly, too.

On a couple of other occasions at Ivy Danny and I found ourselves alone together and we had long, interesting conversations. He initiated them because he was a voracious reader, and he wanted to ask me about what it was like wanting to be a writer and learning the craft. He was working on his senior thesis (which he was writing in French, about Montaigne, and which would earn him highest honors—a "one-plus" in Princeton vernacular). I certainly would never dare say we were friends, but we were quite congenial, and I remember trying my best to sound wise and fascinating with him. He seemed to enjoy my company enough, though, probably because I was so different a specimen from him, and because by then I was chairman of the *Daily Princetonian*, a position that suggested I was achieving in my specialty, as he wanted to in his. Danny Sachs, you see, did not think of college as a place to dillydally. "If we fail to seize the vision now, in the years of intellectual strife when character becomes formed, then we can seldom hope to breathe life into the myth once we take up the tools of the world," he wrote shortly after he graduated.

Who wrote that sort of thing at that age? Who even thought that sort of thing through then?

Well, there was the one other.

Bill Bradley was entering his senior year in high school out in Missouri when Sachs went off to Oxford. By the time he graduated that spring, Bradley had committed himself to Duke, but he broke his foot and, with time on his hands, started rethinking his decision. He had two goals then: to go to Oxford and to become a diplomat. He concluded that he had a better chance to win a Rhodes scholarship at Princeton, so at the eleventh hour he changed his mind, shocking everyone who had told him to go to a hotshot basketball school. As he mentioned to me once, he'd always possessed the sort of perverse independence that allowed him to make the surprise choice. So it was that Bill just sort of showed up on campus, without fanfare; it was around the time Sachs was beginning his second year at Oxford.

In those innocent days, athletes had to play on freshmen teams, and Bradley became an instant sensation, if only on campus. I'd go down to watch him at Dillon gym, where he scored pretty much at will against the other poor Ivy freshmen; or, if they double- or even triple-teamed him, he'd be content to make beautiful pinpoint blind passes to his open teammates. It was a spectacle. But who knew? Who was paying attention to Ivy League freshman basketball? Today there

are actually basketball services that nationally rate—I'm serious—
fourth-graders. Then, basketball was pretty much word-of-mouth.
Even the NBA teams had no real scouts and would draft players
on say-so. When I arrived at *Sports Illustrated*, nobody at America's
sportsweekly had a clue who Bill Bradley was, let alone how good he
might really be.

But Jerry Tax, the basketball editor, finally decided to throw
me a bone and let me try to write a story about the bank president's
son who had turned down Duke and gone to Princeton and might
really be pretty darn good. After all, fish-out-of-water is better than
everything else in journalism except Cinderella and man-bites-dog.
So: my first real chance to shine as a writer. And not only did Bill
Bradley give me my big break, as I introduced him to the wider world,
but because he turned out to be everything I said he was and more,
my stock as a hoop expert soared. Why, I was as much a prodigy in
my line as Bradley was in his. The Kid knew his stuff.

By the time Bill was a senior and became national player of the
year, I had written even more about him. I liked him a lot. Yes, he
was damned serious, an old soul, but he had a good sense of humor.
I remember him paying me a visit at *Sports Illustrated* that summer
after he'd won his Rhodes scholarship. He came into my office and
straight-faced, arching those Mephistophelian eyebrows of his, told
me he was giving me a scoop. Breathlessly, I grabbed for my notebook,
poising my ballpoint. Then Bill told me that he had decided to pass
up Oxford and go right to the Knicks. Startled, I started to scribble it
all down, until he finally roared that it was only a joke.

In fact, it always baffled me why Bill so seldom showed that light
side when he was campaigning. He could be a really funny speaker
on those occasions when he wanted to, but he seemed to keep his wit
in check and be so damn sobersided most of the time.

Late in 1999, as he prepared to run against Al Gore for the
Democratic nomination, I was asked to introduce Bill at a dinner at
the 21 Club. Those in attendance were all his friends and admirers,

you understand, and when I gave him the floor, I kidded him a little and left myself wide open with some self-deprecating remarks.

I thought he would take the opening and lay into me, all in good fun—damn, I can take a punch for the cause—but instead, he just said, "Thank you, Frank," very formally, and then launched into a pro forma stump speech. I honestly thought I might have been out of line with my tone and remarks, but everybody assured me I was fine. It was just Bill being very earnest, in the earnest campaign-issues mode. A few months later he lost the New Hampshire primary to Al Gore by only 4 percent of the vote. If he'd just won that, the history of the world in the early twenty-first century could very well have been very different—and so much for the better. Maybe if he'd just loosened up a little more for the folks. But then, what do I know? I never was everybody's all-American; I never was a Rhodes scholar; I never won an NBA championship; I never won a Senate race.

Bradley had learned about Dan Sachs, the person, when he was at Princeton, and he grew fascinated by what he heard about him. But Bill never met Danny. By the time Bradley got to Oxford himself in the fall of 1965—mission accomplished—Danny was back in the United States, at Harvard Law. They were ships in the night, just passing each other by. Sachs had read history at Oxford, studying Lincoln in particular; he had stayed a third year, too, but for another reason altogether. He wanted to play rugby against Cambridge and earn a Blue, something very few Americans had ever been awarded. He sought that one last chance to play before the crowd before his life necessarily moved behind the dark side of the moon for a few years.

Law school was perhaps the one time in Sachs's life when he didn't excel. He was merely treading water, though, for he had no interest in the law per se, but turned to it only as a sidecar on his political journey. His immediate goal then was to go back to Pennsylvania and eventually represent the state as a Republican senator. By coincidence, in the summer of 1964, Bradley was working as an intern in Washington for Richard Schweiker, a Republican congressman from Pennsylvania who would himself become one of the state's senators.

And it was that same summer of 1964 when Danny Sachs noticed a lump behind his left knee. It was the same place where he had suffered an injury in the Penn game, in that great sophomore season of his in 1957. On July 10, he was told that it was cancerous. The growth was removed in an operation, but the doctors kept it to themselves that it was an incurable cancer, that it was hopeless, that Danny would never live to do any of the things he had prepared himself for. So, mostly, he would only be remembered for having been number forty-six.

Bradley, the best college basketball player in the land, led Princeton to the Final Four that winter of 1964–1965 and was drafted by the Knicks, but instead of turning pro after he graduated, he went off to Oxford, coincidentally assigned to Worcester College, just as Danny had been.

Sachs had fallen in love that spring of 1964, when the cancer was, unbeknownst to him, already spreading. He and Joan would go for long walks along the Charles River as the flowers came into bloom. Sports were behind him, but the whole rest of the world lay spread ahead of him. Even love now, too. One evening, when he was studying, Joan heard him speaking loudly, like an orator. Curious, she came into the room and asked what he was up to. He told her he was practicing a State of the Union speech. "Every man wants to get to the top of his profession," he explained, casually.

But then his health worsened, and he learned of his fatal diagnosis. He did the best with what time was left to him. That September, he was able to walk down the aisle with Joan, and she would bear him a daughter, Alexandra, two years later. He graduated from Harvard, then went back to Pennsylvania, near where he grew up, and joined a law firm. But the pain became intense, and there were more operations, and at last the surgeons took off his whole leg. "If I live, watch me in Pennsylvania," he wrote a friend, with gallows humor. But really, mostly, Danny Sachs prepared, gamely, to die, which he did on

June 20, 1967, when his daughter was only nine months old, and he
had lived but one score and eight. He was buried in a cemetery near
where he grew up, in the shade of a lovely magnolia tree.

By that time, Bradley was back in the United States. He had
opted out of his last two months at Oxford, so that he could get his
six months of military service out of the way and join the Knicks as
early as possible during their season. At the time Sachs died, Bradley
was an officer, stationed in Texas at Amarillo Air Force Base.

Charles Gillispie, Danny's adviser, who had become a father
figure to him, asked me to write a tribute to Danny in the *Princeton
Alumni Weekly*, and it appeared, coincidentally, that autumn, exactly a
decade after Danny had run wild Saturdays on the gridirons in that
sophomore year that belonged to him.

Six weeks later I received this letter from Second Lieutenant
William W. Bradley, who was stationed at Amarillo Air Force Base
with the 3340 School Squadron, shortly before he was mustered out
of active duty and joined the New York Knicks. It is, of course, all
the more meaningful because of what the author became. This is
what it said:

> *. . . Thank you very much for your tribute to Dan Sachs.*
>
> *Unlike you, I never had the opportunity to meet him. Yet his person-*
> *ality, strength and accomplishments have remained before me since my*
> *sophomore year at Princeton. The story of his undergraduate life has*
> *more than once pulled me through a crisis, made me work a little harder*
> *or forced me to disregard the criticism of those whose objections stemmed*
> *from an opposite temperament. Because I had a natural affinity for his*
> *type of character and because I believed life was an eclectic pursuit, as*
> *much imitation as originality, I constructed an ideal for his style of life*
> *and attempted to approach it. It was a respectful emulation, never complete*
> *or unreserved, and known only to me. As I became more and more my own*
> *man it decreased, but for a significant period it was alive and formative;*
> *perhaps so much so that I and the emulation are now one.*

Talking about what Dan Sachs would have done is pointless. I prefer to recall what he did—for me, and hopefully, what the record of his life will do for others. Your words, I think, conveyed very well the debt we all owe him, and focused in a very personal way on the debt I owe him. It is for this reason that I am writing. Thank you.

Yours,

Bill

Years later, when Bradley was running for president, one of the reasons I wanted him to win was that even though he would be his own president, as he had become his own man, at least some of Danny Sachs would have finally made it to the top of his chosen profession.

27

THE MOST AMAZING
FEAT IN SPORT
IN THE TWENTIETH CENTURY

One of the deceits of sports lore, promulgated relentlessly by players'
associations, is that travel is a burden. On the contrary, it is a
Teddy Bear's picnic, with $19 per diem meal money—the games
but interludes in the warm gypsy camaraderie, in the Peter Pan
existence.

"A Teddy Bear's Picnic," *Sports Illustrated*, 1972

It's almost impossible now to explain how little the National Basketball Association amounted to when I first started covering it in 1963. It isn't fair to call it bush, although, of course, everybody did. It was simply so small and insignificant, especially in comparison with what it would become in a relatively short time. This summary is primarily for time capsule purposes.

The league offices, such as they were, were located in the Empire State Building. There may have originally been some symbolism in the fact that the sport for tall guys chose as its headquarters the world's tallest building, but honestly, I don't think there was any evidence of such thoughtful planning by the NBA. It was all much more seat-of-the-pants.

Like this: Wilt Chamberlain was the biggest name in the league. After the all-star game in 1965 in St. Louis, there was a reception at

Stan Musial's restaurant, and all the executives and us writers are drinking upstairs, when here comes a referee named Joe Gushue, and he casually points down to the bottom of the stairs and says, "You know, they're trading Wilt down there." So we all peer down the stairs, and, sure enough, there are the Warrior owners and the 76er owners, working out the deal. The owners traded Wilt, standing there, in a restaurant stairwell.

Walter Kennedy was the new commissioner. He was a very nice man, but invariably defensive, despairing because everybody called the NBA bush. Walter had resigned as mayor of Stamford, Connecticut, to take his dream job. Unfortunately, my first encounter with him was unpleasant, although I was only a blameless accomplice to another's alleged villainy.

My second summer with the magazine, 1963, Jerry Tax got Frank Ramsey of the Celtics—the first famous "sixth man" in history—to agree to do a piece in which he would reveal some of the devious little tricks of the trade. Stuff like surreptitiously holding an opponent's shorts, that sort of nickel-dime thing. Since you couldn't easily photograph such sneaky shenaningans in an actual game, an artist, Bob Handville, was assigned to illustrate Ramsey's devilment. I was sent along, to Frank's home in Kentucky, to take notes. But when we got down there, we realized that, for Handville's photographs, we needed someone to play the dupe to Ramsey's magician, and since I looked like a player, however much I was not one, I was dressed in one of Frank's old uniforms and cast as the foil.

What Frank revealed was hardly earthshaking, but it was real inside basketball for its time, and it made the cover—"Smart Moves That Score Points"—with one of Handville's illustrations of Ramsey outwitting the model DeFord.* Walter Kennedy, who had just taken the job, was appalled that an NBA player would actually go public

---

*I was informed that I was the first Timeinker in the history of the company ever to make the cover of a Timeink magazine, only to be at last joined in that distinction a few years later when Henry Luce died. Still, I remained the only *living* Timeinker cover boy.

about how to (my goodness gracious!) *cheat* in an official NBA game, and called Ramsey in and upbraided him. Frank, who was a smart cookie, acted properly chastened and then went about conducting the same smooth high jinks on the court as always before. As a mere patsy, I was not officially chastised, but now the NBA had its eye on me.

Walter had once been the public relations man for the Harlem Globetrotters, and so he had warm, grandiose dreams that the NBA would someday have worldwide appeal—and, of course, his dream would eventually come true, only long after he was gone. It did not come easily, though. The last year I covered the NBA was 1970, and because Russell had retired, the Knicks had finally risen to the top: Reed, DeBusschere, Frazier, Barnett, and, of course, Bradley. As a consequence, it being New York, all of a sudden the national media discovered the NBA. It was as if the Boston Celtics, the greatest team ever in professional sports, had never existed, and professional basketball had just come into creation that October. Typical New York-centric thing. The Knicks and the NBA were all the rage.

Before the finals, against the Lakers, I was talking to Jimmy, one of the Knicks' PR guys, and he was explaining about all the pressing demands for requests that were suddenly descending upon him. "Hey, get this," he said, "the *London Times* actually called me for a credential."

I was flabbergasted. London swings like a pendulum do, and this renowned epitome of world journalism is actually interested in the New York Knickerbockers! What a great little tidbit that would make for my article. "Where's the English guy sitting, Jimmy? I'd love to talk to him."

"Are you kidding?" he replied. "How many fucking tickets can I sell in London?"

He'd given the credential to some weekly sheet in Jersey instead.

I told the story to Walter Kennedy, and he blanched.

But Jimmy knew that up till now the NBA didn't have much appeal across state lines, let alone internationally. All basketball was local. Several of the eight NBA teams would get their best gates every season when the Globetrotters could be booked for an opening game against their stooges. The Knicks almost always scheduled regular four-team doubleheaders, so that often half the league was in Manhattan at the same time. In fact, there was one bar that a lot of the players favored, so some nights you could find maybe 20 to 25 percent of the NBA personnel drinking together. The camaraderie was real. Most teams only carried ten guys, and few rookies entered the league every year, so there wasn't much turnover and most everybody knew everybody else. The NBA was more like an ensemble than a league.

Race was changing things, though, and anybody with even the slightest understanding of the game appreciated which way the wind was blowing. History has made a lot out of Texas Western winning the college championship in 1967 with five African-Americans start-ing, but at the time, for those of us in basketball, that was nothing remarkable. Red Auerbach had sent out an all-black starting lineup long before that, when he put Willie Naulls in with Russell, Satch Sanders, and the Jones boys for the opening tap, and in an NBA game it was already unremarkable to see nine or even ten black guys on the court. I'd first heard the expression "white man's disease" by as early as 1964.

In the Empire State Building HQ, besides Commissioner Ken-nedy, the only other office belonged to Haskell Cohen, who was the PR man. Every year, Haskell would personally deliver fifths of Scotch to the faithful few writers who covered the league. At Timeink, you weren't supposed to accept any gift above what you could consume in a day, and so I bent the rules to take the NBA's J&B. After all, I didn't drink Scotch. Haskell had an assistant named Connie who handled pretty much everything you needed to know. *Call Connie.* Maybe there were one or two other secretaries in the office opening the mail, but that was it for major league basketball. *Call Connie.*

The schedule was made up by one man, Eddie Gottlieb, who owned the Philadelphia Warriors. Eddie had a Buddha-like figure and a crinkly smile, and because he had also been an owner in the old Negro baseball leagues, he was known as "The Mogul." It was amazing that Eddie could figure out the schedule, for the teams were at the mercy of arenas that also scheduled hockey games, ice shows, 'rasslin matches, Roller Derby, rodeos, and all manner of other indoor divertissement during the long, dark winter months in the Northeast.

The Mogul was officially on the league's schedule committee, but, in fact, as he explained to me once, "I am the schedule committee." Sometimes, Eddie would wake up in the middle of the night with an inspiration, suddenly figure out how he could get Syracuse to play St. Louis after the Nats had a game in Cincinnati. Or something. It was the most incredible feat of precomputer twentieth-century human genius that I've been privy to—Eddie Gottlieb making up the NBA schedule by himself, year after year.

When the Knicks made the playoffs they would invariably get kicked out of Madison Square Garden, even though they were *owned* by Madison Square Garden, because that was when the circus came to town, and it drew much larger crowds. The Knicks would then play their most important games at a ratty old National Guard armory.

Luckily, the Knicks were so bad that after a while this didn't happen very often. When they played regular-season games at the Garden, it always seemed as if the crowd was made up predominantly of gamblers, betting the point spread. The largest cheers didn't seem to be for the home team stiffs; they were for whichever way the spread played out. Smoking was allowed in arenas then, so by the time the nightcap was finishing up a Garden doubleheader, as the haze drifted lower, it was hard enough to see across the court, let alone try to shoot baskets.

I'd be right there in the front row, courting my wife-to-be/bride-that-is with the best seats in the house, because the Knicks, desperate for any ink, gave out passes to writers then for seats that now go to celebrities for four figures.

Actually, The Mogul had been the coach, as well as the owner, of the Warriors, when they became the first NBA champion (although it was called the Basketball Association of America then) in 1946–1947. A hillbilly named Joe Fulks was the team's star, but he's been completely forgotten. Fulks was known as "Jumping Joe"—not because he could jump high (he was, after all, white) but because he was a jump-shot pioneer. He held the absolutely incredible one-game league record of sixty-three points for more than a decade. Fulks died young, killed back in the Kentucky hills over a dispute about a firearm, which was, alas, loaded.

Before Fulks starred for the Warriors in the BAA, The Mogul's team was called the Philadelphia Sphas, which was not a misspelling, but which stood for South Philadelphia Hebrew Athletic Association. Basketball had been heavily Jewish for a period, and at a time when sportswriters dealt generously in stereotypes, this had inspired Paul Gallico to opine: "A Jew, contrary to popular opinion, can take a licking . . . but the reason, I suspect, that [basketball] appeals to the Hebrew with his Oriental background is that the game places a premium on an alert, scheming mind and flashy trickiness, artful dodging and general smart-aleckness."

In 1962 The Mogul sold the Philadelphia Warriors to San Francisco for $850,000. It's the only price I can remember of any franchise sale in any sport, ever, but at the time it astounded us NBA insiders that California guys could get suckered by The Mogul, outta Philly. Eight hundred and fifty g's* for a *call-Connie* NBA franchise that Eddie had bought for $25,000! Can you believe it? Part of the deal, too, was that Eddie had to go out to San Francisco for a couple of years as some kind of transcontinental transition consultant, and so the last time I saw The Mogul in California, he was working the will-call window at the Cow Palace. Then he came back to Philly, still dined at the Automat, and continued making up the league schedule on his kitchen table.

Nobody in the NBA made much money. I could easily get players to go out with me after a game because they knew I had an

---

*Just wondering: why did K, singular, replace g's, plural, for thousands?

expense account so they could cadge free beers off me. Cheap dates. The players doubled up in rooms and, 6-foot-10 though they might be, they flew coach. I can distinctly remember when, in 1967, I was doing a cover story on John Havlicek, on a coast-to-coast flight, he came *forward* to see me, flying in first class for Timeink, and then I went back with him to the steerage part of the plane where the champion Celtics were, there to interview the star.

But John was delighted with the publicity. Are you kidding? The league would do almost anything to cooperate in order to get what was called "ink," then. At halftime, Freddy Schaus, the coach of the Lakers, invited me into the team's locker room, where Elgin Baylor bummed a cigarette off me and then went for another set of double figures in the second half. But then, a lot of athletes still smoked. In baseball, you'd see butts strewn about at the end of dugouts, encased, like amber, in tobacco juice. Hell, athletes made cigarette commercials, just as doctors did.

None of the NBA teams had assistant coaches. Only a couple of teams traveled with trainers. They'd pick up a guy from a local high school to come over and tape ankles. The teams stayed, for the most part, in second-rate hotels. In Los Angeles, they bivouacked at a motel on Olympic Boulevard run by a heavyset* impresario named Pidge Burack, who talked as though everything was on the q.t. and billed himself as "your host on the coast." Pidge commandeered a large chunk of NBA business by installing extra-long beds, and the best room in the house he called the "Polly Adler suite," but he was proudest of his exquisite "flame garden," which diners could view from the motel coffee shop. It consisted of some large rocks and a few well-placed tiki torches. I never think of Los Angeles that I don't think of Pidge Burack's beautiful flame garden.

At least by the time I came to the enterprise, the NBA was using airplanes, but it had only been a few years before when trains were

---

*People politely said "heavyset" for "fat" then, but that's largely gone out.

still in vogue. I remember Tommy Heinsohn telling me that when the Pistons were still located in Fort Wayne, the main line didn't really go *into* Fort Wayne, but trains would agree to stop a few miles outside town at a mail pickup point to allow the players to hastily disembark, like thieves on the lam. Then the team would have to try to scare up cabs from town. I can just visualize LeBron James and Dwayne Wade and company standing by a railroad siding at three o'clock in the morning when it's eight below, while the coach is on the pay phone there ringing up Fort Wayne's only all-night cab company. But there wasn't any choice. That's the only way The Mogul could get all the games in.

On one of the rare occasions when a team used a charter, the Lakers, in 1960, during their last season in Minneapolis, took a DC-3 after a game in St. Louis, back to Minnesota. Unfortunately, the electrical system failed and, essentially, the only thing that continued to work was the propellers. Several of the Lakers told me the story. One was Jim Krebs, who would die only a few years later in a freak accident, when he was helping a neighbor cut down a tree. It's funny the stuff you remember. Jimmy was the last athlete I ever saw in any locker room who wore garters to hold up his socks. Maybe he was the last guy of any persuasion I saw in garters. In any event, besides my father. Except when he was in his feed-the-chickens togs, all of Daddy's socks needed garters.

Anyway, as the Lakers' DC-3 began to run short of fuel, the pilots, who had no idea where they were, finally, gingerly began to take the plane down, until at last they spotted the lights of a little town, which turned out to be Carroll, Iowa. The windows were coated with ice, so when the pilots made out a snowy cornfield they thought they could land in, the copilot had to stick his face out a side window to inform the pilot of their altitude. In the back, the players huddled in the cold, praying, while Elgin Baylor simply lay down, flat out, in the aisle. Hot Rod Hundley remembered hearing the copilot calling out the descending altitude: "Sixty . . . fifty . . . forty . . ." Then, all of a sudden: "Take the sonuvabitch up, take it up!" They were coming in too steep.

The plane soared back up and around, then began to glide down again. "Well, Rod," Slick Leonard said to Hundley, "at least we had some time to smell the roses."

But on this try, the descent was smooth, and, in fact, the plane landed so cleanly in the cornfield that the next day, after it was juiced up, a pilot was able simply to turn it around and fly the DC-3 safely off.

Baylor's been largely forgotten, I suppose, but in his prime he was just fabulous—Michael Jordan before there was a Michael Jordan. Elgin had some kind of nervous twitch, which made it even more disconcerting to try to guard him. One time he went for sixty-three against the Celtics, prompting Hot Rod (who got more free drinks on my expense account than anybody else) to make the famous remark: "Elg and me went for sixty-five tonight."

My first assignment in the NBA was with the Lakers. Young Leggett was going to write a story about the Laker-Celtic rivalry, and since he was going to travel with Boston, I was designated to go along with LA, embedded as Young's reporter. I caught up with the Lakers in Cincinnati, where they were playing the Royals, with Oscar Robertson. The Royals had a PR man named Steve Hoffman, who was a dwarf. This was very convenient because in those halcyon days, the press table was right on the floor, between the team benches, exactly where nowadays the swells pay a king's ransom to sit. So after a quarter ended and Stevie would come by with the mimeographed stat sheets and the play-by-play, he could walk down press row in front of everybody and hand out the papers without disturbing anyone's view.*

---

*In the area of whatta coincidence, yet another major-league team, the Milwaukee Braves, also had a dwarf for a PR man, but unlike Stevie, who was a sweetheart of a guy, the Braves' dwarf, Donald Davidson, could be cantankerous, and he had a foul mouth. One time he was on the elevator with a player who didn't like him, and because Don wasn't tall enough to reach his high floor's button, he had to ask the player to punch it for him. "Fuck you, Don," the player said, exiting the elevator and leaving little Davidson adrift.

Anyway, I was supposed to officially meet the Lakers in the hotel lobby the next morning, where we would jam into cabs, our long legs all entangled, and go to the airport. I was scared to death. This was, if you will, my debut as a traveling sportswriter. I remember picking out my best shirt and tie. I think I slicked down my hair with both Vitalis and Brylcreem. I put on my fancy new checked sports jacket and a pair of horned-rims in a vain effort to make myself look just a little older. In the lobby, I tried to appear as unobtrusive as possible, but Baylor spied me right away. You've got to understand, Elgin was not only the star of the team then but the leader and, as well, a very good straight-faced comedian. Loudly, in his deep voice, staring directly at stylish me, he says: "I didn't know Ralston-Purina was making sports jackets these days."

All the Lakers roared.

Welcome to the big time, DeFord.

Hot Rod Hundley did make me feel a little better later, when, over a couple of Cutty Sarks on me, he told me that the beat writer with the *Los Angeles Times* had bad teeth, so Baylor had tagged him "low tide at Santa Monica."

Hot Rod revealed this to me at our destination—Detroit—where the Lakers were going to play the Celtics in the lidlifter of a double-header. That's right: because the Pistons were struggling at the gate, the NBA had awarded them the league's best attraction, the Lakers-Celtics, as the undercard. I guess the Globetrotters were otherwise occupied.

Both the Lakers and the Celtics (along with Wilt Chamberlain and the Warriors, who were playing the Pistons) were staying at a hotel that was also holding a hairdressers' convention. Now try to envision this: thirty young guys, most of them extremely tall and randy, a lot of very gay hairdressers, and plenty of beautiful models with blue hair and pink hair and whatnot stuck all together in one hotel. And it is something like ten degrees below zero outside, so nobody is going outside. And I'm buying drinks on the Timeink expense account and

picking up the hoop skinny, and, coincidentally, providentially, because of said expense account, I am very popular with all and sundry
of both genders.

   This, I believe, was when I decided that maybe I really did want
to be a sportswriter for a while.

28

HUB TALES

New England is a singular place. Everybody thinks of the South as the most distinctive American region, but since air conditioning, the people in Atlanta and Charlotte are from Cleveland and New Jersey. New England is the other way around. There was never any cult about New England. In the South, the thinkers wrote about the South, and glamorized it; in New England, the thinkers started schools. New England was a place unto itself, and it still is. The people prize their own.
    "The Kid Who Ran into Doors," *Sports Illustrated*, 1975

As ordinary as some of the chosen NBA hotels were, none compared with the Hotel Madison, the dump that many teams used, for convenience, in Boston. Not only was the Madison dirt cheap, but it saved the teams cab fare, because it was located, like the Garden itself, as an extended part of a railroad depot, the North Station. Especially since it was taken as gospel that the Boston coach, Red Auerbach, bugged the visitors' locker room—and anyway, the guest accomodations were, for a fact, kept either boiling or freezing—teams preferred to dress in their uniforms in their dingy, double-up, cubbyhole accommodations at the Madison and then dash through the station, snaking by the degenerates and riffraff, to reach the Garden proper. Outside a saloon, the Iron Horse, I would hear patrons scream, "Hey, you faggot cawksuckers" and other friendly epithets as the players scurried, be-uniformed, toward their engagement with the Celtics on the distinctive parquet floor.

Press row at the Garden would be filled because there were still a great many Knights of the Keyboard, still a veritable surfeit of dailies in the Hub: the *Globe* and the *Evening Globe* and the *Herald* and the *Traveler* and the *Record-American* and the *Quincy Patriot-Ledger*, not to mention the *Christian Science Monitor*.

In the whole NBA at that time, though, few newspapers staffed the home team on the road. The *New York Post* was the leading NBA source in the nation. Leonard Lewin was the top beat writer, but there were also Leonard Schecter and Leonard Koppett and Leonard Cohen and various other Leonards I've forgotten. The gag was that if you walked into the *Post* newsroom and cried out, "Hey, Lennie," the whole newspaper would grind to a halt. But the *Post* was an exception, NBA-wise.

However, once the playoffs started, the multitude of Boston papers would take to the road en masse with the Celtics. Howie McHugh, the PR man, would even splurge and take a hotel suite in every town, so we could all drink there after the game. Sometimes a Celtic player or two would drop by, just to grab a free beer and shoot the breeze with his newspaper buddies. It was a happenin' place, for along with the beat guys there'd be some of the top columnists, and maybe a writer from far off Providence or Worcester, too. Maybe even Portland! It was the closest I ever came to the legendary press box days of yore, when newspapers were legion.

In point of fact, the playoffs were pretty much the only time the Boston fans would also appear in abundance. The Celtics might have been champions, but even though basketball was created just out there in Springfield, New England barely knew what basketball was back then. When the Celtics had first come to town in 1946 the players had been required to go around to the schools that didn't even have courts and give a little show-and-tell with basketballs. *This is how you dribble. This is called a bounce pass.* What have you. No, in wintertime, Boston hearts belonged to the Bruins, who invariably sold out ("banged out," in Boston vernacular) the Garden, even though they finished dead last most years.

One time, Red Auerbach told me he'd had to pledge his personal credit just to keep the phones working in the champions' musty old office somewhere in the intestines of North Station. But every spring, when the Celtics would get into the playoffs, the writers would hit the road with the team. This elite journalistic ensemble was led by a writer named Clif "Poison Pen" Keane. He had been so christened on a bumpy airplane ride with the old Boston Braves. As the plane pitched and yawed, one of the Braves, Earl Torgeson, began to imitate a radio broadcast, announcing loudly that the plane had crashed, all hands lost. The players groaned. Then Torgeson said, "The first person identified at the crash site was Clif Keane of the *Boston Globe*. Keane was immediately recognized by the poison pen clasped tightly in his hand."

I was amazed at how Clif got away with tormenting the players he covered. "There's more dog in you than an Airedale!" he'd holler. "The SPCA shouldn't let you play here."* The players would just laugh and insult him back. Clif was a great mimic, too. So was K. C. Jones. One time, I remember, while we were waiting for a connecting flight in the middle of the playoffs in the middle of the night in the middle of the country somewhere, Clif and K.C. entertained us for about half an hour doing imitations of other players and referees. It's a common refrain how players and writers don't get along as well as they used to nowadays. I just think of Clif, and the rapport he had with the young men he covered, of him and K.C. working up an impromptu act together at midnight in an empty airport somewhere, and I know how true that is, that it's just not the same anymore.

In 1964, when Tony Conigliaro was a hotshot hometown rookie with the Red Sox, I was sent up to do a piece on him. The kid was tired of reporters, and he had all the ink he needed from the plethora

---

*My favorite inside newspaper story about Clif was how he upset the dog-show crowd. While covering a big show, a popular dog died, but Keane only mentioned that fact deep into his story. His editor, responding to the criticism, asked why. Clif replied: "A dog died. I buried it."

of hometown papers in the Hub, so he blew me off. Poison Pen was furious. He personally dragged me back down to the clubhouse and, with me standing sheepishly beside him, confronted the rook. "Hey, what the hell's the mattah with you, Tony?" he snapped. "This man has come alla way from Noo Yock to do a story on you. Now, the least you can do is be polite and tock to 'im."

So, grudgingly, Conigliaro gave me an interview. But can you imagine any writer talking that way to a player today? Can you imagine any player doing what the writer told him to?

I laugh now, too, at all the Red Sox Nation crap, the myth that all New England has always worshipped the Sawx through thick and thin, forever held them to its ever-lovin' bosom. I remember one gorgeous spring afternoon at Fenway, when the attendance was so small ("A lot of people came dressed as empty seats today," Poison Pen observed—first time I'd heard that old saw) that all over the park you could hear one loud fan screaming at a visiting (happily married) infielder on the other team about the babe he'd picked up the night before in some bar. The fan was so distinctly loud and the Fens was so deserted that you could see the infielder's face getting red. Boston was fed up with the Sawx then. They were losahs. The Patriots were bush, in what was always called the "Mickey Mouse League"—the AFL—and the Celtics had too many black guys and only drew for playoffs, so the Bruins, losahs though they may also have been, were the only team anybody in Boston really cared about.

In those days, virtually all the players in the NHL were Canadian, and as rotten as the American athletic system is to kids, it was even worse up there in the cold Dominion. There, hockey prospects would be divvied up among the six NHL franchises barely after their voices changed, taken from their families, and schooled on the ice in some provincial jerkwater. It was called Junior A hockey, adolescent servitude. But so it was, as the Bruins finished in the cellar year after year, as the Celtics made the playoffs and I drank in Howie McHugh's suite with the Boston writers, late at night, in hushed voices, I would be told the tales of the Canadian Christ ice child who would someday be the Bruins' savior. It would be only three more years now . . . two . . .

The teener's name was Bobby Orr, and he was playing Junior A hockey somewhere up in Ontario. So, now, even though I don't know a hockey puck from a quoit, I realize that I have got me another Bill Bradley. For a sportswriter, this is the equivalent of stumbling on two Lana Turners, back-to-back, at Schwab's drugstore. As a consequence of this secret scoop of mine, in the summer of 1966, when Orr turned eighteen and was finally old enough to play in the NHL, I traveled up to Parry Sound, Ontario, with Leo Monahan, a hockey writer from the *Boston Record-American*. In the coffee shop, we asked the waitress if she knew the way to the Orr residence.

Well, yes, as a matter of fact she did, inasmuch as she was Bobby's mother.

So I wrote the first national story about Bobby Orr, and he went on to become by far the finest defenseman in the history of the game, and my reputation for discovering phenoms increased apace. Orr was sensational right off the bat. "I don't think most people can understand what little pressure I felt out there," he told me years later. "It was like I was skating in a little balloon. Only you can't take that balloon anywhere else with you."

That's about the best definition I've ever heard of what it's like to be blessed with great talent in one particular glamorous thing. Imagine being a kid and finding out that you're in that balloon. But also imagine how hard it is to understand that you're in the balloon only when you're on the blue line or in the batter's box or on the eighteenth green, whatever. And imagine what it's like when you're still playing, but you're older and all beat up and the balloon is starting to deflate. And then you're not even middle age in real life and the balloon is busted. That's what it's like being a great athlete.

Twenty-two years after Parry Sound, I was doing a story on Larry Bird (whom I did not discover), and a big dinner was held in his honor in Boston to unveil a statue of him. By now, Orr was long gone from hockey. He never even broke a tooth all the years he played, but his knees went on him, early, so he'd lost his reservation in the balloon. But he continued to live in Boston, and he came to the Bird soiree, and when it was time for dinner, we sat down together.

When Bird got up to speak, he started talking about what it was like to play in Boston Garden, and about how, before every game, as he stood there during the national anthem, he would look up at all the championship banners hanging from the ceiling. And, Larry said, he always focused on one. There was a pause. "Number four," he said. Everybody is trying to remember what great retired Celtic was number four, when Bird paused, perfectly . . . then added, "Bobby Orr."

Even before he said the name, Orr caught on. His face had frozen in shock. The two players had barely ever met, and Bird had never told anybody this before. And when he pronounced the name and started talking about how he idolized Orr, this guy from a different sport, Bobby's hand reached over on the table, and he almost involuntarily grabbed mine, stunned, his fingers tightening over the back of my hand. "Oh my God, Frank," he whispered. "Oh my God."

29

MY MAN

If he won, so what—he should have. If he lost he was a loser. It was his function to be played against.
"A Team That Was Blessed," *Sports Illustrated*, 1982

Most players—even some of the biggest stars—quickly disappear from our journalistic purview once they're put out to pasture, but there was one exceptional athlete whose relationship with me changed considerably for the better over time. That was Wilt Chamberlain, a singular man of manifold contradictions, who also remains, in my mind, the most imposing physical specimen I ever encountered upon this earth.

I'm sure Wilt's great size—or more to the point, how everyone he met reacted to his great size: *how's the weather up there, yuk, yuk, yuk*—affected him from early on. It was not just that he was tall. Good grief, Manute Bol towered over him, but poor, sweet Manute was just a noodle on end. I was never awed in Manute's company, merely charmed to be in the presence of something so exotic.

Wilt, though—he was somehow a force for size. Like Lorna Doone's brothers, he appeared to block out the sun. Bill Russell told me he was convinced that Chamberlain was honestly scared of how he might accidentally hurt someone, and so he always played a bit timidly. I'm just not sure that Wilt ever could make up his mind about his body. His freakishness certainly didn't make him withdrawn, however. In fact, unlike so many American athletes, whose interest in geography is pretty much circumscribed by the length of the Las Vegas strip, Wilt spent much of his free time abroad. Had he been self-conscious about his height, he never would have ventured so far afield. Indeed, even as a civilian, in middle age, Wilt favored clothes that called attention to his body: tank tops, tight pants, and (even on city sidewalks) bare feet.

But here was his professional bugaboo: expectations. He was so overwhelming, so good at almost everything he tried, athletically, that he could never please people. I think this was at the heart of the unease he often exhibited. One night, late, he told me that he'd managed to fall in love only once in all his life, but he never really contemplated sharing his life for long with anyone. He probably feared that he would let his wife down, the way everyone else had always expected too much of him. There was even a theory that subconsciously he made himself miss so many free throws because that would show folks that there was some one thing he couldn't do in sports. I ran that by him. He just said, "No, it's just totally a head trip." So: maybe.

Anyway, I didn't like Wilt when I first started covering him. Part of it is that I liked Russell, and the basketball world then was absolutely divided into Russell People and Wilt People. The Russell People said their man was bright and sensitive, a team player invested in winning, while Wilt was a dullard and a loser, only interested in piling up his personal point total. The Wilt People retaliated that he was misunderstood, lacking good teammates, so he wasn't vain and selfish, only forced to do it all by himself, because, after all, one-on-one he was bigger and better than Russell.

But despite my misgivings about Wilt's dedication, I think I pretty much treated him with distant appreciation, until, in 1968, at the age of thirty-two, he got traded from Philadelphia to Los Angeles. A couple of months into the season, I was assigned to write a cover story on how things were working out, especially with respect to the two incumbent Laker stars, Elgin Baylor and Jerry West. This would turn out to be the only time in my life that I personally influenced an athletic event.

I had pretty good contacts on the Lakers, and I wrote that Wilt and the coach, Butch van Breda Kolff, were not getting along, and that while West had graciously accepted Wilt as a teammate, Baylor and some of the others hadn't. In fact, they laughed behind his back, said that he smelled, and called him Big Musty. Also, displaying my heavy inside hoop expertise, I wrote (on deep authority) that Wilt wasn't going to the basket enough and added, "There is a growing school of thought that he no longer possesses sufficient moves to make him a bona-fide high-scoring threat." After all, whereas not so long ago he had averaged fifty points a game for a whole season, it had been more than a year now since he'd scored so much as fifty in a single game.

Oops. Promptly, as soon as the article came out, the very next game, Wilt answered *me* by scoring sixty.

Later that season, when I was covering the Lakers in the playoffs against Boston, I was in their locker room before the game. Jerry West came over to me. Jerry wrote recently that he was chronically depressed, but no one could have guessed that. He had always been very friendly with me, as he was with most writers. The Lakers called him "Tweety" for his high-pitched chatter and "Louella" for his constant dispensation of gossip. Once, after I wrote a long profile on him, he even sent me a thank-you note, which—trust me—is pretty unusual for athletes, even the ones who might have stationery. Anyway, on this occasion Jerry was obviously uncomfortable, for he said he had been delegated by Wilt to tell me that he didn't want me in the locker room, and I should depart forthwith.

I didn't have to, of course. Every locker room was open to the press, but the last thing I wanted to do was make a scene, and I could tell that Jerry was embarrassed enough by the role he'd been cast in, so I quickly took my leave. Wilt averted his eyes as I walked past him. You see, he really didn't like confrontation, and that was why he'd deputized West instead of approaching me directly—which he certainly had every right to do. After all, I'd written that his teammates said Wilt was a guy who smelled.

I covered the NBA for one more year, that season of 1970, which ended when Willis Reed of the Knicks, playing center against Chamberlain, famously came back from injury to send Wilt the Stilt to yet one more defeat. Good riddance.

And the years passed.

Now, by coincidence, one of my closest friends is Tommy Kearns, who had, by the by, been the playmaker on the undefeated 1957 North Carolina team that had beaten Wilt's Kansas team in the NCAA triple-overtime final in Kansas City. Not only that, but at the start of the game, since Carolina didn't possess a starter over 6-feet-7, and had no chance to win the tip against Wilt, the Carolina coach, Frank McGuire, had sent out his smallest starter to jump against Chamberlain, to mock his height, embarrass him.

Thus the Tarheel assigned to jump center against Wilt was Kearns, who stands maybe 5-foot-11. And it was he who was in possession of the ball as the clock ticked down, Carolina up a point. As the frustrated Kansas players rushed to him, Tommy simply heaved the ball high. By the time it came down, the game was over and Wilt Chamberlain had been tagged a "loser." He would walk the streets of Kansas City alone, disconsolate, after the game.

Kearns was drafted by Syracuse, but after he was cut,[*] he became a stockbroker, and as an indication of his superior salesmanship was able to convince Chamberlain, the man whom he'd helped make a figure of fun, to let him be his broker. They became good friends, and occasionally Tommy would advise me that I ought to reconsider my assessment of Wilt, that he was a good guy.

The Kearnses and Defords liked to travel together, and late one night, at a bar in Punte del Este, Uruguay, of all places, I agreed with Tommy's suggestion that if Wilt was up to it, when we got back to the United States the three of us would go out together. Wilt accepted

---

[*]Kearns played in one game, took one shot, and made it, retiring from the NBA with a 1.000 shooting percentage (you can look it up).

Tommy's invitation and we three went to a track meet at the Garden (Wilt loved track), and had dinner, and, yes, Wilt and I, though shy and tentative at first, actually got along quite well. To cap the evening, he demanded that he pick up the dinner tab. (Most athletes, having been fussed over all their lives, do not consider that as part of their MO.)

A couple of years later I called up Wilt and went out to Los Angeles, where he lived in a custom-made house with special facilities that accommodated his height, there to do a long story on him—to celebrate the fiftieth birthday of a physical marvel. It struck me almost immediately how content he was now. When he was playing, he had often said that his happiest year had been the one when he had traveled with the Harlem Globetrotters before he joined the NBA. Now, he was even more at peace. In fact, I'm not so sure that there's ever been a great star athlete, besides Wilt, who was so uncomfortable when playing and then so much happier retired. (I also think he would have been much more satisfied if he'd played an individual sport, so he could have been responsible just for himself and not have had to worry about the Team. You can't call an individual-sport athlete "selfish," because that's the whole point: to be selfish.)

Anyway, in Los Angeles, as Wilt neared his fiftieth birthday, our rapprochement was complete. He even started calling me "Frank," instead of "my man," which was his preferred manner of address with almost everyone; remember, *everybody* knew who Wilt the Stilt was, so he could hardly be expected to reciprocate by remembering the names of the whole human race. We had a few laughs together. Nothing amused Wilt more than the glad-handing phonies who would corner him and tell him how they had been right there, cheering him on at Madison Square Garden, the night he scored a hundred points against the Knicks. Wilt would just nod and grin. That game, you see, had indeed been against the Knicks, but it had been played in Hershey, Pennsylvania.

We also could laugh together at people like flight attendants who always tell tall people to "watch your head" *even when you are staring, eye-level, at the top of the airplane door.* Little people like to tell tall people to watch their head, even though, if they thought about it, they would realize that, being tall, you learn to naturally watch your head. Wilt and I also talked about how it's also true that little people are never embarrassed about asking tall people exactly how tall they are—even though no one would ever ask a short person how short he is or ask a fat person how much he weighs. Not only that, but then they don't believe you. They always say, "You're taller than that." I'm 6-feet-4. In my entire life, the hundreds, maybe thousands, of times people have asked me how tall I am, and I've said, "Six-feet-four," no one has ever said, "No, you're not that tall." Instead, people always say, "You're taller than that."

Another thing. Since I've been on National Public Radio, when I meet people who know me only by my voice, they all think I should be shorter. It's a strange phenomenon. I don't know whether I just plain sound short or there's a general belief that tall people cannot possibly be on the radio. Even people who have *seen* me on television are taken aback at my height when they encounter me live, in person. I think there is a general assumption that everybody on television is exactly the same size.

And more years passed.

And then, yes, Wilt made a complete ass of himself by writing a book, boasting that he had slept with twenty thousand different women. Oh, my man, how could you? But, in a way, it was in keeping, for if Wilt took pride in how tall he was, then it followed that everything else must be tabulated to prove its value. He'd always been measured by numbers. Be the tallest. Score the most points. Grab the most rebounds. Hand off the most assists. Make the largest salary. And, yes, screw the most women.

It quite surprised him that his sexual braggadocio did not impress people but, rather, put them off, even disgusted them. Here he had become, if not a grand old man, the grandest old man of height-sensitive commercials, and he'd frittered it all away on a stupid boast. Wilt Chamberlain was now thought of as, for lack of a better word, a slut.

In 1999, specifically as the century wound down, Bill Russell was himself coming out of the shadows. He'd spent much of the past years, if not in seclusion, then certainly out of the spotlight. Friends began to point out to him that he was being forgotten. Never mind that he'd won twelve championships and became the first major-league African-American coach, but in a world where even black baseball players admitted that they didn't know who the hell Jackie Robinson had been, Russell was being lost. So he agreed to something of a comeback coming-out party.

I happily did my part by writing an article in *Sports Illustrated,* for a cover that proclaimed him the greatest team player of the century, and then I also helped with an HBO special. Russell began to make appearances, even to sell his autograph, which he'd always famously resisted giving away (even as he'd stand politely and take far more time to explain why he was opposed to the practice than it would've taken to scribble his name).

As a culmination of his reentry into celebrity, Russell came back to Boston, to have his numbered jersey—six—officially retired to the heavens of Boston Garden. It was a huge affair, and Chamberlain graciously agreed to fly across the country to help honor his old rival— even though he knew he'd be the designated villain at the celebration.

He showed up in the most dazzling, outlandish outfit I'd ever seen him in, reminding me of one of those double-colored Popsicles. At a party after the ceremony, Wilt spied me and beckoned me over, and after greeting me nicely, he forced himself to confront me, stuttering a complaint. "My man, what's this I hear about you criticizing me for the way I played Willis Reed in that game?"

He was referring, of course, to that famous 1970 playoff, when an injured Reed, shot up with God knows what, had limped out on the floor and immediately scored a basket against Chamberlain that lit up the Knicks and inspired them to victory. And yes, I had indeed mentioned that episode in the article I'd written about Russell, but it was not me tendering criticism. Rather, I was quoting Russell, who claimed that had he been Chamberlain in that situation, he wouldn't have backed off the wounded Reed, but would've gone right at him, again and again. Oddly, too, in a way, it was a sensitive, backhanded tribute to Wilt, pointing out again how reluctant he was to exert his great strength against a gallant foe.

So, rather testily, I replied: "Hey, Wilt, come on, *read* the damn article. I didn't say that. I was just quoting what your skinny friend over there told me." And I pointed at Russell, across the room, surrounded in glory, absolutely drinking in the accolades.

Wilt looked over, enviously, at Russell. Here his rival was, after all these years, the conquering hero once again. Wistfully, Wilt then turned back to me. "You think you could do me a favor?" he asked, almost sheepishly. I don't think he was used to asking for favors.

"Sure. What is it?"

"You think you can do one of those HBO things on me that you did on Bill?"

"Sure," I said. I was pretty certain HBO would be delighted.

"I could really use that," Wilt said—and maybe for the first time I realized how beaten down he had been, how much he'd been mocked and humiliated by his claim about the twenty thousand women.

"I'll give you a call," I said.

"Thanks, Frank. I'd appreciate that."

"OK," I said. "Now, watch your head." He laughed.

And I did run it by HBO, and the network was all for it, and I called Wilt, but all I got was a phone machine. Maybe he was out of the country. It was a bit later before he called me back, but he got my answering machine, and—my fault—I didn't get back to him right away, and then, of course, he died, only age sixty-three.

I should've made a point of reaching him right after we spoke in Boston. Some friends thought he understood he was dying, and this made me feel even more guilty. All the amazing numbers that he did put up, those meant so much to him, but the idiotic twenty thousand is the one that still lives on after him.

30

ANGLOPHILE

All I know is that the main difference between men and women is that men just assume that what they own will look good on them—otherwise, why did they buy it?—but women assume just the opposite.

An American Summer, 2002

By good fortune, I arrived in sports just as the logjam was breaking up. *Come back, Paul Gallico, we're improving February!* Jackie Robinson, of course, had been the first break in the wave, but just think of all the revolutionary stuff that began happening a few years later: the NFL exploded, pro basketball and hockey moved up from bush, college basketball became truly national, franchises shifted, leagues expanded and whole new leagues were created, free agency blossomed, players struck, collegians won the right to turn pro, Billie Jean King spearheaded the women's movement, Title IX was signed, domes were built, Astroturf was grown, the Olympics were politicized, amateurism started cratering, agents surfaced, money proliferated, and, above all, television brought it all to you, right into your own family room.* *Tastes great! Less filling!* Good grief: sports was a fascinating, whole new, larger arena.

As a matter of fact, sports today isn't nearly as interesting as it was a generation or two ago. The revolution is over. Oh, there are plenty of games to write about. There have never been more stanzas,

---

*Or "den" or "club cellar," as a family room was known then.

more frames, more tilts, more playoffs. But every day it's pretty much just more of the same, and everything is on ESPN, so, in extremis, there is a natural disposition, in print, to look more and more inward, endlessly analyzing, dissecting, predicting, enlarging minutiae. No wonder a whole profession missed steroids; we were too busy studying the animal entrails of drafts. Besides, everybody genially accepts that a considerable portion of popular American sport—college football and men's basketball—is an outright fraud, so that makes it so much easier to abide deceit in all the other precincts.

There's always talk about what constitutes "The Golden Age" of sports, but whenever it was, I'm convinced that The Golden Age of Writing About Sports began just about the time that I, providentially, came into the vestibule. Not coincidentally, it was precisely this period that my old friend David Halberstam called "The Golden Age of Magazines"—that airy time before color television and before all serious large-circulation magazines gave up the ghost and became weekly versions of *USA Today*. But ah, back then: during those years there was simply more varied fare to delve into and write about—and there I was, right smack where sports flowed into the golden-hued magazine delta.

Then too this was the ante-software era. That world I stumbled into in 1962 was not quite yet being manhandled by technology. The late Neil Postman, who was a brilliant social observer, once wrote, "Education as we know it began with the printing press. It ended with television." So now, I suppose, we could say: Journalism, as we know it, began with the printing press. It ended with the Internet.

But ah, back then, in those Proterozoic times, you still needed paper. When you were on deadline, you'd ask the local Western Union office to have someone stay on late duty. Then, after the game, you'd go back to your hotel room and type out your piece. Typewriters were loud—especially when everyone else was trying to sleep. Sometimes the poor people in the next room would bang on your wall, or they'd get the management to call you up. There were times when I'd go into the bathroom and turn on the shower, to mask the sound of typing on the bathroom floor. At last, story finished, I'd drive down to Western Union, physically hand over those actual pieces of paper, go back, and catch a little shut-eye before flying home. For sportswriting, this was the equivalent of working in a foxhole with mortar shells whizzing overhead.

Of course, as with war correspondents, institutionally there was always everywhere real camaraderie to be found amongst sportswriters, for more than other journalists, we traveled so much together and then regularly gathered together in the press box to cover the action. We are also, of late, generally distinguished by an inability to dress with any style. Most sportswriters don't know how to mix and match, only to mix and mix. John Kruk, when he was playing with the Phillies, once allowed, "It's easy to be a sportswriter. All you have to do is put on forty pounds and wear clothes that don't match."

Now Kruk is an analyst on ESPN, a journalist himself, and he proves his point every time he appears on the air.

Particularly because I was so young when first I would go out representing *Sports Illustrated*, I always made it a point to dress up. But, then, probably because I was so impressed by my father's good taste, I do like handsome clothes. Bryant Gumbel, my elegant host of *Real Sports* on HBO, says I dress like "an English fop," which he means as a compliment. I wear a lot of purple. I just like purple. Once I even had a plum-colored overcoat, which I bought for a song at a contraband warehouse in Naples when I was traveling with the Harlem Globetrotters, and one of them, Nate Branch, had the right commercial contacts in that dodgy town. Still, for goodness sake, I don't want to wear purple all the time. Then, rather than a preference, it would be an affectation, like guys who wear hats indoors.

Bespoke attire aside, England did have a more substantive influence upon me when I was a young writer and first went there, to cover Wimbledon, in 1966. The London newspapers were a revelation to me. I wouldn't say they influenced me so much as they buttressed a style I already believed in. I simply had established the opinion that American journalism in general was stodgy and guarded, and that our sportswriting in particular had grown too dependent on feeding our readers quotes from athletes that were merely obvious and self-serving. This view was certainly shared by the British. As Henry Fairlie, the wise British newspaperman, wrote, baldly, "That most American journalists have yet to learn to write is an accepted fact of American journalism, of every kind and at every level."

As much as I had first been taken by the *Herald-Tribune*, encountering the British newspapers enamored me. The writing was sharp, and the sportswriters, in the tradition of Bernard Darwin, were not afraid to put forth their opinions, rather than hiding behind wishy-washy neutralism: what the Japanese call *ademonai, kodemonai: on the one hand this, on the other hand that.* Instead, insipid quotes from vapid jocks were held to a minimum. It was, in fact, during this summer, when England was about to take on Germany in the World Cup, that a British reporter, Vincent Mulchrone of the *Daily Mail,* wrote the greatest sports-page lead ever: "If the Germans beat us at our national game today, we can always console ourselves with the fact that twice we have beaten them at theirs."

In the United States, Dick Young of the *New York Daily News* was the one sportswriter who could, at least in his own rough way, match the English candor. You had to read his stuff, for Young was as good a reporter as ever there was in sports; he waded in, fearlessly. His style was sometimes compared to that of Walter Winchell, the dot-dot-dot gossip columnist, but Young was accurate with his jabs whereas Winchell would swing wildly for effect. And as direct as he was with his opinions, Young could slip a little out of the side of his mouth, too. For a game early one season, he wrote, "It was so cold out here today even the brass monkeys stayed home."

Young was a prickly guy, though; when I was younger, I always gave him a wide berth when we passed on the baseball field before a game, because I knew he didn't suffer anybody but the daily press—and, really, just the muscular variety, i.e., anything like his own *Daily News*. Everybody else was bush. Even though he professed to admire Red Smith, Young thought the real reason the *Herald-Tribune* had gone out of business was that the writing—especially the sports section—was too prissy. Young decried "literature" in journalism. Also: "sociology." He was very leery of colleagues who used high-falutin stuff, like, say, adverbs. Bush. And, as you might expect, *Sports Illustrated* was fit only for dilettantes. Bush.

Of course, we were also new competition, and in that regard, Young had a lot of company in keeping us down. *Sports Illustrated* even had a devil of a time getting permission to so much as use the press box to officially cover baseball games. The press box may have been a part of a team's stadium, but it was the local papers that controlled access—sort of like diplomats existing above the law in a foreign land.

Young also warred against the broadcast media. He hated Howard Cosell most, because Cosell became even better known than writers, Dick Young prominently included. And, of course, much wealthier, too. At press conferences, when television was first allowed in, Young would stand, truculently, his head with its silver pompadour held high so as to block the camera's view. In the locker room, when some poor radio spaceman would stick his microphone in while Young was interviewing a player, Young would spout vulgarities into the offending microphone, ruining the poor guy's tape.

The player being interviewed would look on with the greatest amusement as Young screamed a purple array. I thought it was funny, too. Young, though, was at war. He told me once that the radio guys were "parasites who pirate our material, then beat us to the public with our own stuff."

Young became, unfortunately, something of a caricature in his last years, guilty of the same sort of hypocrisy he had so long inveighed against. He also grew hidebound—dismissive of the new generation of sportswriters, the Chipmunks and their ilk—no less than he frowned on the new breed of ballplayers. Perhaps he was stuck in time, bullheaded in the same way that some old people maintain that they're as principled/progressive/sensitive as ever, only it's just that everybody younger is dragging our culture into the abyss. Certainly, Young's prose, ever as direct and rugged and untainted by sissy adverbs, pretty much held its own to the end, but somehow the devil-take-the-hindmost guy himself grew crotchety. No, nobody had ever expected Dick Young to grow old gracefully, because he'd never been graceful in middle age—three different Dodger managers barred him from the clubhouse—but it was a shame that he went out shrill, for he had been an original who had as much effect on American sports reporting as any other, ever. Of course, he never won a Pulitzer; probably he never even got an early call at the clubhouse turn. But then, I'm sure that two of the three newspaper writers in America critiquing architecture got so honored.

Young was of a species that once peopled the sports pages: the raw, unschooled type who learned the craft as an apprentice, picking up writing—and in his case a style, as well—by osmosis. Copyboy? Young had to be *promoted* to copyboy. He had departed the CCC in the Depression, talking his way onto the *Daily News* for a messenger's job, only finally finding his way up to print, to sports reporting, during the war, when staffs were depleted. He covered the Giants at first, but really found himself with the boys-of-summer Dodgers in 1946. He was already feeling his oats, writing his most memorably caustic line that year, as the Dodgers gave way to the Cardinals: "The tree that grows in Brooklyn is an apple tree."

Baseball was Young's baby. Boxing for the big bouts. Football as the NFL grew in popularity. Maybe a bit of basketball during the playoffs, when it became the topic du jour in the right saloons, when they were not singles bars but still places to drink doubles. But that was it. Ice hockey wasn't big enough to take up his time, and he didn't give a flying fuck for horse racing, even though it was still big in his heyday. Young only wanted to cover the human shot-and-a-beer sports, and he went to his grave (in 1987) convinced that no real fan could possibly care about pussy crap like golf or tennis. And let's not even get into soccer. When the Olympics came to his backyard, Montreal, in 1976, Young called up (probably under duress from his editor) for a credential, expecting it to be OK'd over the phone, no different from asking for a press pass for some Knicks-Bullets game, and he went berserk when he was actually advised that he had to apply in writing, send in passport photos, etc. *What the fuck is it with these people?* That was another thing. As Young often took pains to regularly point out to the poor, stupid bastards in the hinterlands (say, little burgs like Philadelphia or Los Angeles), New York was the only place where they knew how to do things right.

But just as no one in the fraternity had ever let envy intrude upon the wholesale affection for Grantland Rice, when he was the most consequential sportswriter of his time, neither would even the most pained rivals of Dick Young ever shrink from praising his industry —even though he had few real friends among his colleagues. Young, you see, really did change the way business was conducted. While sportswriters had long been allowed in locker rooms, it was usually just to chew the fat with coaches, but Young pioneered the art of haunting the players' sanctuary, picking up grit and gristle. Before him, reporters for morning newspapers would hunker down, keep score, bang out their accounts of the game right after the game, hand their copy in to the telegraph lady, and go get a Seven and Seven. But Young would arrive early, work the locker room, return after the game, and fill his game story with the skinny and knowing quotes. Soon, in order for the other beat writers to compete with him, clubhouses became chat rooms, as well. The downside was that now everyday quotes, scribbled by journeymen reporters, began to proliferate, often, alas, choking out literature and sociology.

The whole idea of journalists going into the locker room remains, so far as I know, strictly an American idiosyncrasy. I can remember being in Barcelona, at a Davis Cup match in 1965, when Bud Collins and I waltzed down to the Spanish locker room. It wasn't just that we were barred. The Spanish sentinels looked oddly at us, no less than if we had tried to enter the ladies' room. Really, though, I understood. I've never felt altogether comfortable in a locker room. Trust me, nothing in your upbringing prepares you for carrying on a conversation with another person when you are fully clothed and the other is naked as a jaybird.

Beyond that, I always simply feared that I was intruding on someone else's privacy. (They even call it a "clubhouse" in baseball, as if to remind you that you, buddy—yes, you, in the jeans and New Balance sneakers and the ugly Walmart plaid shirt—you, kiddo, are not really part of this particular *club.*) In fact, I was always envious of the writers who seemed so at home in those sweaty environs. I guess I've been weird for a sportswriter, because my idea has always been to get any athlete I was writing about as far *away* from the locker room as possible.

The point was really brought home to me when I went to do a story on the Boston Celtics the year after John Havlicek retired. He had come to this, the opening game, as a civilian, and we were standing outside the locker room. As I started to enter, John touched my arm. "I'll see you later, Frank," he said. "I can't go in there. I don't belong there anymore."

Excuse me: John Havlicek didn't belong in the Celtic locker room, but I did? No.

31

REMEMBER
"CONSCIOUSNESS-RAISING"?

*Athletes and pretty girls share too much, so that it would be hard for
them to contribute anything but sex to one another.*
Everybody's All-American, 1981

Of course, much was made about women infiltrating the locker room
when females first began to enter the profession. But, then, more so
even than the rest of journalism, sportswriting truly was a male com-
monwealth. Locker rooms? Why, women weren't allowed to sully
press boxes. (Well, unless they were Western Union teletype opera-
tors; those, however, didn't count as females—or as human beings,
for that matter.) Locker rooms? As late as 1973, a colleague of mine,
Stephanie Salter, was thrown out of the huge annual banquet of the
Baseball Writers Association that was being held in a public hotel
ballroom in that liberal bastion New York.

Indeed, if there's one regret I've had as a sportswriter it's that
sport is so predominately male that you don't get much opportunity to write about females. That's unfortunate for a male writer
because (1) men aren't inclined to open up to another man as much
as women are, and (2) except where sex is involved, I think men and
women are programmed better to talk honestly to each other. There's
a sort of instinctive flirtation built in that advances the conversation.
Grown-up interviewing is basically only what you learned going out

on high school dates; it's all just *What kinda music do you like?* taken to a somewhat higher degree.

But then, the only time I was physically frightened by a subject, it happened to be a woman and probably the smallest person I ever interviewed. Robyn Smith, who would, in a subsequent life, become Mrs. Fred Astaire, was much the best female jockey at that time, and in the process of doing a piece on her, I discovered a few, let us say, benign fibs that she had conjured up to make her life seem more enthralling before she became a jockey. We were sitting alone in a barn at Belmont when I confronted her with these impolite facts. She was holding a rider's crop in her hand, and as I proceeded, most politely, to inquire into these discrepancies, she started to slap that whip across her palm—glaring at me all the while. Any moment, I expected to find out what it feels like to be a horse's withers. Mercifully, however, after our painful little chat concluded, Robyn allowed me to leave the barn unscathed.

This did not, however, mean that she was pleased with me. When the article—complete with a lovely cover shot of her (with the beguiling tint of a smile that would surely have made the Mona Lisa see red)— appeared, she took the time to go right to the top and write a facetious note to Hedley Donovan, the editorial director of all Timeink:

Dear Mr. Donovan:
Please thank Mr. De Ford for the lovely article he wrote about me. I only hope I can live up to everything he said.
Best wishes,
Robyn Smith

Notwithstanding the paucity of women in sport, in one major respect I was tremendously fortunate: I was covering a lot of tennis when Billie Jean King took the bull by the horns. Remember that old expression "consciousness-raising"? Well, it was Billie Jean more than anyone else who raised my consciousness. I consider it one of my finest professional compliments that Billie Jean still says I "got it" before most all my other male colleagues did. But, then, that may be damning me with faint praise, because the vast preponderance of sportswriters had no more professional connection with women than they had with Mongolians or antelopes.

Billie Jean, though—man, but she was amazing. Here she was, virtually running a sport, getting up at six o'clock after a night match to make an appearance on *Sunrise in Cincinnati* or *Hello! Omaha!* in order to hype the tournament, and yet she was also serving as a symbol for a whole movement—and taking a lot of crap from people who didn't appreciate her—and still winning championships on the side. A little while ago, when we had dinner in New York, I asked her what she best remembered about those days. She smiled. "Just that I was sleepy all the time," she said.

I *knew* she would beat Bobby Riggs. There've been only two or three times in my life when I was dead sure of an outcome in sport, and that match is at the top of the list. I made a nice bit of money from men, betting on her. Apart from the fact that Billie was obviously so much better than Bobby then and so well equipped to handle the pressure, she was really a lot like him—and she'll be the first to admit this. They both knew how to work a crowd, and they both enjoyed working a crowd; only Bobby was in it for the con, and Billie for a cause. Honest to God, there are still old cronies of Riggs who will swear that he had to have thrown the match so he could make even more in a rematch.

I was on a television panel with Riggs a little while after the match. Bobby was wearing his yellow Sugar Daddy jumpsuit and his big carny grin. I was sitting next to an old comedian, Henry Morgan. When we got up to leave, Morgan said to me, "You know, I've been in show business all my life. Anybody who gets up onstage, on television, whatever—you gotta have a big ego." With a mix of wonder and admiration, he nodded toward Riggs. "But I've never seen *anybody* in show business with half the ego of this guy." What Billie Jean had, though, was pride.

Several years after the Riggs match, when Billie Jean was near the end of her career, she was outed by a woman named Marilyn Barnett, who was seeking money in what was described as a "palimony suit." It's difficult to understand, perhaps, but Billie Jean needed money to fight the case. Unfortunately, like a lot of athletes, she had not invested wisely. Unlike a lot of athletes, however, she had lost much of her wealth nobly, investing in a cause, backing a magazine called *womenSports*. It was a fine idea, but, well, idealistic. Even now, as more and more girls and women participate in sports, they don't yet seem to possess the sports-*watching* gene that we men do. Women may play sports now, but—*vive la différence*—they don't *follow* them as we men do.

Except for golf, where the possibility for tedious instruction seems infinite, and where golfers will indiscriminately devour it endlessly, in the self-improvement mode of dieters or born-agains, sports journalism is all about being a fan. More and more, as a matter of fact, it's about celebrities, and when most women want to read about celebrities they want to read about entertainers, not athletes. So, at least for now, any journalism about women's sports is pretty much doomed to suffer small audiences.

It's also true that the most popular spectator sports are team sports, in which people have a lasting, even constitutional, rooting interest; and women's team sports have never been as popular as women's individual sports—starting with Olympic figure skating. I can even remember Billie Jean presciently telling me, years ago, that for all Title IX had done (and for that matter, unsaid: all Billie Jean had done) to promote women in sport, women would never begin to approach athletic equity with men until their team sports had become popular.

Anyway, Billie Jean had lost a bundle on the magazine that meant so much to her and in a couple of other well-meaning ventures like a smokeless ashtray (let's not get into that), and when Marilyn Barnett went public, Billie Jean was not only mortified but jeopardized financially as well. To make some money, she decided to write a book and asked me to be her collaborator.

It was so sad. Billie Jean may be the most enthusiastic person I've ever met. There seems to be nothing she involves herself with that she doesn't commit to completely. But she was only writing this book for the money, and the subject matter was difficult, so she was despairing, and it was like pulling teeth even to get her to sit down and talk. Besides, I was myself heartsick about what she was going through. I didn't find out till I was finished with the work that she hadn't been able even to bring herself to read much of the material I had sent her. And then, irony of ironies, just a few weeks before the book was published, a judge not only summarily threw out Marilyn Barnett's suit but excoriated her for even attempting to squeeze money out of Billie Jean.

Notwithstanding, great public relations damage had been inflicted upon Billie Jean. She was left all but bereft of product endorsements. At least, though, after all the pain she endured, she was freed of her secret, and she could get on with her life, with her terrific life partner, Illona Kloss. Before long, and especially as society became more accepting of gays, the dispiriting episode was forgotten, and by the end of the century, she was being celebrated for what she is, an important and inspirational cultural figure. I was never so happy for an athlete winning anything as when she was given the Presidential Medal of Freedom in 2010. There is no doubt in my mind that Billie Jean King and Jackie Robinson matter far more significantly than all other American athletes, ever.

32

FUN IN THE SUN

Beauty is in the eye of the ticket holder. Skin deep still counts.
"Advantage, Kournikova," *Sports Illustrated*, 2000

I learned to sympathize with female athletes. Whereas it's always been accepted that it is manly for a boy to participate in sport, it has, at least until recently, been the case that an athletic girl—do we still say tomboy?—is at cross-purposes with femininity and, very likely, suspect in terms of her sexuality. Herewith, from *Women's Sports: A History*, way back in 1901, a time when women were first venturing onto the playing fields: "How can we admire a girl, however beautiful she may be, whose face is as red as a lobster, and streaming with perspiration, whose hair is hanging in a mop about her ears . . . and whose general appearance is dusty, untidy and unwomanly?"

Or from Paul Gallico in 1938, as he took his leave of sportswriting: "Unattractive girls are comparatively good sports. Pretty girls are not. This might be simply enough explained. An attractive woman hates to be made to look bad, and no one looks his or her best taking a licking at anything. The ugly ducklings, having taken to sport as an escape and to compensate for whatever it is they lack, sex appeal, charm, ready-made beauty, usually are too grateful to be up there in the championship flight to resent losing too much."

Although it is now so common, even natural, for girls to grow up as athletes, for a long time it was customary to view women athletes as oddballs. To psychoanalyze my own gender, I would say that much of it has been sheer envy. Or fear. What is the worst thing you can say about a man? That he got beaten by *a girl.* We have countered by trying to deny those who could defeat us their sexuality, making them neuter. If only symbolically, this dates all the way back to the Amazons, who were supposed to have cut off their right breasts, their womanhood, so that they could draw an arrow as well as the men they battled.

Nevertheless, in curious contradiction, despite ourselves, we men have always deigned to give special dispensation to an annointed few gorgeous female athletes—admiring their womanly *figures,* not their athletic *bodies.*

Probably the first sportswoman who was also allowed to be enticing was Annette Kellerman, an Australian swimmer and diver who toured the United States in 1907, performing in a daring short-sleeved bathing suit. Generally, though, it has been the besequined figure-skating dolls who have most often been permitted to revel in their sexuality. Sonja Henie even became a top-rank movie star, Dorothy Hamill was accepted as the absolute all-American-girl model for her coiffure, and both Peggy Fleming and Katarina Witt were revered for their classic western looks—as Kristi Yamaguchi would be no less renowned as an Asian beauty. Occasional swimmers—notably Eleanor Holm, Esther Williams, Donna de Varona, and Natalie Coughlin—have escaped the criticism that swimming enlarges women's shoulders and achieved crossover status. However, in researching my latest novel, *Bliss, Remembered,* whose main character is a cute backstroker who goes to the 1936 Olympics, I was surprised to discover that when silk suits came into vogue back then, they were so sheer they provided the most revealing displays of feminine assets this side of burlesque theaters. Many embarrassed young swimmers would have helpers posted at the edge of the pool, so when they emerged from the water they could quickly be wrapped in the modesty of a large beach towel.*

---

*The beautiful Eleanor Holm, who won a gold medal in 1932, was signed to a Hollywood contract, and later starred at the 1939 World's Fair in her husband Billy Rose's Aquacade, did not avail herself of these towels. Eleanor was thrown off the 1936 team for misbehaving

Other sportswomen who have, in the past, been ordained as sex symbols were Flo-Jo, the sprinter; two golfers, Laura Baugh and Jan Stephenson; and two tennis players, Gorgeous Gussy Moran—she of the famous lace panties—and Karol Fageros, who was known as the "Golden Girl." However, except perhaps in the athletic hinterlands of beach volleyball and softball, team sports have never produced famous crossover femmes fatales—well, at least until Brandi Chastain took off her shirt at the Rose Bowl when the United States won the women's soccer World Cup in 1999. For whatever reason, women's team sports just don't lend themselves to babe status.

Of course, when it comes to women and *Sports Illustrated*, we have been known more notoriously as a pinup calendar than as a showcase for female athleticism. People would always say to me, "The swimsuit issue? What kind of a sport is that?" Hah, hah, hah. As if they were the first in the world with that line.

Or, just as brilliantly: "I guess you do that to sell magazines."
Yes.

However, so far as I can tell, while women can be portrayed as sex objects in almost every magazine in America, if you put a sexy lady in *Sports Illustrated*, women will have a fit. It is a somewhat contradictory reaction, but at a time when female athletes have finally begun to be accepted as perfectly normal representatives of their gender, many women have taken the position that women athletes may be portrayed only as *athletes*, that any reference to their appearance is ipso facto sexist. I appreciate that this is a backlash against all the sexism that has gone before, but, still, it's too defensive by half. You can call

---

on the ship going to Germany, charged with playing cards and drinking excessively with newspapermen—and perhaps sharing carnal knowledge with a gentleman other than her husband. When Eleanor was in her eighties, I was with her at a reception at the White House that the Clintons gave in honor of an HBO documentary I had written about great American female athletes. Eleanor spent most of the evening flirting outrageously with President Clinton, at one time cooing to him, "You are one good-looking dude." Without embarrassment, Eleanor wondered out loud whether he might sleep with her.

a woman athlete smart or funny or sweet (or not so sweet, for that matter)—anything but that which hints of the physical.

In 2000, after I had returned to *Sports Illustrated* on a contract basis, I pointed out to Bill Colson, the managing editor, that Anna Kournikova was absolutely phenomenal. Not only was she the most downloaded athlete on the Internet, with more than twenty thousand Web pages devoted to her, but she ranked nineteenth among the most searched-for items—men, women, or *things*—in all the Internet world. It was estimated that Anna—an athlete!—was photographed more than any other living female. She had appeared on the international covers of *Esquire, Vogue,* and *Cosmopolitan,* and in the United States as the cover girl for *Forbes*—*Forbes,* for Chrissake—where she was ranked right behind Colin Powell on the worldwide celebrity power list. She had even (get this) made the cover of *Sports Illustrated for Women.** She was hauling down a cool $10 million a year in endorsements, exponentially more than any female athlete, ever. Indeed, it was fair to say that there had never been another athlete in the world like the luscious Anna Kournikova.

I thought: Hey, this is a valid story. So did Colson. And if I do say so myself, I was tailor-made for the job. Anna was a tennis player, and I had long covered tennis. In fact, I had written two books with women Hall of Fame tennis players—Billie Jean King and Pam Shriver—and, holy of holies, I had once even been named Writer of the Year by the Women's Tennis Association. But Anna was also a beauty, and it just so happens that you are also talking about a credentialed beauty expert here. After all, I had judged Miss America four times.** Surely, seek high

---

*Alas, like Billie Jean King's *womenSports* and Condé Nast's *SPORTS for Women,* this also has bit the commercial dust.

**Before my first Miss America pageant, I was a bit nervous about judging, but then a wonderful Miss America maven, Eleanor "Big Momma" Andrews, explained that it was really very easy. "Honey," Big Momma told me, "don't worry about it. All you have to know is that the women judges just vote for the girl that reminds them most of themselves, and the men judges just vote for the one they'd most like to sleep with."

and wide, and you are never going to find another expert writer the equal of yours truly with feet in both the tennis and the pulchritude camps.

And so I did the piece. Reaching for my best *Vogue* prose: "On the court Anna is like a trim sloop, skimming across the surface, her long signature pigtail flying about like a torn spinnaker in the wind."

And so did the wrath of women sportswriters and women sports fans come down upon me. Never mind that Anna was a cultural marvel. Never mind that she was a *Forbes* pinup. Never mind that she was the most popular woman athlete in the world and carrying all of pre-Federer tennis on her trim sloop. No: how dare you, *Sports Illustrated*, and you pig, Frank DeFord. Kournikova is ranked fifteenth in the world. You should be doing a story on number one (whoever that was). It was even snarkily suggested in some sewing circles that this was really nothing but a scheme on my part to seduce Mademoiselle Kournikova.

Now, at this time, I was already pretty long in the tooth and Anna was still a teenager, and while I am many things, some of them lustful and leering, never once have I been mistaken for Silvio Berlusconi. But so—to the vast amusement of both my wife and my daughter (who is about Anna's age) and, I'm sure, Anna herself—ran the scurrilous chatter.

Poor Walter Iooss, the photographer, suffered as much calumny. Walter, who had spent years photographing gorgeous models for the swimsuit issue, was only now revealed as a dirty old man. The funny thing is, too, that when we arrived in Florida, where Anna was playing in a tournament, Walter told me that what he had in mind was to do the unexpected and shoot Anna in action playing tennis. That would be the cover shot.

Only, guess what. Anna would have nothing to do with this altogether original, innocent idea. While she finally agreed to grant me a few precious minutes for an *exclusive* intimate tête-à-tête in a noisy hotel lobby, she (and her mother) would simply not allow Walter a photo session—on the court or anywhere else. Then, weeks later, out of the blue, Anna's agents called Walter and told him that if he flew to Majorca, where Anna was vacationing, she would agree to pose for him there.

And so he did. And when he arrived, he told her what he had in mind—beautiful action shots on the court. Anna would have none of it. She demanded that the whole session be done in her boudoir, with her looking tawny and come-hither. And then poor Walter was pilloried for taking such demonstrably lustful pictures of a *tennis player*!

If women only knew that theirs is the same sort of prudish attitude which had created the notorious swimsuit issue. It began innocently enough, back when *Sports Illustrated* still ran travel and lifestyle stories. Since, as we know, there was just nothin' cookin' in the sports world from the bowl games on New Year's Day till the pitchers and catchers reported, *Sports Illustrated* would invariably run a tedious tropical travel piece during these winter doldrums. Usually, in poetic desperation, it would be hopelessly entitled "Fun in the Sun."

In 1964, Laguerre chose to put funinthesun on the cover in the person of an attractive young lady standing ankle-deep in still water. She was by no means seductive—more preppy, I would say—certainly not at all buxom, and in a bathing suit more burka than bikini. But sure enough, a few letters of shock and protest came in, one in particular from a librarian declaring that such outright pornography certainly had no place in her pristine sanctuary. Laguerre, who was invariably vexed by American Puritanism, merely mumbled something like, "Well, wait'll next year," and thus from little acorns do big oaks grow. Soon enough, there was Cheryl Tiegs in fishnet.

When I would go out on stories, men would invariably ask me—wink, wink—what it was *really* like hanging out with all those beautiful models. Reluctantly, I had to explain that Cheryl and her ilk never even graced the office, let alone in fishnet. It was only the photographers, like the suave and handsome Iooss, who got to consort with the models. Immediately upon this revelation, I could, in the eye of the beholder, see my stature rapidly declining.

Then in 1989, the silver anniversary of our sin in the sun, the folks in the business department decided to really blow it out. They shot a fancy video and gathered up several of the models, and along with Jule Campbell, the lovely editor who'd always assembled the issue, took a swimsuit dog and pony show on the road to play for advertisers. I, the erstwhile Miss America judge, was invited to go along as the emcee, which, with great reluctance, I agreed to do. Good company man, you understand. We were given the Timeink company plane, and here we flew away, just us, across America: the likes of Elle Macpherson, Kathy Ireland, Carol Alt, Rachel Hunter, Jule, and me.

We bonded, the girls and I. Elle had a spot of man trouble, and it came to a head in Chicago, and we all tried our best to console her. Then, as it happened, on Valentine's Day we played Detroit, cozying up to the automobile boys. Being both the only writer and the only man in the troupe, I wrote out personal valentines and read them out loud to my girls at the luncheon.

But all too soon our road show closed, and since I don't hang out in the right circles, I quickly lost touch with my pretties. Except that years later, outside on a beautiful soft night, dining at the Villa d'Este on Lake Como, I looked across the lawn and spied Rachel. In that instant, she saw me too, and we both rose as one, and, our eyes only for one another, her long auburn hair glimmering in the starlight, my dimples deepening, we quickly closed the distance, until at last we stood together again and exchanged a sweet kiss.

Then she took me over to her table and introduced me to her husband, Rod Stewart. He did not rise, nor did he express the slightest interest in who I might be or where his wife and I had once spent a cold and innocent Valentine's Day together. And so I returned to my table, to my patiently waiting wife, never to see Rachel again.

Ah, but I thought: We'll always have Detroit.

33

SUMMER SONGS

If it's possible to argue that sport brings us together, that when whites cheer for a black man on the field it makes it easier for them to accept blacks at church or on a bus, then it's just as possible to argue that sports makes a handful of blacks into municipal mascots, which, in turn, allows whites to put aside the more delicate tangles of brotherhood.

"40 Christmases Later," *Sports Illustrated*, 1986

Athletes remain our touchstones of memory. As we get older, we associate our youth with the boys who were playing back then. In that sense, athletes are analogous to oldies but goodies. When I was doing a story on Al McGuire, we were in a nightclub in Toronto one evening. Al was no book-learner, but he was a truly wise man, who probably saw the odd connections and disjunctions of life better than any other person I've ever known. The band struck up a song, "Cherry Pink and Apple Blossom White." Al turned to me and said, "More people will dance now."

"Why?" I asked, bewildered at his total assurance.

"Summer song," Al said sotto voce. "This was a summer song. People remember summer songs better."

Instantly, the dance floor was thronged.

And, in the same way that we have *our* songs from summers past, we have *our* athletes, too, whom we connect with a season from long ago. In my own case, for example, no one is more associated with my youth than was Johnny Unitas. He meant so much to Baltimore. As a card-carrying sportswriter, though, I seldom covered football, and so I never met Unitas until late in his life, when I was introduced to him at a reception. When he said, "Hello, Mr. DeFord," it was competely discombobulating. I wanted to say: *No, no . . . you're the mister. I'm just a teenage kid named Frankie.* For me, forever, Johnny Unitas was a summer song.

Once, however, you begin to deal with athletes professionally, they primarily become product, and thereby do they lose so much of their aura. After a while, it took a great deal to impress me. I suppose the last time that happened was when I was interviewing Sir Edmund Hillary in 1999, for an end-of-the-century story. He couldn't have been more laid-back. It was at his house in Auckland, and his cat walked all over him while we were talking, and he wanted me to just call him "Ed," but still, here was the hero who had conquered the last bit of planet Earth, here was a gentleman whose face was on his country's five-dollar bill. There was a sense of chatting with Thomas Jefferson.

But, from the very start of my career, it was almost natural for me to be casual, even smug, about whom I might be interviewing, because working for such a prestiguous journal made it so easy to obtain access. Now, at least I always appreciated that edge. I understood I was only incidentally Frank DeFord. I was foremost just a hired hand from *Sports Illustrated*. People would talk to *Sports Illustrated*. People would call *Sports Illustrated* back, and there I'd be on the other end of the phone.

Also, back then, there weren't as many other credentialed journalists, and athletes weren't yet in thrall to television. I still remember so well that in 1968, after the Celtics again won the championship from the Lakers, I went into the Los Angeles locker room and spoke alone with Jerry West for about fifteen minutes, and then went over to the Boston locker room and had the same sort of intimate one-on-one with Bill Russell. Today, the modern versions of Russell and West would address the assembled press, mobbed, in a special interview room. So, in a way, the more the media, the more we get the same wholesale stuff.

Being privileged also helped me, over time, appreciate how the high-and-mighty press rationalizes in a skewed way. It came to amuse me how people from important institutions, like, say, Timeink, would be horrified if, say, the *Inside Blabber* paid money to someone for information. But here's the reality. A source who would approach the *New York Times* (or me at *Sports Illustrated*) didn't make that effort out of the goodness of his heart. He did it because he had an ax to grind or was looking for the most effective place to present a story that would shine the best light on him. Now, this will surely make me look like an apostate in the eyes of much of respectable journalism, but: what difference does it make if a source chooses instead to *sell* privileged information? It's the same thing—you're just leveraging what you have, and, to my mind, whether you do it for vengeance or for publicity or for money, it's essentially the same self-serving motive.

When I ran the *National*, some hanger-on came into possession of a transcript of an investigative hearing that baseball had conducted into nefarious goings-on that George Steinbrenner, the Yankee owner, had participated in. The guy shopped the transcript. We bought it for $7,000. OK, I felt sort of naughty, doling out seven grand in $100 bills to a small-time hustler in my apartment, but I'll tell you: it never left a mark on my conscience. In fact, I rather enjoyed it when the *Times* got all high and mighty and sniffed at what a lowlife rag we were for *paying for news*. Heavens to Betsy!

At high-toned *Sports Illustrated,* the currency I dealt in was power; at the nouveau *National,* cash. Today, ESPN gets athletes to make commercials for it because the athletes know they're getting the best stage—and getting on the good side of the most powerful source in American media. So what if cash money doesn't change hands? Television news shows pay sources for "licensing" the use of photographs, when, of course, they're really buying exclusive interview time. I'm sorry, but it's all the same. Journalism is noble, but it's also barter. Your words, your story, your likeness in exchange for vanity, for publicity, for vengeance, for money. The only real difference is that money leaves a trace that emotions don't.

In a sense, journalists are not unlike the NCAA, which claims that amateurism is wonderful because it's pure. In fact, athletic amateurism is wonderful for the NCAA because then its member colleges don't have to pay for the unique services of their athletes. Likewise, in journalism, the support of the principle of keeping inside knowledge on an amateur basis is wonderful because then the big, respectable media companies don't have to pay for the unique services of their sources.

One of my ace "exclusive" interviews came early on with Lew Alcindor. When he went to UCLA, back in the time when freshmen could not play on the varsity, Alcindor was completely sequestered from the press, as he had been in high school in New York. The quarantine had to be lifted when he would play varsity as a sophomore, so UCLA made the decision to let his first interview be a national one, with—not surprisingly—*Sports Illustrated*. I drew the assignment simply because I was the magazine's basketball writer. As it would turn out, though, the interview with Lew developed into a most strained— and then upsetting—assignment.

I picked up the young Alcindor after practice and took him out to dinner. *Uncomfortable* would not do him justice. He had been schooled to be wary of reporters, and it was immediately apparent that he was suspicious of me—if, indeed, he plain didn't like me. It was a painful evening, although I kept telling myself that he was still a teenager and that I was charged, in effect, with introducing him to an unknowing public that was fascinated by him, and so I must accord the young man every benefit of the doubt in his debut profile. I tried to keep the conversation in areas where he might possibly be interested, even, pray, forthcoming.

At one point we discussed his heritage, for although I am indeed genuinely interested in people's genealogy, I was going out of my way to give him, a descendant of African slaves, the same opportunity I might give any descendant of white European immigrants: *And where, Mr. O'Brien, did your family come from in Ireland?*

Indeed, it was a subject that finally animated Alcindor somewhat, and he told me that his family had come from Nigeria. Well, obviously Nigeria did not exist at the time his forebears were captured and enslaved, and so in the article I worded it that the Alcindors "believe they can trace back to present-day Nigeria." All right? I believe I can trace my ancestors back to present-day France, although they might have lived in what was then Burgundy or Aquitaine.

But Alcindor then wrote me a long accusatory letter, of which this was the centerpiece:

> *Mr. De Ford,*
> *I am writing this to let you know of the extreme dishonor you have done both myself and my family. In your article you made it seem as if there was much doubt as to the validity of my family heritage. . . .*

And so forth.

I wrote back, trying to explain my choice of words, but he never replied. I must say that later, given the gift of lapsed time, when we encountered each other occasionally after he became a pro with the Milwaukee Bucks, our relationship was cordially distant, and he never again brought up the subject of his discontent. Nevertheless, while I certainly did manage to upset a number of athletes with my sharp choice of words, I'm pretty sure young Alcindor was the only person who ever went to the extent of accusing me of dishonoring him and his race.

To be frank, though, during that time, given the existing journalistic mores, a great many white reporters were something of default racists. It was accepted then that the private man was generally off-limits when you were writing about the public person (see: Kennedy, John); and so too were indelicate opinions expressed about sensitive subjects, such as race, embraced in that, uh, gentleman's agreement. In sports, the racial hypocrisy was perhaps more prominent, though, because we were white reporters with white coaches, at precisely a juncture when it was dawning on the coaches that, to win, they needed these Negroes, who were quicker and jumped higher than the incumbent slow, gravity-afflicted white boys. As the expression went (with a chortle): "You start two at home, three on the road, and play four when you're behind."

Some coaches who had black players would even, privately, laugh and call forth stage "Rastus" dialect. Understand, it was understood, a compact. People would never have spoken so in front of me if they believed I would report them. That was the way of the world of American journalism—sports and otherwise—that I was introduced to and that, yes, at that time of my life, the way of the world that I accepted.

By chance, on the day Martin Luther King was shot, I was in the office of an owner of an NBA team that, of course, featured star black players. Also there with us were the owner's wife and another team official. The owner's secretary came to the door and said: "I just wanted to tell you, sir, that the official word just came in that Dr. King has died."

The owner's wife immediately said: "I'm glad the coon got it."

Inevitably, the white stars were disappearing. Jerry West was the anomaly. Oscar Robertson, his contemporary, had been better when they started out, but Jerry was his superior at the last, the best player in the world by the end of the 1960s. Havlicek was an athletic freak of nature, and when he learned how to shoot, too, he became genuinely great. Rick Barry is like Baylor—people have forgotten how terrific he really was. But that was about it, the last hurrah for Our Crowd except for Larry Bird later on.*

---

*Europe still produces some very good white basketball players, and this can best be explained by the fact that the European whites grow up playing pretty much against themselves and thus develop without being intimidated by black competitors, and without being constantly reminded from an early age that they possess inferior bodies. Also, the coaches impart fundamentals better in Europe; this is likewise part of the reason why we also don't produce any more good tennis players.

God knows the NBA tried to hold back the obvious. At first, only the very best African-American players could make the rosters. Then, well . . . if you were good enough to start. It was so transparent. A bunch of white stiffs would be cluttering up the bench, getting the dreaded DNP in the box scores: Did Not Play. But who were the owners kidding? Did they really think that white people would be satisfied to keep on shelling out for tickets to watch blacks play so long as a bunch of white kids in sweat suits dressed up the bench for forty-eight minutes? Come on.

At *Sports Illustrated,* Andre Laguerre suffered some of the same fears the team owners did. He worried that if he kept putting black stars on the cover, it would turn off his white readers. Owners, editors, writers, PR people, broadcasters, and advertisers excused it as being *only* commercial racism, not your traditional immoral kind, you understand. Don't take it personally. But, of course, racism is what it was, and the end result was the same: blacks suffered. They didn't get the chances they deserved. Second-rate white players would get the commercials. The hunky Jantzen International Sports Club, featuring all-Americans in bathing trunks, was for white stars only. White players tended to get drafted higher; black players made less money. *Be grateful we let you in, kid.*

I fought to finally get Baylor on the cover in 1966. At that time, Jerry Krause, who would become the superb general manager of the Bulls (he stole the unknown Scotty Pippen to give an ungrateful Michael Jordan the running mate he needed to win), was scouting for the Baltimore Bullets. Jerry worked the hinterlands. He kicked over all the rocks out there. He told me that the two best NBA prospects in the country were Walt Frazier at Southern Illinois and Earl Monroe at Winston-Salem State.

Except for the hoop cognoscenti, hardly anybody had heard of Monroe, who was playing at an HBC, a historically black college. So I went to see Monroe play a game at Winston-Salem, where I was probably the only white person in the whole gymnasium, as the crowd chanted "Earl, Earl, Earl the Pearl / Earl, Earl, best in the world." And if he wasn't quite that good, even I could tell that Monroe was surely the real deal.

When Krause's Bullets drafted him first in 1968, I helped convince Laguerre to put the unknown Pearl on the cover of the basketball issue. Earl is quite dark-skinned; he was shot twirling a basketball against a stark white background. Laguerre got a blistering note from one of the top Timeink editors saying that it was "one of the ugliest, most unappealing covers that I can recall ever having on one of our magazines." But it also turned out to be one of the best-selling issues of the year. Clearly, the white audience was beginning, however grudgingly, to accept the reality that black athletes were starting to dominate their favorite sports. Take it or leave it. And sure enough, Earl, as a rookie, finished fourth in the league in scoring, so thanks to Jerry Krause we looked like pretty knowing hoop savants.

Nonetheless, a few months later, when Laguerre wanted to do a lead story on the Atlanta–San Francisco playoff series, he was getting chary again about the African-American dominance of basketball, and he advised me that what he had in mind was a split cover which, by a wild coincidence, would have two whites on it: Jeff Mullins of the Warriors and Richie Guerin, the player-coach of the Hawks. I blanched. Mullins was the leading scorer on his team, a legitimate cover subject. But on a team whose rotation was virtually all-black, Guerin seldom even played anymore. The choice was just too egregiously racially bent. I politely suggested to Andre that I thought he ought to change the cover. OK, Mullins—but at least bump Guerin. He found me insolent and growled that he'd made up his mind. So I said that then I was sorry, but if that was the cover, I couldn't do the story.

"That's the cover I want," he snapped at me. (No familiar "Frankie" attached this time.)

"Then, I'm sorry, sir, but I can't do it."

"All right, I'll get someone else," he said, flatly, waving me off.

And he did. And the cover ran. And he never said another word about it. And certainly neither did I.

I'd like to say that this bold confrontation of mine proved what a principled stand-up guy I was, that I was the Atticus Finch of sports journalists. Rather, I suspected, as Bill Russell would affirm to me later, that it was already a common view amongst African-American athletes that *Sports Illustrated* practiced a double standard of race with its covers. So, honestly, my bold objection was mostly based on the fact that I couldn't imagine myself going back out on the road after my cover story ran and seeing all the black players I knew, whose trust I had earned. When it came down to it, I could face my boss before I could face my contemporaries.

For whatever it's worth, on the next NBA cover, a month later, Laguerre ran an action shot of Russell.

I've always found the expression that somebody "changed with the times" backward. Rather, it's the other way round: the times change only because we who inhabit them do the changing first. It is not the times that are accepting gay marriage nowadays. In my life span, people have surely changed most dramatically in their racial attitudes. This is all the more impressive to me because it isn't that simple to shuck off the biases that you grew up with, that you were inculcated with. As per Rodgers and Hammerstein, you've got to be taught to hate, but, of course, people almost never think that they do hate. More accurately, you're taught to discriminate, and that's so much more tolerable to slide along with. Still, in my lifetime I've seen so many ordinary folk who've been able to dial back their bias. That should count for something, so I do get a little irritated when people today look back on generations past and judge those people unsympathetically, by current standards, without the context.

Sure we were more racist, more sexist, more homophobic, more biased about a lot of different groups than we are now. *What are they saying about the Spic up there?* But certainly, for those of us white guys actually in sport, in one way or another, we were forced to confront race directly. That was new for a lot of us. A time of transition is always trying; but it was transforming, too.

Years later, as the new century turned, I was at Bob Cousy's home, interviewing him about those days of long ago. Now, Cousy had been an absolute prince among men to his African-American teammates. He was one player who didn't have to be taught anything about brotherhood. Indeed, in 1950, when Chuck Cooper, the first black player to be drafted by the NBA, joined the Celtics, Cousy immediately befriended him and looked after him. When the Celtics were playing an exhibition in North Carolina and Cooper wasn't permitted to stay in the team hotel, he decided to return to Boston. So Cousy, who was just a rookie himself, declared that he would skip the game, too, and, instead, he rode the train north with Cooper.

And so we were talking about that time, when Bob suddenly stopped. Then he began to cry, softly at first, and then with really hard, deep sobs. "Bob?" I said. "Bob, what is it?"

He finally got hold of himself, but the tears were still coming some when he said, "It's just that I should have done so much more. I've never forgotten that. I should have done more." He who had done so much. So, yes, we all should have.

34

ROADIE

*Wherever I go, in what is called the heartland of America, I am
told not to fear because "there is Interstate all the way." I have
heard this so often that I am convinced that if the road to hell were
made Interstate before heaven became that accesible, most Midwest
Americans would gas up and join the devil.*
   "In Search of Naismith's Game," *Sports Illustrated*, 1967

As I watched from the press box, what I saw television do to sports was
to make athletes into personalities—not just the distant performers
outlined against the blue-gray sky that they had been. Television gave
sports what the movies had given actors: close-ups. And whereas actors
were, as everybody knew, acting, players were actually performing for
real. Slowly then, athletes became more human and thus potentially
more heroic. Besides, many of us had played sports as kids, so we at
least thought we knew what it might be like to be a star athlete. We
could identify better with athletes than with actors. Or anyway, we
could dream better.

    The pendulum has begun to swing back the other way recently,
because the paparazzi and the fanzines now cover the private lives
of actors (and musicians) more closely—and their private lives are
real now and not those gauzy ones that had been made up by the
studios. We know who's screwing who in show business better than
we do in sports, and that makes a big difference. As a consequence,
now more people connect with entertainers—dream along with
them—than they do with athletes, who hide their private lives in

gated communities (except when they go out to clubs and get involved in gunfights). Then too reality shows make very ordinary people into celebrity "performers," so there's a sense that we're all just a step away from being the American Idol. But that sort of daydreaming can't possibly make any average person believe he could be a star athlete. We'll watch someone who can't really dance well try to dance. We'll never watch somebody who can't hit a curveball try to hit a curveball.

This one particular time back in the 1960s, when I was the *Sports Illustrated* basketball writer, I was covering a college game somewhere, on deadline, and after I sent in my story, when I called in the next morning, the editor said, sure, we got the story, but why didn't you write about such-and-such a strategy? Well, I knew this editor didn't know jack about basketball himself. But I quickly surmised that he'd seen the game himself on television and was regurgitating what the "analyst," some failed coach, had proclaimed. So it was: the scales fell from my eyes. Very simply, as a consequence of television, sportswriters had lost their original reason for being, which had been to tell you, the reader, about what happened at the game that you didn't see. I thought: you know, I'm redundant now. Yes, we could still be sportswriters, but it was all over for *games*writers.

So there. That was another good reason why I began to spend a lot of my time away from the reaches of television, chronicling unusual personalities or athletic exotica, the Americana of sports, out on the fringes. In a sense, I got to go back into time, to see the way it had been, bush, before television and the big money, when a great deal of sports meant hustling and scuffling, when there was a vagabond spirit and a quaintness to it all.

Of course, if you have the temperament and the curiosity, being a writer alone on the road is a fascinating existence. After all, I've never been very good at being a grab-ass, one of the fellas. I think the reporters who succeed best covering teams are the ones who have that kind of *belonging* team personality themselves. Besides, while the thought is hardly original with me, in dealing with people as subjects you must be something of a chameleon. The people you're meeting to interview don't know you, and so you try to emphasize the facets of your personality that most please them—and you can't very well pull that little deception off if you're writing about the same people on a team day in and day out. A writer alone can better be something of an actor, and I guess I have a bit of that in me.

And so, I looked for what was real and unusual, athletic quaint. I went to the Soap Box Derby, which is on a hill in Akron, Ohio. I traveled with ice shows. I covered Joie Chitwood's thrill car-driving rodeo and big trucks racing and I wrote about alligator wrestling and the waterskiing extravaganza at Cypress Gardens. I judged a cheerleading contest. I flew with the Thunderbirds precision jets and took g's. I rode a thousand miles in a truck with a guy named Jerry Malone who towed around a whale named Little Irvy, charging 35 cents a head for folks just to see Little Irvy lying there, frozen dead. I loved stuff like that. It was YouTube, only in person. It's mostly all gone today, vanished. You see, by now all the memory lanes are interstates.

Well, the Harlem Globetrotters still thrive out there. It's the one goofy thing television hasn't been able to kill. I played against the Globies in Bologna. This violated my promise to myself that I would never, on a story, try to do with any of my subjects what they do for a living. Leave that amateur hokeyness to the local television reporters. I'd learned that lesson all too well when traveling in an elongated station wagon with a wrestling bear named Victor. This noble ursine treated me with respect until I too wrestled him, and he pinned me in about eight seconds. Thereafter Victor not only disdained me but cuffed me around whenever the spirit moved him. He even knocked a Coca-Cola bottle right out of my grasp because he liked to drink Coke himself. You stay in character, you can deal with a bear, but you get down to the bear's level, and sometimes the bear will eat you.

But then, later, when I was traveling with the Globies in Italy, they kept urging me to suit up as one of their patsies on the New York Nationals. After all, the Nationals were tall and slow and white, and thus a perfect fit for me. Finally, my vanity got the best of me and I agreed I'd do it, but only once, on my last night with the team. Hey, if the Globies made too much of a fool of me, I was only playing a one-night stand, and Bologna would be in my rearview mirror by morning.

As it was, the Globies decided that discretion was the better part of dealing with a guy writing about them; they treated me with kid gloves, and I went for a huge eight points. *Double figures* were within my grasp! But Marques Haynes dribbled out the clock. As I left the court, the very idol of Bologna Jerry Venable approached me. "Next time, Frank," he said, "it's your ass."

"Don't worry, Jerry," I assured him. "There'll be no next time." At least I had learned that if you do wrestle the bear, only wrestle him once.

Of course, this does allow me a response when people say, "Gee, you're tall, did you ever play basketball?" I can say, "Well, yeah, I played a little pro ball in Italy."

I spent a lot of time going all around Robin Hood's barn with the Roller Derby. They were about the best people I ever met in all of sport. They were so grateful just to be making a living, to be skating, to be out there on the glamorous road—and the heroes of adoring fans, to boot. Plus, the guys could make extra money putting the track up and tearing it down, moving on to the next stop. They were like the elephants in the circus.

Ann Calvello played the villain on the women's side. She would dye her hair all sorts of colors, till it possessed the consistency of Brillo. She'd wear huge hoop earrings that didn't match—like, say, one big red and one big blue. She carried a king-size chalice with her, and would slam it down and ask the barkeep to fill it up. Which he would do, to the brim. How do you say no to a loud woman with pink polka dots in her green hair who carries a chalice with her? She had one rule: "No skating talk while drinking." Ann was one great broad.

Joanie Weston was her opposite, the heroine, blonde and rosy-cheeked, Catholic-schooled, skating lead with the beloved Bay

Bombers. Joanie might've been the best woman athlete I ever met, but there wasn't much chance back then for a lady to make a living in sports, and so she had to settle for the Roller Derby. When I was driving with her and her little dog, somewhere in Dixie, she got wistful all of a sudden, and she said, "You know, Frank, all I want out of the Derby is to make good money, get out of it in one piece, and years from now, when I say I was in the Roller Derby, I want people still to know what it is. I want that."

Joanie's dead now, much too soon, but this is just to let some people know a little about what the Roller Derby was when Joanie Weston was the star.

Joanie herself took advantage of having to skate all over America by doing some sightseeing, but most of her colleagues only wanted to get from Arena A to Arena B as quickly as possible—especially if they were the guys who were paid to put their track up for the extra money. One time, though, she prevailed upon several of them to divert a little out of their way in order to actually see the Grand Canyon.

To her chagrin, when the skaters got there, they did not seem much impressed. They just kind of stood around, looking out vacantly into the great chasm. Finally one of them asked Joanie: "Where are the bears?"

"What bears?"

"You know, Joanie, the bears. The famous bears."

At last Joanie caught on that he must've meant the bears at Yellowstone Park. This was just the Grand Canyon.

"You mean we come all this way out of our way just to see a hole inna ground?"

Joanie glumly nodded, they got back into their cars, and they headed to the next appointed arena, forthwith.

Unlike the Globies, the Derby skaters were unaware of the protocol that you should play up to a writer from a national magazine, even pretend that you are enchanted by his company. After all, if the Grand Canyon doesn't impress you, then Frank DeFord from *Sports* fucking *Illustrated* magazine is just another chump, too; the Derby skaters felt no compunction about publicly embarrassing the interloper who would be their biographer.

It happened thus: one of the more prominent skaters—let us call him Donnie—was flamboyantly gay, and late one night in Minneapolis, when I was seated with Calvello and her chalice and several other skaters in the dark hotel bar after a game, he made a rather overt move on me. Such was duly noted by those in attendance. As the plot would have it, I had already arranged with Donnie to interview him, riding with him alone to Duluth the next day. Likewise: duly noted. And those who had gone unnoted were assuredly brought into the loop by Calvello.

When the game began in the packed Duluth arena, I was seated by myself at the press table. After all, Roller Derby: bush. What real sportswriter would descend to cover such a lowly sport? After only a jam or two, the Bay Bombers called time-out and skated over to a position just above me, and there, a cappella, led by their fabled captain, Charlie O'Connell,* the Bomber men looked down upon me and, in chorus, sweetly sang "Here Comes the Bride."

Alone there at the press table, I was mortified, and surely red-faced, until it dawned on me that none of the baffled Duluth patrons understood what was going on, and so I blew kisses to the Bombers, and the game resumed. Well, that was the one time in my career when I stopped a game.

In the event, it's ironic, but in a profession where we necessarily bunch up and hang together, I became a living oxymoron, the lone-wolf sportswriter. Research a subject, make phone calls and reservations, go out somewhere alone, scout about, interview, return home, write, visit the office, and turn the story in. Then back out. Long-term parking, aisle seats, shuttles, rental cars, motels, interstates,

*Always referred to as "Bomber Great Charlie O'Connell," as if Bomber Great were part of his name.

cheeseburgers and fries, minibars, Magic Fingers. I wasn't just writing about Americana. I was Americana. I began to collect hotel shampoo bottles. Indeed, I now own the largest collection in the world (I don't believe there's a number two). It's on display in my garage on little shelves my son Christian built for me. I've got up into the five hundreds by now—no duplicates—although to my surprise I've learned that shampoo in those little bottles evaporates. Who knew?

35

WITH EASE OR ANGST

*It has always been my impression that few top athletes are avid
sports fans. These fellows succeed so easily at games—and from an
early age—that they have no need to transfer any of their sporting
interest to the performance of others. This is the reason, I think, why
so few of them can comprehend the manic affection in which they
are held.*

   "A Time for All Us Children," *Sports Illustrated*, 1978

As the 1960s flowed into the 1970s, we became blasé about our success
at *Sports Illustrated*. Not long before I arrived they'd had a pouring for
the golf writer Alfred Wright,* simply because he was going to take
a transcontinental flight for a story in far-off California. Godspeed,
Al. But soon enough, the writers were flying hither and yon without
so much as a fare-thee-well. The magazine started to make money,
and then we were rolling in dough. *Life* staggered to its knees, then
folded. The end of an era. *People* hadn't been invented yet. So *Sports
Illustrated* was, if only by default, suddenly the cat's meow at Timeink.

   This did not mean, of course, that we received much acclaim.
In the Time-Life Building, we were still looked upon as a rude jock
journal, and in the wider world, during this golden age of magazines,

---

*Al had been married to Joan Fontaine, the movie star. He was a nice enough guy, well
bred and tweedy, but with a butcher's face, and I just could never, for the life of me, figure out what a genuine movie star had seen in him. But then, at that time I didn't know
any movie stars, and it did delight me that at least one of them had seen fit to actually
marry a sportswriter.

when there was breathless talk about the so-called New Journalism, we remained very much below the salt. For some reason, with the literary connoisseurs, sportswriting was never new enough journalism.

Likewise, when great editors of that era were deservedly praised —Harold Hayes at *Esquire*, Clay Felker at *New York*, Willie Morris at *Harpers*, Osborn Elliott at *Newsweek*—Laguerre, as the racetrack chartmen say, never got a call. But then, that has been the way of our world. Red Smith didn't get his Pulitzer till late in life, at the age of seventy-one, after he'd been picked up by the *New York Times*. That presumably finally made him worthy—because of the new company he kept. Likewise, the Pulitzers were about thirty years late in recognizing Jim Murray of the *Los Angeles Times*.

It wasn't only the good writing that was ignored. Serving as art director under Laguerre was Dick Gangel. He was a former World War II fighter pilot, tall and thin as a pencil, a very enigmatic guy, perfectly genial, but even though I played doubles tennis with him for years, he was hardly one to reveal himself. Dick knew what he liked,* though, and under his aegis *Sports Illustrated* was running more first-rate art than any other magazine in the country. However, only the artists and illustrators beating a path to his door seemed aware of it.

As good as the magazine's writing was, too, for the first time I began to understand that few people can bring themselves to compliment sportswriting the way they do other written work. It's still true, too. If people are nice enough to appreciate something I write, they'll invariably say to me, "Frank, that was really good. In fact, it was so good, it wasn't sportswriting." Ergo, if it's bad, it's sportswriting, but if it has any merit, then it can't *be* sportswriting. Anyway, I know by now people *mean* this as a compliment. It's like spelling my

---

*If you don't count Bellows's boxing and Degas's horses, Leroy Neiman is by far the most famous sports artist ever (lovely man, too), but Gangel thought Leroy's work was garishly abysmal, and it never once appeared in *Sports Illustrated*, even though people were forever telling me how much they loved Leroy's work in *SI*.

name DeFord; they just can't help themselves. I merely say, Thank you very much indeed.

But as the magazine prospered as a product, it lost its special camaraderie. It had always been the Timeink way of life that writers stayed in the nest, there in the building, under the thumb of editors, on the proper floor. As that was the way it had always been at the flagship, *Time*, and then at *Life*, then, by God, that's the way it had started out at *Sports Illustrated*. So, in the beginning, all the writers lived around New York and were supposed to come to the office and kick the tires even if they weren't writing a story. But *Time*'s writers were basically rewrite men for the far-flung correspondents who sent their copy in to be putty in somebody else's hands, and *Life*'s writers were glorified caption stylists, waiting for the photos to be selected so they might compose. We were 100 percent honest-to-goodness writers; we wrote whole real stories all by ourselves. Poor Roger Hewlett, who had been a writer at *Time* and then had come to our place as an editor. "Just my luck," he told me once, with equal parts wryness and wistfulness, "that I was a writer on an editor's magazine and then an editor on a writer's magazine."

So after a while, as the magazine evolved under Laguerre, our writers started "working at home," and stopped bothering to come to the office or hang out at the bar, and then Andre let guys live wherever they wanted to, all over the country.

By now Dan Jenkins had become the most famous writer on the magazine. He had a wonderful sense of humor, writing shit-kicking, colloquial Texas prose, which was distinct and funny—and nobody had seen that kind of belles lettres beyond what is now called the Metroplex. Certainly *Sports Illustrated* had never had an original talent like that before. Then, too, Dan wrote a big best seller, *Semi-Tough*, which was really amazing, because sports fiction rarely sells. The sports books that make the best-seller lists are invariably worshipful autobiographies and insider tomes. If you like sports, what do you need made-up stories for when you can watch the real thing in the comfort of your man cave?

Think about it this way: Lawyer books are the inverse of sports books. Whereas real sports is exciting, real law is boring—plea bargaining and appeals and writs and stuff—so lawyer fiction is much better than actual real-life law. You're crazy to try to write good sports fiction if you can write run-of-the-mill lawyer fiction.

In fact, even if you should write sports fiction, people are bound and determined to believe that true sports is too exciting for you to make up imaginary sports. *What's it based on, Mr. DeFord? Who is it, you know, really?*

When I wrote *Everybody's All-American*, the hero—an old jock named Gavin Grey who can never stop reliving his glorious gridiron years—was a composite of many guys I'd known. He could have been from any sport. I chose football simply because, especially in college, it's the most glamorous sport. I put it in the South because the South cares most for college football and because the hero was married to a beauty queen, and the South cares most about beauty queens. I put it at the University of North Carolina simply because I was familiar with Chapel Hill from writing *basketball* stories, and a couple of good friends had gone there and told me some good anecdotes about the place. In other words, Gavin Grey was a complete fabrication, and I had him go to the University of North Carolina for a lot of utterly random reasons.

As soon as the novel came out, though, the good people of North Carolina decided, arbitrarily, that the hero of *Everybody's All-American* must be based on one Choo-Choo Justice, who had been a flesh-and-blood Tarheel all-American. I had never met Choo-Choo and knew nothing about him. Never mind. When I protested, wounded North Carolinians told me that I was lying, and that I should be ashamed for expropriating their hero and holding him up to ridicule.

A few years later, Hollywood was going to make a film of *Everybody's All-American*, with Kevin Costner in the title role. Naturally, they wanted to shoot it at Chapel Hill. One day I was at home when I got a call from the site producer. This is the way the conversation started, word for word:

"Hello."

"Hey, Frank, who the fuck is Choo-Choo Justice?"

That's all the poor producer had heard ever since he'd arrived in the state, and, indeed, the university would refuse to let us shoot the movie at Chapel Hill because it would defame a beloved real Tarheel, even though he had nothing to do with my made-up novel. Kevin Costner moved on to star in *Bull Durham,* and my movie went into "turnaround," which is Hollywood's purgatory, because once a film is turned around it's a loser and nobody turns it back.

But, miraculously, a couple of years later, the film project was revived by Taylor Hackford,* with Dennis Quaid cast as the new leading man (opposite Jessica Lange). However, since it was verboten to shoot the film in Choo-Choo's state, Taylor went looking for a new location. Florida State, Ole Miss, and Louisiana State were the candidates, and for whatever simple reason involving the best deal, LSU was chosen. Again, pure, dumb circumstance. And again, immediately, the good people of the Bayou State (who had obviously not read the book) decided, with no evidence whatsoever, that the film hero was based on Billy Cannon, an old LSU all-American.

As with Choo-Choo, I had never met Cannon and had never used one smidgen of whoever he was to form the character of Gavin Grey, but by now it's an article of faith that I stole Billy Cannon's soul for my own selfish purposes.** By now, though, when confronted, I tend to let it go. Whenever anybody asks me why I based Gavin Grey on Billy Cannon, I say, "No, he's actually based on Choo-Choo Justice."

Anyway, *Semi-Tough,* which was about imaginary players on the New York Giants, had sold a hell of a lot better than *Everybody's*

---

*Taylor gave me a small speaking part, too. I played a racist café owner who is furious, enduring a sit-in. It was an art-follows-life moment. A couple of the black extras sitting in at the lunch counter across from me were the children of African-Americans who really had sat in at just such a place a few years before.

**One day, exasperated, I finally went into Wikipedia and rewrote, removing the canard that *Everybody's All-American* was based on Billy Cannon. Last time I checked, Wikipedia still believes me on the subject of me.

Jerry Tax is with Red Auerbach and me on the parquet. Jerry was essentially the whole basketball staff at *SI* when I arrived.

I modeled as a foil for Frank Ramsey and became the first Time Inc. employee to make a Time Inc. cover.

Payola: the Harlem Globetrotters sent me my own uniform after I played against them in Bologna, Italy. Then when people ask me, since I'm tall, if I ever played basketball, I can answer: "Yeah, a little pro ball in Italy."

FRANK DE FORD   1973

That seventies guy, Frank DeFord. This is the fetching photo used for my first novel, *Cut 'n' Run.* As usual, my name was misspelled.

With my daughter Alexandra, who died of cystic fibrosis in 1980, a couple of years after this photo. No, you don't ever get over it.

JOHN READER

I'm next to Arthur Ashe on a State Department tour of six African countries in 1970. Stan Smith, who was Wimbledon champion at the time, is on my right, the journalists Richard Evans and Bud Collins to Arthur's left.

The acme of my career as a thespian came in this Lite Beer commercial with Billy Martin and Marvelous Marv Throneberry. Marv wised me up how to get a free sports jacket.

I also was an extra for several alumni commercials, trilling (either) "Tastes Great!" or "Less Filling!" The All-Stars were a wonderful group of guys (well, except for the all-jerk Rodney Dangerfield).

On a spring training story, my son, Chris, was most enthralled by the delightful Bill Veeck—especially the ash tray Bill kept in his peg leg.

Jimmy the Greek and me at Saratoga. It was a difficult story, for we both were fathers who had lost children to cystic fibrosis.

My daughter Scarlet, whom we adopted after Alex died, joins me and the girls on the swimsuit issue PR tour that I emceed.

Pete Rozelle was great company and the most successful of commissioners,
but everybody's somebody's fool, and as Pete revealed to me, Al Davis tied him in knots.

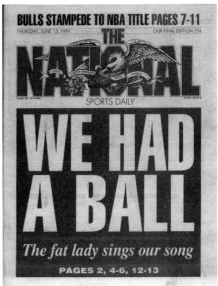

Well, we did. We also lost $150 million
of Emilio Azcárraga's money in eighteen
months of publishing. Good product,
bad business.

Peter Price, a friend from *Daily
Princetonian* days, was the publisher
of *The National,* who brought me on
board as the editor.

I love this picture. I was in a bar in Cameroon when the home team scored the first goal in the quarter-finals of the '90 World Cup, and the fat lady grabbed me to dance. Alas, Cameroon went down to defeat.

The infamous Anna cover by Walter Iooss. We became dirty old men for daring to report on the most famous athlete in the world.

This was Carl Lewis's last gold medal in '96, but his anchor run in '92 remains my most memorable moment as a sportswriter.

For a story on the Air Force Thunderbirds, I took a few Gs myself. Athletic talent of any sort amazes me. I've always enjoyed doing stories on the fringes of sport, but I'm a writer, not a doer. I just want to go along for the ride.

I loved the Aussie tennis players when they dominated the game. Here from the left: Ken Rosewall, Ross Case, Owen Davidson, Yank Writer, Fred Stolle, Rod Laver, and the American player, Dick Stockton.

American soccer fans expressing their First Amendment rights at RFK Stadium in Washington. Soccer people can't understand why discriminating types think other sports are more entertaining. I believe this game ended one-nil.

© RICARDO BARROS

A man's garage is his castle. I'm terrible about saving important memorabilia, but midst my effluvia you may see part of the world's largest collection of hotel shampoo bottles. Also for the sharp-eyed: a naked autographed picture of Blaze Starr.

All-American would, and although Dan Jenkins had grown up in Fort Worth, he had soon qualified as a certified man about town. He became known as Broadway Dan, this being the age of Broadway Joe Namath. He and June, his BW—which is what a tabloid columnist named Earl Wilson called all celebrities' better halves; BW meant "beautiful wife"— who really was beautiful, lived on Park Avenue and were around and about at all the right places like P.J. Clarke's, Elaine's, and what have you.

Besides college football, Dan covered golf, which he also played (it being required in our profession that all golf writers play golf and *believe in* golf), and he played it exceptionally well, so he was popular in those right circles, too. Let me tell you: Dan Jenkins knew how to be a *Sports Illustrated* writer better than anybody else ever has. It went this way: Dick Young was exactly what a tabloid sportswriter was supposed to be like, and Herbert Warren Wind was exactly what a *New Yorker* sportswriter was supposed to be like, and Grantland Rice was exactly what a Grantland Rice was supposed to be like, and Dan Jenkins was exactly what a *Sports Illustrated* writer was supposed to be like (but none of the rest of us were). We were all insanely jealous of him.

Dan was also as delightful personally as he was in print. You would expect that to be the norm, but, with writers, it ain't necessarily so. Jim Murray, for example, was the wittiest sports columnist ever, and although Jim could be the best company and could get a lot of smiles out of you, he was much more entertaining with his fingers doing the talking. As a general rule, don't talk a good game before you actually write, because then editors will expect more and be let down. Always tell editors how you're struggling, but you're sure you'll "bring it together" and pull the fat out of the fire at the eleventh hour.

Anyway, all the time I was out plying the back roads by my lonesome, Jenkins was at the head of some table in some fine barroom somewhere—like at the Masters or the Cotton Bowl or Innsbruck.*

---

*See, he also took chalets and covered skiing between the golf and the football. Skiing, for Chrissake. Who would think of covering skiing? But: chalets, roaring fires, hot buttered rum. I guess.

For a few years Dan and I had cubicles literally right next to each other, cheek by jowl, but I don't think we ever crossed paths there in the actual office during that whole time. So the same people who were disappointed in me because I didn't hang out with the swimsuit models were also let down when I would tell them I really didn't ever see much of that famous writin' raconteur Dan Jenkins either—let alone run with him.

My fondest memory of Dan is one time when we somehow came across each other three thousand miles distant from our abutting offices, in LA, and I joined him and his assemblage for drinks at the Polo Lounge. He was at the head of the table, presiding. Dan was the only person I ever encountered who drank Scotch and coffee together. I don't mean mixed together, but in tandem. Sip of Scotch, drag on his cigarette, sip of coffee, then do it all over again. He was a marvel. He made it all look so easy.

And could he turn his stuff out. Dan wrote *Semi-Tough* in three months. He never took a note, operating on the theory that if he couldn't remember it, it wasn't worth putting in his story. And I thought I was old-fashioned, just using a little notepad. He loved deadlines. He loved being exactly what he was, better than anybody else in the business at what he did. Hell, Dan played golf with Ben Hogan when he was a kid, and Hogan said he could help teach Dan to be a pro, and Jenkins just said, no thanks, I wanna be a sportswriter. Imagine Johann Strauss telling his father, Johann Strauss Sr., thanks for the help at the piano, but, really, I wanna be a showbiz *reporter*. Bud Shrake, Dan's bosom buddy, who came up from Texas to *Sports Illustrated* a few years after Jenkins, summed it up best: "Being another sportswriter in the company of Dan Jenkins can be a humbling experience."

When I think, though, of my earliest days when writers were still together in the office, there in the labyrinth of cubicles of the twentieth floor, the writer I remember with most clarity is Mark Kram. He, you see, was at the other extreme from Jenkins, the most tortured writer at the magazine. Mark was also the only one on the magazine who ever carried the potential of real genius. His story on the Thrilla in Manila is, simply, the finest piece of writing, ever, about any one specific event—in sports or anything else.

Mark and I were close for several years, and although our friendship was bolstered by the fact that he too came from Baltimore, we barely shared that municipal geography any more than we did temperament. I was from a green-leaf neighborhood; Mark had come from the other, gritty, industrial side of white-stoop Baltimore. In 1966, when the Orioles made their first World Series, Laguerre, to my despair, gave Kram the assignment to write an article on our hometown. Mark took for his scripture H. L. Mencken's bittersweet ode: "If, after I depart this vale, you ever remember me and have thought to please my ghost, forgive some sinner and wink at a homely girl." Baltimore, you see, became Kram's homely girl. It did not make him popular with his old neighbors who read the piece.

But then, in the working-class family Mark came from, reading —let alone writing—held no favor. Growing up, he himself barely cracked a book, but at his Catholic high school, Calvert Hall, he was a superb all-around athlete, best at baseball, a talent that took him into the minor leagues after his time in the army. When he failed as a pro, though, he came back to Baltimore, and after a desultory period working in a factory, he somehow completely, incredibly transformed himself. He began to read, eclectically, deeply, especially haunting the Mencken Room at the main branch of the library, breathing in every nuance of the great Baltimorean cynic. Although Kram had never really written anything before, he willed himself to be a writer and managed to wangle a job on the sports staff of the *Baltimore Sun;* the editor remembered him as a high school hero, and Mark satisfied the academic requirement with a forged telegram attesting to a college education.

Soon enough, though, he became what he'd imagined, and he began writing columns; just like that, Laguerre brought him to *Sports Illustrated.* It was a magical ascent, all the more amazing in that he was otherwise so undisciplined. Mark was torn by fears and social insecurity, was too often in his cups, and was given to inexcusable bursts of temper and even an occasional show of cruelty fueled by paranoia. One bad transatlantic flight made it all but impossible for him to get back on an airplane—a considerable disability in a profession where travel was requisite. Well, for that matter, Mark simply never bothered to learn how to drive, either. He grew more exasperating with time—so it was all the more confounding to me that he had once been able to completely refigure himself.

Kram's work could be positively luminous, though. It was, however, the sort of brilliance that only came from standing too close to the fire, so you never could be sure where the flames would light. To Mark, writing was a laboratory science more than a craft; he could not write the second word till the first word was perfect. He also believed that he was like a female holding a finite number of eggs—that he had only so many words within him.

Back when we still worked in our offices, you could hear the tap-tap-tap . . . tap of Kram's typewriter keys, then nothing, maybe another tap-tap. Nothing again. Well, maybe moans. Then Mark would appear in the hall, monkeying with his pipe—which, appropriately, like his typewriter, he could only work intermittently—complaining how impossibly hard writing was, cursing his plight ever to think he could write, ever fearing that maybe that bucket of allotted words had all run out in the very middle of his last paragraph.

It was painful to hear, to watch, but when he was at his best, Mark made all us sportswriters so proud. When Ali and Joe Frazier fought the first time, in 1971—The Fight of the Century!—*Life,* which was struggling, down to its desperate star-fucker stage, hired Norman Mailer to write the story and Frank Sinatra to photograph the action ringside. Mark had only an hour to turn his piece out on deadline, rushing back to the office on a subway from Madison Square Garden. Mailer had days to fashion his epic for *Life* magazine, which was hyped to the heavens.

Kram's short piece was vastly superior, however, to Mailer's celebrity bloviating and, properly, received much more acclaim. So it was that shortly thereafter the two men happened to find themselves at the same party. A furiously jealous Mailer insulted Kram, and then Mister Macho Author head-butted him. Kram fought back, and when Mark—who was a tough cookie, stocky, that former minorleague baseball player—started to get the best of him, Mailer, the self-proclaimed hard case, bit his arm. Kram had to get a tetanus shot because Norman Mailer took a bite outta him.

Unfortunately for Mark, when things were not working well in the laboratory, as was increasingly the case, the fire singed his neuroses, and he was never able to approach the heights that towered within his talent. He came to believe that writing, which had lifted him above his dull destiny, had also transformed his soul for the worse, and once he began to believe that, his work became more than his challenge. It became his enemy.

Eventually, Mark gave in to temptation and went on the take with Donking. He'd always had the shorts, always been scuffling for walking-around money, fancifully padding his expense account to cover his bar bills and pay back whoever else he was into. Of course, part of the Timeink lore then concerned the many wildly improvisational expense account stories, but among those crocheted expense reports, Mark's classic is a masterpiece of the succinct. When, unwilling to fly, he took an ocean liner to and from England, he simply submitted his report this way:

"BOAT . . . $10,000."

So, even now, as I look back on that time, when men in cubicles pounded on Royal typewriters in the company of their neighbors, my everlasting vision is of Mark Kram, pacing, fitful, struggling; at last: simply tormented. If only he could've just been able to sit down and write. I told him once, "You know, Mark, you're like one of those pitchers who can throw a hundred miles an hour, but you have to aim every pitch. Don't always aim. Sometimes just throw the sonuvabitch."

He shook his head. He knew he couldn't. Too bad. Otherwise Mark would've died great and not just might-have-been.

36

LOST IN TRANSLATION

We aren't dominated by one team game. That's why we can have our own American dream. The dream of most other countries is simply to have their national soccer team do well.

"Team Up," NPR, 2011

After I give a speech, and I solicit questions, invariably somebody will want to know something about what's up there at the top of my all-time lists: my favorite all-time game list or the most all-time inspiring athlete list or the all-time hardest story I ever did list. It's a list-centric world. I also get this question: how do you write?

You mean like: in the morning after breakfast, in my office, on a computer. That's how I write.

Oh.

All are terribly disappointed when I tell them that. But I understand. Because writing is such a personal endeavor, people are curious as to exactly how you go about it. I don't think people ask, say, what captains of industry do in their offices. How do you talk on the phone? Tell us, Mr. Insurance Agent, how exactly do you go about selling life term policies? But it's flattering that people want to *visualize* you writing. I'm always sure to tell them how Victor Hugo would give all his clothes to his valet every morning and then write naked, so that he couldn't go anywhere until he'd written his quota for the day. I don't know if that's true, but I read it once, and it's certainly more interesting than how I write, fully clothed, without a valet, so it's a good answer, even if a lot of people don't any longer know who Victor Hugo was.

But lists are very important now. Rankings are too. Once, we all knew poems and nursery rhymes and history. Now we know rankings. So given the popularity of lists, to satisfy inquiries, I have had to make up my own lists; I have decided, for example, to declare that at the top of my all-time interview list, worldwide department, was Sadaharu Oh, the great Japanese slugger. Domestically all-time: Mickey Mantle.

Mr. Oh first. I went to Tokyo to do a big cover story on him. It was all arranged ahead of time by the Timeink bureau in Tokyo, and so I flew over with my wife.* Every day I would go to the ballpark and bow to Oh-san and he would bow back, and every day I sort of *expected* the translator to say that today we'd have the interview, but it just never seemed to happen. Japanese demurrals are more vague and obtuse than even the best of our demurrals. Carol got bored and took the bullet train to Kyoto. Finally I had to tell the translator point-blank that I had come ten thousand miles to see Mr. Oh, and, really, pretty please, I had to have that little chat with him.

"But you can't just talk to Oh-san," the translator replied.

"No?"

"Oh no. For such a man as Oh-san, you must take him out to dinner."

"Well, that's terrific," I said. "I'd much rather go out to a restaurant with Mr. Oh than just interview him at the ballpark."

"No, no, no, you can't just take Oh-san to a restaurant."

"I can't?"

"Oh no, that would not be worthy of Mr. Oh's stature."

"So?"

"No, if you are to take Oh-san out to dinner, you must reserve the whole restaurant."

Well, luckily the yen hadn't yet gone sky-high against the dollar, and I was able to compromise on renting merely a whole *floor* of a

---

*Carol accompanies me when I do stories in places like Tokyo or London or Paris. She has not yet, however, made the NCAA regionals in Indianapolis or Charlotte.

restaurant as being a fair enough measure of Oh-san's stature. Mr. Oh brought about fifty of his friends, who gorged themselves, while we sat in the corner with a translator, as Oh-san supplied canned answers to my hopeless attempts at assaying searching questions.

It just never works with translators. I believe somebody said: something is lost in the translation. Before the 1994 World Cup, which was held in the United States, I went to Italy for *Vanity Fair* to do the exclusive American story on Roberto Baggio, who was then the best soccer player in the world.* The last thing he wanted was to waste his time with some strange American reporter, but Roberto was represented by IMG, which thought it would be good for his endorsements, so grudgingly he went along. *Va bene.*

This time, though, I had a beautiful translator named Patrizia, and when Roberto saw her he was suddenly singing a new tune. He and Patrizia would babble on gaily for a few minutes, smiling, gesticulating, carrying on like old buddies, and then I'd break in: "What'd he say, Patrizia?"

"Roberto says, 'I am training very well.'"

And then they'd chat happily for another five minutes, and Patrizia would turn to me and breathlessly reveal, "Roberto says, 'I am looking forward to coming to the United States.'"

Lost.

The last time I used a translator was to interview a hockey goalie for *Real Sports* on HBO. On the side, the goalie had robbed banks in Budapest, so we were in a Hungarian jail. I didn't get much out of that either, but at least he wanted to talk. It kept him out of his cell for a while. I think he's still there in the pokey.

In 1996, before the Atlanta Olympics, I went to Switzerland for *Real Sports* to interview Juan Antonio Samaranch, the old Franco spear-carrier who ran the Olympics like Boss Tweed. At Olympic

---

*Typically, Graydon Carter lost interest in an actual sports story and ran a piece about an obscure columnist friend of his. Then Baggio turned out to be, as I ballyhooed in the story, the most intriguing A-list personality in the World Cup. *Vanity Fair* blew a sports scoop!

headquarters, the day before the interview, I made the point of asking his PR woman if His Excellency—Samaranch preferred to style himself that way—would rather speak with me through an interpreter, in Spanish. Oh no, she assured me that His Excellency was a regular linguistic whiz, who was perfectly at home in English. Which he was indeed.

However, when Samaranch pretty much came across as a pompous jackass, saying things like, "We are more important than the Catholic Church," I was accused by his defenders, such as Dick Ebersol of NBC, which drank deep at the Olympic trough, that I had unfairly taken advantage of the wonderful old gentleman, by forcing him to communicate in an unfamiliar language. Of course, on television it was altogether apparent that His Excellency had full command of the English language. Still, when he got to the United States and was questioned about the indelicate put-down of the Catholic Church, he simply denied ever saying it. Never mind that it was on tape. Nothing must sully humankind's glorious Olympic *movement*!

The Olympics did expand tremendously during Samaranch's corruption-riddled reign, and, of course, he was given full credit for their success by his Olympic toadies. The greater truth is that Peter Ueberroth, the impresario of the Los Angeles Games of 1984, was the man who saved the Olympics, by showing Samaranch the way they could be run; then by Dick Pound of Canada, Samaranch's point man for television and almost everything else that mattered, who was the brains of the whole enterprise.*

All that said, I give Samaranch full credit for one important change. Realizing how impossible it was any longer to even pretend that amateurism, a failed idealistic vestige from the nineteenth century, could continue to be propped up in the major commercial sports, he summarily ended the hypocrisy, decreeing that the various Olym-

*When he was forced to retire, though, Samaranch just baldly betrayed Pound and told his sycophants to vote for a bland Belgian named Jacques Rogge to make sure that the IOC power stayed in Europe. Dreadful man, Samaranch—commonest European I ever met.

pic sports could make their own rules of eligibility. Thus did honest professionalism enter the Games. Tennis had opened its championships up to pros in 1968, and rugby, the last official international amateur redoubt, would become pay-for-play in 1995. As a consequence, today, in all the world of big-time commercial sport, shameful amateur servitude still exists only in the United States, in college football and basketball, where coaches make millions and colleges make millions and television makes millions and sportswriters make a good living . . . and the players make nothing except on the cheat.

Oh, well, it's good for our profession, keeps the wolf from our doors. I imagine, from kindergarten through college, K–16, about 99 percent of what is written about education in the United States is written about sports in education. Of course, that doesn't help American education at all—this is one reason why it's going to hell in a handbasket—but college sports amuse the students and purport to keep the alumni involved with their alma mater's mission.

Now, as for interviewing Mr. Mantle. I was doing a story on Billy Martin, when he was manager of the Texas Rangers in 1975, and since his old buddy the Mick lived in Dallas, I asked Billy if he could get Mantle to agree to speak with me. Billy immediately picked up the phone and put Mantle on. Mickey said he'd be delighted to talk to me about Billy, but he was playing golf tomorrow morning, so could I drop by his house beforehand? Sure, Mickey, when? I'm figuring ten/ten-thirty.

How about seven-thirty?

I don't think I'd ever interviewed anybody, live, so early, but, despite this being pre-GPS when you actually had to locate houses on your own hook, I arrived at what I deduced to be the dark Mantle residence and, nervously, rang the bell. Nothing. All was silent. Could I have the wrong house, and was I going to wake up some stranger? Or had Mantle forgotten and was he sound asleep—or, worse, would he come to the door, furious about this ungodly early intrusion? But no, just as I was about to depart, a very wide-awake Mantle comes down the stairs in his wrapper, cheerfully admits me, and escorts me to the kitchen, where we might talk convivially over a cuppa java.

Whereas I had participated in madhouse group interviews of Mantle many years previously after big games, we had never formally met. I had, however, been privy to a rather fascinating assignation he had enjoyed some years earlier when I was an occasional observer of the Baltimore demimonde on the Block. My favorite hangout there was a joint called the Club Trocadero ("When you go, go Troc"), whose emcee was a squat, raucous lady known as the Gorilla Woman. She would announce shows with these pointed words: "Showtime! Showtime! All the pussies onstage." As a budding journalist, anxious to perfect my interview techniques, I became friendly with several of what were discreetly referred to as "exotic dancers," one of whom was known as Fern the Flower Woman.

So it was that when I arrived at the Troc after an absence of several days, the Gorilla Woman informed me that exciting things had happened. The Yankees had been in town for a series a few days earlier and Mantle and a couple of teammates (including the next day's starting pitcher) had come by to imbibe and enjoy, for their viewing pleasure, the pussies onstage. Indeed, so taken had Number Seven been with Fern that he had invited her to take her leave with him, thereupon to retire to his hotel room.

I approached Fern for more embossed detail. "The sonuvabitch," she said ruefully. "I spend the whole night with him, and I know how good it was because he gave me a hundred. So I figure anybody who spends that kind of night with me is not going to be playing much good baseball the next day. Plus, I seen the pitcher have a few drinks, and I know because it's the Yankees, we're giving them good drinks here. So I take the hundred, bet it all against the Yankees, and what does Mantle do? He beats the Birds with a home run."

Proof again that there is never a sure thing in sports.

While I remembered this example of Mantle's prowess, I thought it best not to bring it up as an icebreaker, especially as the missus lay asleep just upstairs. Instead, as soon as Mickey had prepared the coffee, we began to talk about Martin. He was enthusiastic and expansive in chatting about his old pal, and seemed in no hurry to dismiss me, and so the conversation began to range some. It had been seven years since he had last played, so I asked him if he missed the game. What a stupid, clichéd question. But Mickey didn't mind at all. "Oh yeah," he said. "Alla time."

To my amazement, he became downright wistful, talking about how much it hurt him that he could no longer play. "I miss the crowds applauding. I miss the big ovations." I was caught up in his reveries, even touched by then. Then, because he was sitting right there in his nightclothes, it occurred to me to ask Mickey if he'd ever dreamed that he was playing again.

Immediately, I was embarrassed that I had asked such a hackneyed question. It was so childish: what do you dream? When I'd been a Miss America judge, I cringed when other judges asked idiotic questions like that. If you were an animal what would you be? A tree? If you could have dinner with four people in history who would they be? To myself, I called them "desert-island questions," as in: If you were stranded on a desert island, what . . . ? And here I'd gone and—

"Oh yeah," Mickey said, grinning. "I have the same dream lotsa times. I'm in the Astrodome, and I'm at bat . . ." and with great relish he told me how, in this recurring dream, he hits a home run and jogs around the bases, listening to the crowd roar again, touching home plate, tipping his cap—all with fine detail, all the while smiling as sure as if it were true.

"You dream that often?"

"Oh yeah."

"And it's always the same?"

He paused, but for only a few seconds. "Yeah. Just about."

I came back to being a real journalist. This was years before there was interleague scheduling. "But you never played in the Astrodome."

"Yeah, I did," Mickey said. "When they opened it, they had the Yankees play an exhibition there."

"And you hit a home run?"

Almost shyly, he said: "Yeah. It was the first one there."

The episode only convinced me all the more that players—or, at least, the great ones—are never really able to put the glory out of their mind.

"I tell you," Mickey went on, "when Aaron hit that home run last year that broke the record, I had goose bumps. I knew just how he felt."

It also, despite myself, encouraged me to put aside my bias against dreams, and I remain as amazed as I was that morning in Mickey Mantle's kitchen to realize how many people do have some significant recurring dream. Most strange was Larry Bird. We were having lunch in Seattle, where he was playing on the road, and without my even bringing up the subject of dreams, he started talking about one that he'd had repeatedly when he was growing up in a rather impoverished family back in French Lick, Indiana. I have no idea why he volunteered it to me. It's funny what people will suddenly tell you sometimes, completely out of the blue. And this was late in his career, and Bird had never told another writer (or maybe he never told anyone else at all). But, he said, rather touched by the memory, the dream he had when he was a little boy was that he had found $1 million in cash and hidden it in a hole under his front porch, and he was just sitting down there, hiding, with all this money, while his brothers kept going up and down the stairs, never knowing that little Larry had a stash of $1 million, just beneath them, in a hole.

"I had that same dream over and over," he told me, rather in wonder.

When people tell you their dreams, it's a pretty good sign of a topflight interview. However, boy, do I hate dream *sequences* in movies—or books or plays, wherever. They're made up by directors, so they're forced, pretentious crap.

Mr. DeFord, what is your favorite sport to write about?

Well, it really doesn't matter, as long as it's a good story.

In fact, while it confounds me that soccer is still so popular a spectator sport around the world, nothing touched me so much as when I went to Cameroon during the 1990 World Cup. I wanted to do a story from the point of view of the people down there, when poor, little Cameroon was playing England in the quarterfinals. The place was so impoverished, so desperate, and nothing good had ever really happened there, and here was Cameroon's chance . . . at last. Its one day in the sun. Cameroon scored the first goal, too, and in the bar where I was watching, a short, fat lady next to me grabbed me and started dancing with me, and if only you could've seen the unbounded joy on her face. The photographer who was with me took a picture of that moment, and it's the only sports photograph I keep in my office. It tells you better than anything else about the joy of sports—and the power, too, I suppose.

Cameroon lost, though. Their players didn't understand that when you get ahead in a soccer game, you're supposed to fall back into the equivalent of a fetal position, bore everybody to death for seventy-two minutes, and *go through** one-nil.

I caught a Sabena milk-run plane at three o'clock the next morning to get to Brussels just in time to connect to Rome in order to see the Italians lose on TV to Argentina in Naples. I was watching that at a bar, outside. When the Argentines scored the winning goal, the bartender, without a word, walked over to the television set and flipped it off, and everybody there just immediately got up and quietly drifted away, stunned. That was something of a record for me: two losses for the home country, consecutively, back-to-back, on two

---

*"Go through" and "results" are my favorite foreign sports expressions. Nobody gets *bad* results, though. When a player told me he'd had some results, invariably he meant he'd won. It took me a while to figure that out. It's like saying just "Morning" when we mean "Good morning." I also very much like "level," meaning "equal," but if I wrote that the Yankees and Red Sox were level at three through six innings, nobody around here would know what I meant. Instead, our sports announcers like to say "knotted," a word never otherwise employed that way in normal discourse.

different continents. At least Cameroon sort of expected to lose. But the Italians were convinced their Azzurri would win, and they were absolutely destroyed. Really, nobody said anything. Rome was a tomb.

I've especially liked the World Cup—its wonderful flavor and passion and its consummate global embrace—but soccer is, on balance, bad for the world, precisely because it does matter too much to too many people in too many countries. Critics complain about how the United States is too sports-minded, but the fact of the matter is that everybody everywhere is too sports-minded, only most people are really just too soccer-minded. The most salubrious aspect of American sport is that we spread our interest around, so that if your football team is lousy, you can turn to your basketball or hockey team, and then to baseball. In most countries, though, if your soccer team is a bummer, that ruins you for the year. Sometimes for all your years. Not freaking out over soccer is one of the best things about American sport.

However, American soccer fundamentalists are the most defensive sports adherents in the world. Look, it never bothers me that other people don't like, for example, baseball, as I do. I understand. It's only a matter of taste, and the luck of nativity. If I'd been born in São Paulo or Torino instead of Baltimore I'd probably hate somebody else's national pastime and think one-nil is the way the sporting life should be. But because soccer is not preeminent here as it is elsewhere, soccer Americans seem to feel that they've let the god of soccer down. As a consequence, they get terribly upset with those who aren't true believers. *It is the human condition to like soccer!!! What is wrong with you?*

There must, after all, be a good, authentic reason why we good Americans have chosen to prefer other sports instead of soccer, and the obvious conclusion (which no soccer people want to hear) is simply that most of us Americans think soccer is, by comparison, an inferior entertainment. Soccer has, in fact, had every chance to take hold here. Kids have been playing it for generations now. After all, all American babies born are weaned by what?

Soccer moms!

But then, after playing soccer as a tyke, after being immersed in it, most of us grow up and, exercising free will, choose other adult athletic amusements where the participants are actually allowed to use their hands—those most exquisite, divinely human instruments that God gave us to separate us from the beasts of the field. (Imagine, please, the ceiling of the Sistine were God touching Adam toe to toe.) Americans also grow up being used to the big play—to the home run, to the hundred-yard kickoff return, to the fast break. That's our meat. In soccer, that's offside. Blow the whistle, bring it back. Soccer is the coitus interruptus of sport.

I had a great friend named Jack Winter. He was brilliant. He entered Harvard when he was sixteen, with, as he described it (without vanity), "an IQ that was twice my body temperature." Jack thought he was the youngest boy in his class, but years later a classmate, one Ted Kaczynski, came into some unfortunate publicity and thus Jack learned that he was second youngest . . . after the Unabomber. Oh well.

Jack had entered Harvard as a math wizard, but he switched to philosophy, then spent most of the time at the humor magazine the *Lampoon*, where he became the president. He developed very eclectic interests, the four most prominent being the following:

- Frogs. He smuggled some exotic ones into the country (before 9/11) and always kept a large number of various species in the bathtub of his Manhattan apartment.
- Basketball, for which he wrote long (and quite unlike him) boring treatises to prove conclusively that it was the best sport in the world. Unfortunately, I was required to read these monographs and discuss them at tedious length with Jack because I had once covered basketball and therefore was among the few authorities allegedly capable of discussing the sport's sublime intricacies with him.
- The Taj Mahal. Jack would get misty just thinking about it and went to his grave distressed that, although I had traveled

in much of the world, I had never been to the Taj Mahal and therefore really hadn't seen anything worth seeing.

- Pygmies. Jack flew to an outpost in the Congo and then somehow got out into the bush to spend quality time with them. What he liked best about the Pygmies was how they smiled.

Jack, you see, liked laughter. He had become, by profession, a writer of comedy, first as a prodigy, making up jokes for Jackie Gleason, later as a sitcom writer. As with his views on frogs, the Taj Mahal, basketball, and Pygmies, he had very firm opinions about comedy. Sometimes when I would tell him how I'd laughed at a joke, he would say, "But, Frank, that isn't funny."

And I would say, "But I laughed, Jack, so, you know, it was funny to me."

That was not good enough. Jack would just shake his head at me, and explain why the wannabe joke wasn't funny despite the mirth that I was convinced it had elicited from me.

The reason I bring this up is that Jack was so special and I miss him, I still think often of him, and one day it occurred to me that Jack was to jokes as I am to soccer. Soccer is not entertaining. Yes, I know it entertains billions of people around the world, but it doesn't really, because it is not entertaining.

37

THE ANCHOR LEG

Athletes get frozen in time. They get attached to a certain year.
People say, "Oh yeah, that was his year." "That was Walt Dropo's
year." "That was Dick Kazmaier's year." "Wasn't that Tom Gola's
year?" Nobody ever says that about other people. Nobody once ever
said that 1776 was Thomas Jefferson's year. Maybe just athletes
have years—and very few of them; usually, just the kids.
"The Kid Who Ran Into Doors," *Sports Illustrated*, 1975

Happily, unlike everybody else, we Americans don't get all worked
up over international sport. The Big Ten or the American Football
Conference North means much more to us than the world something-
or-other. Who gives a fig whether we beat Bolivia? Who even cares
if we beat China? What bowl game did those mothers ever win? The
only time international sport really mattered to us was at the 1980
Winter Olympics when we beat the Soviet Union in hockey. Why?
Because that was the one and only time when we, the mighty United
States of America, were the underdog—our innocent little downy-
cheeked college boys, amateurs all, praise God!—up against the big
bad grown-up professional commie scum. Just for once we weren't
the monster villains. Just for once, we were Cinderella.

Of course, the 1992 Olympic basketball Dream Team interested
Americans, but not in an athletic sense. It was more just a reality show
that could've been entitled "Basketball with the Stars." It happens to
be, though, the only time when the outcome of a game personally
mattered to me, because I had a lot riding on the outcome.

I was, after the *National* folded, working as a contract columnist for *Newsweek,* where the editor was Maynard Parker. He was especially competitive—well, downright combative—with the Timeink magazines. With the Dream Team, he desperately wanted to have its first cover story for a national weekly, so he had Larry Bird, Magic Johnson, and Michael Jordan pose for the shot. Now, *Newsweek* came out on Monday each week, as did *Time. Sports Illustrated* was first available on Wednesday. But to publish on Monday, *Newsweek* had to finish printing its cover on Saturday. Ah, here was the rub: the Dream Team's first exhibition game was on a Sunday, against Brazil, which was one of the better national teams, and Maynard didn't want to wait a week; he wanted to hit the newsstands that Monday when that first game was still hot news.

Maynard told me he'd print the Dream Team cover—and man, did he *want* to print that cover—but only if I could promise him that the United States would win. If we lost, it would be too late to change covers, so the Dream Team's loss would be huge news and *Newsweek* would be a laughingstock, with a "Dewey Beats Truman" kind of cover, going out to millions of American households. Could I absolutely "guarantee" him an American victory?

I was sure the Dream Team would win, but it was the team's first game, the players' first real time together. Funnier things have happened. But what the hell—in for a penny, in for a pound. "Maynard," I said, "if this were a game in an individual sport—a tennis match, boxing, a race—you could never be sure, because all you need is one injury to one man. But no, I can't visualize the U.S. *team* losing."

"You guarantee me?"

"Come on, Maynard, nobody can *guarantee* a thing like this. But I'm sure they'll win."

"Dead sure?"

I thought for a moment. "All right, dead sure." I paused. "Because if I'm wrong, I'm gonna wanna be dead." He didn't smile much at that. "All right, Maynard, I'm sure."

"OK," he said then, without any further pussyfooting, "we'll go with it."

And, yes, the Dream Team beat the pants off Brazil: *Newsweek* came out with my story with Michael, Larry, and Magic on the cover the next day; Maynard looked like a genius, and he felt like that cat that ate the canary. *Sports Illustrated*, beaten, never did run a Dream Team cover.

Next question.

Mr. DeFord, who is the best athlete ever?

I think I'm supposed to say Michael Jordan.

Then again, time's a-passing and before long it will be so long ago when Jordan played that he could no longer be considered all that good against the current crop of immortals. Nowadays, it's an article of faith that only today's athletes can be the best ever. It is true, of course, that in those sports where performance can be measured, the statistical best is now. Hello! Records are made to be broken! Johnny Weissmuller's fastest times would leave him gulping for air, meters behind adolescent girl swimmers. Jesse Owens would barely be out of the starting blocks by the time Usain Bolt hit the tape. And, yes, today's athletes are indisputably bigger and stronger. Red Grange would be a nice Division III wideout. But I've always thought it's fair to judge an athlete only by how he measured up against his contemporaries, rather than to take a star from the past and plunk him down now, when everybody is bigger and training is improved and conditions are advanced and certainly the illegal drugs are better, too. It's just not a fair fight. It's a little like dismissing Alexander the Great and Napoleon as top generals because those ancient idiots didn't know how to employ airpower.*

---

*Conversely, it always amuses me that whereas only modern athletes can possibly be considered the best ever, no living members of the other arts—painting, writing, composing, whatever—are ever ranked ahead of Rembrandt or Shakespeare or Beethoven or others of the classic past. In everything but sports, once you get to the top, you're there forever. In sports, you've got till next Tuesday to stay number one.

Actually, my own best guess is that Jackie Robinson was the finest athlete of all time, but that always confuses young audiences because if they know him at all it's just because of his race, and they haven't a clue that Robinson may well have been more proficient in football, basketball, and track than he was in baseball, where he was merely Hall of Fame.

In any event, notwithstanding who may be the best, which can never be anything more than a good barroom argument, the athletes who have always most intrigued me are jockeys and baseball pitchers.

Pitchers fascinate me so much because a live arm is such a capricious possession, such a dicey thing to depend on; and jockeys interest me primarily, I suppose, because I'm tall and they're such brave little people.

I remember being at the Preakness Ball in 1972 the night before the race. I was standing at a urinal when I looked over, and next to me was Ron Turcotte, who was riding the favorite, the Derby winner, Riva Ridge, the next day. He looked up at me. "Hey," he said, "how 'bout giving me a couple inches off your top, eh?" (Ron was Canadian.)

"If I would," I said, "you wouldn't be riding Riva Ridge tomorrow."

He laughed and nodded, ruefully. He didn't win that Preakness, but he won the Triple Crown the next year on Secretariat. Then, only five years later, Ron went down in a spill, and he's been paralyzed, in pain, ever since. I've always wondered whether he would've liked making that deal with the devil, taking some of my height, and, for it, never having the glory, never having Secretariat, but always having his legs, having peace.

Mr. DeFord, who is the most interesting person you ever interviewed?

It's probably Teddy Tinling, but nobody's much ever heard of him and everybody wants to hear about a big name, so if it's old people I'm talking to, I say Bill Veeck, and if it's young people I tell them Arthur Ashe or Billie Jean King and hope they're still remembered.

Veeck, of course, had a wooden leg, wherein he kept an ashtray, hollowed out. Of all the places I took my son, Christian, and all the big stars I introduced him to when he was a kid, what impressed him most was when he was sitting at spring training with Bill Veeck and Bill lit up a cigarette and started using his peg leg as an ashtray. Kiss my ass, YouTube. You'll never see that again.

I am generally reluctant to believe people who boast that they only need four or five hours' sleep except in two instances: Bill Veeck and Jerry Jones, the owner of the Dallas Cowboys. Because of his war wound, Veeck was almost surely in discomfort, if not in at least a bit of pain, all the time. They kept cutting off his leg, higher and higher. He drank beer to dull the pain, but still, he didn't sleep well, so he would stay up either reading or talking with people late into the night. When he owned the White Sox, he would host something of a salon after a night game in his apartment at Comiskey Park, and into the wee hours whoever was there would drink beer with him and discuss great books, great people, great ideas, and baseball of all sorts. Bill would gleefully moderate.

I always prided myself on being able to keep up, socially, with the more worldly folk that I wrote about, especially because it is, in fact, often late at night, after a few beverages,* that people might very well relieve themselves of interesting thoughts they otherwise might keep to themselves. But Jerry Jones ran me to ground. It was around one o'clock, and we were in yet another establishment, and the beers were lining up before us, and the waitress asked Jerry to autograph her breast, and he, being an impeccable host, suggested to her that it would be impolite not to let his guest autograph the other.

Especially, he added, since I was a writer by profession.

So she proffered the second one to me, and I obliged. It was the only time I've done that. Sportswriters, as a general rule, are not often given that opportunity.** But it was my last hurrah of the evening. Shortly thereafter, I told Jerry that I was sorry, but I just had to

---

*God, but I hate that word. Nobody ever actually says it in real life except flight attendants.
**Actually, come to think, I don't imagine many owners are, either.

go to bed. He was a little disappointed in me. Himself, he had to be up at something like six to take his plane out to West Texas to see somebody about an oil well.

Mr. DeFord, what star's performance moved you the most?

I would have to say it was a sometime race-car driver named Paul Newman. Yes, that Paul Newman. He lived for many years in my town, Westport, Connecticut, where he was our most honored and beloved citizen. I only met him a couple of times, but one night a few years ago, strictly by luck, at a small musical show in Westport, Carol and I had the two seats next to those assigned to Paul and his wife, Joanne Woodward.

He had cancer then and had but a few months to live; he was frail, but the glorious blue eyes still had a glow to them, and when he sat down next to me he gave Carol and me the best that remained of that you-never-know smile of his. Joanne had been waylaid by some friends at the back of the hall, but Paul recognized me, and so then he groused, good-naturedly, about how isn't it just like a woman to always be talking. Yeah, ain't that the truth, Paul? Uh-huh, you can't take 'em anywhere. Every damn time. And so on. Husband chitchat.

The lights blinked. Joanne bade her friends good-bye and rushed to her seat. The lights dimmed, lower. Out of the corner of my eye, I sneaked a look to my right. The instant it was dark and the music started, Paul reached over and, like a teenager, took his sweetheart's hand in his.

I only waited a second. If Paul Newman, the handsomest, sexiest man in the world, age eighty-two, married half a century, could . . .

I reached over and took Carol's hand, and the four of us held them like that while the music played. Double date.

Mr. DeFord, what was the best game you ever saw?

Truthfully, of games, I retain a few select beautifully vivid memories: a cavalcade of games with Russell's Celtics playing Baylor and West's Lakers; the magnificent Borg-McEnroe final at Wimbledon in 1980; a New Zealand equestrian rider named Mark Todd riding a black horse named Charisma to victory for a repeat Olympic victory in the Three-Day Event at the Seoul Games. Yeah, funny the stuff that stays with you. An equestrian competition is embedded more in my memory than any single baseball or football game I can recall. I can still see that little horse jumping the most incredible hurdles up there by the DMZ. And of all the beautiful arching jump shots I saw, swish, at the buzzer, still, my clearest basketball memory ever is of Sam Jones of the Celtics, using the backboard to bank shots in. Nobody does that anymore; nobody knows how to *kiss* the backboard with a ball the way Sam did fifty years ago.

So, no, it doesn't always get better. And, yes, I'm afraid that the games do blur so when you have a press pass round your neck and you're taking notes and you've seen it all before. I'm sorry, but you do get jaded.

In fact, the single most glorious vision that remains uppermost in my mind took place at the Barcelona Games of 1992. It was barely an instant in game time—less than ten seconds. Carl Lewis had been sick when the sprint trials were being held and so he only managed to make the team, after he'd gotten better, as a long jumper. But during the Olympics, one of the American sprinters who'd qualified suffered an injury, and suddenly Lewis, as great a sprinter who ever lived, was *substituted* onto the 4×100-meter relay team. Furthermore, what an irony: the lowly substitute, being indisputably the fastest, was assigned the anchor leg.

I went down and stood by the track, where I watched the U.S. team pull away from the competition. By the time Lewis started prancing forward and then, at cruising speed, reaching back and taking the baton, the race was already settled. It was just a private exhibition, Carl by himself, those long legs of his kneeing up and stretching out to glory, a medley of grace and strength and speed. It was only a few seconds, of course, but in my mind's eye, it is always there, the one most fetching moment I retain of sport—Carl Lewis on the cinders at Barcelona. There are perfect swings of the bat, down oh-and-two on the count, with the bases loaded; there is Unitas standing in the pocket; there is McEnroe flicking a volley; there is Nicklaus sinking a long, curling putt, then holding up his putter, one-handed, like a saber; there is Sam Jones working the glass—so many, many special moments when an athlete did precisely what he had to do to win, and did it with surpassing beauty. Notwithstanding, for whatever reason, Carl Lewis, gripping the baton and gliding to the tape in muscular élan is the portrait supreme in my mind of the human as athlete, as performer, as epitome.

But then, I understand. You had to have been there, as I was, right by the track, overwhelmed, not jaded, not at all, but instead: a child again.

38

THE SWEETEST THING
I EVER SAW AN ATHLETE
DO FOR A MEMBER
OF THE FOURTH ESTATE

... where the longitude of majesty and the latitude of grace meet.
"Talk About Strokes of Genius," *Sports Illustrated*, 1984

The first game the Dream Team played at Barcelona in the 1992 Olympics was against Algeria. It was no contest. The highlight, such as it was, was when Charles Barkley clobbered some skinny Algerian player for no good reason, and then explained afterward that he had to do it because, who knew, the guy might've had a spear.

Nevertheless, the official postgame press conference was packed to the gunwales, because this was before the Internet and blogs, and the Dream Team was all anybody with a credential was writing about. Those were the old days of consensus and critical mass. However, only the American coach, Chuck Daly, and one designated player were escorted into the interview room. The player chosen was the team captain. That was Magic Johnson.

There are always Olympic functionaries who run these press conferences, and they are usually officious and invariably patronizing. So too here. The media factotum, swollen with power, condescended to allow a few questions, and then, while the beseeching masses raised their hands like little children at a magic show, pleading to be the next chosen one, he summarily announced that he would permit only one more question. He anointed the lucky devil, and, after Daly answered his question, the media enforcer began to annouce that the proceedings were thereby, as he had summarily warned us, officially closed.

But at that point Magic gently laid a hand upon the man's arm and silenced him. "No, wait," he said. The Olympic apparatchik stiffened, looking at Magic in surprise.

Magic simply nodded and said, "You see, Mr. Jim Murray, the great columnist for the *Los Angeles Times*, is right over here, and he has to be allowed to ask his question."

Magic and I have had our differences, but I was never so taken by such a lovely public gesture from an athlete on behalf of a sportswriter. Jim seemed as surprised as the rest of us. He was seventy-two then. He had recovered his sight after working for several years blind. He was a dear person, actually beloved, and he had finally won the Pulitzer Prize a couple of years previously. But this was quite an extraordinary moment, surely different from any other he had ever experienced in all his years working with athletes.

I don't remember what question Jim asked. Anyway, it wasn't particularly memorable. What mattered is that, because of an athlete, he had been allowed to ask it, in a particular instance of grace and reverence.

39

YOU WON'T BELIEVE THIS

It's damned if you do, damned if you don't. The U.S. Open is like a flea market, but Wimbledon changed its clock—its clock, for God's sake—and was accused of blasphemy.
"A Club Like No Other," *Sports Illustrated*, 1982

I came into tennis through the back door, because it was such a rinky-dink, hypocritical enterprise that no sportswriter worth his beans wanted to cover it. After all, the pros, the best players, were outlawed from the best tournaments, so all the championships were for amateurs —or "shamateurs" as everyone called them, because they had to take money under the table in order to make sure that amateurism in tennis remained pure. As a consequence, tennis was bush. I'm sure Jimmy Cannon had some dandy "Nobody Asked Me But" citations for tennis, probably involving tea and crumpets.

But I'd played a little tennis as a kid. You know, at least I knew what "love" and "ad out" meant. Good enough. So, whereas I'd never been to a tournament before, when I got the chance to write a couple of short pieces on some kid players, I jumped at it: beggars can't be choosers. Presto: all of a sudden, I was a tennis-writing prospect. So it was I who was assigned to do a major feature story on Roy Emerson, the Aussie who was then the shamateur champion of the world.

And where was I sent to meet Emerson but Mexico City, where he was playing in the Davis Cup against Mexico. Here, the scales fell from my bright, young, brown eyes. I'd never even been out of the country before, and what had brought me to an exotic foreign land? Tennis.

Tennis may be bush, but, as it dawned on me now, it was international. And unlike basketball, where big games were in Lexington, Kentucky, and Bloomington, Indiana, tennis was invariably contested in the likes of London and Paris. And instead of at smelly gyms: at lovely country clubs. Hey, who's bush? Besides, as I quickly learned, the tennis players were generally great guys. The players in secondary sports are, in point of fact, inclined to seem like great guys, because they're desperate for publicity, so they play up to you, but I hadn't figured that out then. I just assumed the tennis guys liked me as a person.

The Aussies were genuinely nice to just about everybody, though. They traveled all over the world together from the time they were teenagers, rarely getting home. After all, they weren't making more than "expense" money, so they couldn't afford just to grab the next Qantas and fly back home, Down Under. Along with the tennis tournaments themselves, a staple then were elegant tournament parties,* and one of my poignant memories from those years was walking along the beach on a starlit night after a fancy bash at the Caribe Hilton in San Juan with Margaret Smith (later Mrs. Court) and Lesley Turner (later Mrs. Bowrey). They were the best two women players in the world then, yet mostly what they talked on and on about was how sad and lonely they were.

Here I was, about their age, thrilled to be at a fabulous sunny Caribbean resort in the middle of the winter, and they were so tired of it all, so desperately lonesome for home—or even for someone just to talk to about something besides forehands and second serves. That, I suppose, is why they were walking along the beach with me. They were international stars, heroines, and I was just a kid with a typewriter, and I was the happy one. And I was getting paid on top of the table, too.

It was easier for the Aussie men, of course. There were plenty of them, after all: mates. They were tanned and charming, and there

---

*It's like now, when there are always great parties at bowl games. When you're not paying the athletes, you can treat yourself, do it up brown.

were beautiful women at all the tournaments, and beautiful women as often as not like athletes. The boys drank lots of Foster's beer— "tasties"—with one another, helped one another out when their games went bad, and enjoyed themselves immensely. There were authentic stories about Aussie roommates making the finals of a Grand Slam, partying together the night before, getting, as they would say, pissed as parrots; then, the next morning, making breakfast for one another, before going out to play against one another for the great title. You see, there was no real money, after all. It was just a carnival of a sport: expenses and travel to nice places, and maybe you could meet some rich executive who could get you a grown-up job in his company when your shamateur career was over.

In all countries, tennis was run in smoke-filled drawing rooms by stuffy gentlemen in black tie—"high-noters" or "lardies" in Aussie lingo. If the mob had boxing, society had tennis. Same thing. The only difference was that the high-noters didn't have to pay their athletes or suffer hoi polloi. As late as 1983, when I went to Wimbledon to do a story on the All-England Club, the chairman, one Air Chief Marshall Sir Brian Burnett, GCB, DFC, AFC, FAF (Ret'd), could not be bothered so much as to speak with me, a grubby member of the press. I had lunch at the club, and Sir Brian sat catty-corner from me at the same table, but he still so much as refused to even acknowledge my existence. It was during the Falklands War. I found myself starting to root for the Argentines.*

At least tennis had gone honestly professional by then, but back when the sport was still shamateur, the lardies in charge were convinced their sport was superior for keeping its players in an indentured

---

*But make no mistake: in my experience, our own Augusta National, which runs the Masters, is a far snottier outfit than the All-England. The All-England accepted women half a century ago; Augusta National still hasn't. Maybe Sir Brian wouldn't talk to me, but at least his minions let me in the joint and graciously accepted me and answered all my questions. When I did a story on the Masters for HBO, I was denied entrance to the club, and no officer would agree to speak with me, nor was any of the paid help allowed to. We hired a helicopter and flew over the course just for spite. Cold comfort.

state. They thought their sport was classy while, in fact, it was really only shabby and deceitful. But, hey, I was just the piano player in the whorehouse, and Melbourne sure beat covering basketball in Evansville in February, staying at the Come-On Inn, Room 417, with the musical stylings of the Bonnie Belle Trio downstairs in the famous Hi-Lite Lounge.

In my experience Aussies and Filipinos are the most nickname-inclined people in the world. Almost no Aussie player went by his square name. Instead: Muscles and Dibbles, Emmo, Newc, Nails, Fiery, Dave-O, Rocket. And so all the boys from Down Under went in a squadron, bouncing hither and yon throughout the world, looking out for each other, sharing. If you were cheap, if you didn't pick up your share of checks, you had "short arms and long pockets." Women were sheilas. Another round was a "shout." No matter how badly injured you were, if you played, you weren't injured. No excuses. *Good game, mate. Let's have a tastie. Your shout. Where's the sheilas?*

Actually, Emerson brought me up a little short when I introduced myself to him in Mexico City and told him I'd come all this way to do a story on him for the big hotshot American sportsweekly. I figured he'd really be impressed. Instead, he just asked me straightaway: "How much will you pay me?"

I was flabbergasted. Of course, I was still a babe in the foreign woods and didn't realize yet that that's the way it worked in a lot of the world—perhaps especially with amateurs, who had to get everything off the books. When I finally regrouped, I had my wits about me sufficiently to stutter that I thought Joe Cullman wouldn't be happy to learn that his prize employee had passed up such a good chance to give Philip Morris some publicity.

Cullman, you see, ran Philip Morris,* and Emerson was on retainer as something of a goodwill ambassador for the company. Now I

---

*He'd become even more famous in tennis a few years later for bankrolling the first professional women's tour with another of his brands: Virginia Slims.

had Emmo back on his heels, and he mulled my remark over. "Lemme talk to Hop," he said at last.

Harry Hopman (or, colloquially: 'Arry 'Opman) was the Australian team "captain" (as in Bligh). Now, of course, *he* was paid, and he was an absolute monarch, a total taskmasker and a Class A son of a bitch. I remember that after Fred Stolle won the five-set match against Dennis Ralston in the 1964 Davis Cup to bring the cup back to Australia, Hopman was mad at the press for some slight he'd personally suffered, so because *he* was irritated, he wouldn't let Stolle talk to me and get a little more acclaim for himself from *Sports Illustrated* for his victory. Hop ran the show. Several Aussie players left the country and settled in Italy, Hong Kong, South Africa, wherever, because Hop didn't like them. You had no chance in Australian tennis if he alone didn't approve of your game. Or you. It's no different now, in our colleges, where the football and basketball coaches run their shamateurs off the team so they can have another scholarship to play with.

But, luckily for me, in Mexico City, crabby old Hop agreed that Emmo, the amateur, should consent to a free interview, and he thereupon became putty in my crafty reporter's hands. Of course, Emmo was that rare athlete: not only the best in his sport but also the absolute most popular person in his sport. One night I interviewed him in what turned out to be a gay bar. I'd never even heard of gay bars before. Here I am on foreign soil, discovering exotica, to boot! *Hola! Dos mas cervezas, por favor!* And London and Paris are on the horizon. Country clubs! Sunshine resorts! Maybe even Down Under! I am definitely a *tennis* writer.

Emmo appreciated the story I did on him, so when next I saw him, he gave me a carton of Marlboros. Remember now: at Timeink, you were supposed to accept only what you could consume in a day, but, what the hell, I'd already sold out to the NBA for a bottle of Christmas Scotch, so I took the smokes, too.

Soon, as if it established my credentials as certified tennis writer, Bud Collins introduced himself to me. It was in 1964 at the National

Indoors, in Salisbury, on the Eastern Shore of Maryland. The reason the second most prestigious tournament in the United States was being held at a backwater on the Delmarva Peninsula was because tennis was so down in the dumps then that a charming hustler named Bill Riordan, who lived there, operating a dress shop, had convinced the U.S. Tennis Association that he could run the Indoors in a high school gym in Salisbury better than anybody else in a real city in a real arena. Which, in fact, he could.

Bill was more accurately a boxing promoter who had somehow gotten sidetracked into tennis. He liberally quoted Shakespeare, but he loved Evelyn Waugh best—especially Waugh's novel *Scoop*, which is a satire about a newspaper reporter, and which Bill thought all tennis writers should study. But then, Bill might have been one of Waugh's characters himself, if only Evelyn Waugh had ever thought to set a novel on the Delmarva Peninsula. Bill talked out of the side of his mouth, especially when he was dishing out cash to the players under the table, as if they were splitting the loot up after a heist, saying things like, "Here's a little extra, kiddo," as he slid him another ten-spot.

Bill also himself invented a tennis player, naming him Stanley Stampenzak. As Bill explained, Stanley was a Nazi sympathizer who was the Polish junior champion, given as much to punching out opponents as beating them on the court, a proclivity which, you see, kept him in stir behind the iron curtain. Otherwise he would come to the free world and mop up all the pussies on and off the court. Many players truly believed that there was a Stanley Stampenzak who would someday emerge. Hey, in a madhouse of a sport, like shamateur tennis, it was certainly within the realm of possibility.

After tennis went pro, Bill became a real players' manager, handling Jimmy Connors. He fronted Jimbo like a pug. He claimed that he and his meal ticket were very much alike, the only difference being that "when I started out and had a choice between good and evil, I picked good, but this kid went the other way." Bill liked to preface remarks by saying, "You won't believe this." As in: "You won't believe this, but Jimbo told me: 'Get me Laver.'" Nobody in his right mind believed Connors had said that, but it got Riordan a big-money Vegas TV match for the young Connors, rampant, against the aging Laver. It and subsequent matches starring Connors were ballyhooed by Riordan as "winner take all." You won't believe this, but they weren't. The players had guarantees. By then, in tennis, as in other real sports, nobody did anything on the cuff. However, at some point, Riordan and Connors fell out, and Bill sued his old pal Jimbo. He was usually suing someone or other in tennis. The last time I saw Bill, he had moved on from tennis and was hustling teenage skateboarders. He was ahead of the curve there, too. Oh, what Evelyn Waugh missed by not booking a trip to Delmarva.

In any event, back when I first met Bud Collins at Riordan's Eastern Shore show, old Al Laney and old Allison Danzig were still around, but there were so few other American tennis writers that Bud sort of welcomed you in, as if it were Skull and Bones. At Wimbledon, he would greet all Yank newcomers and show them the foreign ropes. Bud's the most generous journalist I ever met. And I can't believe that any writer, in any sport, ever knew so many people in the sport—and for decades now, too.

Nevertheless, while Bud was that rare American reporter specializing in tennis, the British press swarmed over the sport. Another reason to be impressed by London sportswriters: they were smart enough to see that even though there were no British tennis *players* worth a damn,* tennis was still a dandy thing to cover. The British tennis beat writers had, in fact, become like a global, corporate Grantland Rice, because if they weren't covering a tournament, then it really didn't count. As a consequence, just as the players were paid expenses to travel to a tournament, so were the British writers comped plane fare and hotel costs by the promoters to appear. You'd be in Philadelphia or Dallas, and the Baltimore paper or the Houston paper

---

*Well, no males. Virginia Wade was very good, and since she was all England had in that line she was always called "our Ginny."

wouldn't be there, but all of Fleet Street would. If you didn't know any better you'd think a snooker tournament had come to town.

The Brit brigade dressed well, puffed thoughtfully on pipes, and drank whiskey neat; also, most of them had names that seemed to have come right off West End marquees: John Barrett, David Gray, Barry Newcombe, John Parsons, David Atkins, Lance Tingay—are you fucking putting me on: *Lance Tingay*?—Richard Evans, Rex Bellamy, Laurie Pignon.

I did a little story on Laurie once for HBO, and we had Pimm's Cups in his perfect English garden at his perfect English house with his perfect English wife, whom he affectionately called "the Dragon." Laurie had been covering tennis since before the war, during which, unfortunately, he found himself a POW in Germany, working as slave labor for several years. He returned from captivity to write for the *Daily Mail,* which is a tabloid in the middle rank, but Laurie outdressed all his broadsheet betters. Usually, he wore bow ties with his pinstripes and held his curly pipe just so. "The ultimate joy," Laurie liked to say, "is to sip green Chartreuse from a woman's navel."

But somewhat before my time, there was one old-time British tennis writer who is supposed to have cast the widest net. According to Teddy Tinling—the designer most famous for fashioning Gorgeous Gussy Moran's lace panties, a man who brought as much art to hyperbole as he did to ladies' undergarments—this most intrepid of journalists kept a detailed journal of the menstrual cycles of all the best women players; then, he could bet against the ones who had their period.*

---

*No, Teddy did not explain to me how the reporter obtained this critical personal information, but there was a football player for the Baltimore Colts named Alec Hawkins, aka Captain Who. One night Alec did not manage to arrive home till breakfast, and when his wife inquired of his whereabouts that night, he replied that he had come back late, and so, as not to disturb her, and the night being of a nature both gentle and mild, he had gone to sleep in the hammock out back. Replied Mrs. Hawkins: "Alec, we haven't had that hammock out there for years." Undeterred, Alec said: "Well, that's my story, and I'm sticking to it." Likewise Teddy Tinling's tale of the old tennis writer with the menstrual chart: that was his story, and he was sticking to it.

Keep in mind, now: this was before we had statistics on everything, so you had to look harder for an edge.

Teddy was English, but he had grown up on the Riviera, where,
as a teenager in the 1920s, he had pretty much been the personal
chair umpire for the first great tennis diva, Suzanne Lenglen. Teddy
informed me that there were occasions when after a match Suzanne
entertained the press in her bath. Also, he told me both her breasts
would, one at a time, regularly pop out of her tennis dress when she
was on the court. I wasn't inclined to believe that, but photographs
of Suzanne do show that she leaped about energetically, and Teddy
assured me that the exposures happened so often that the fans had
given Suzanne's boobs names—Jane and Mary. Jane was the left one.
Teddy told me that, on the way to see Suzanne play, Riviera intimates
would opine: "I wonder if it'll be Jane or Mary that we shall see today?"

So, I had to believe him. Nobody, not even Teddy, could make
that kind of detail up.

Individual sports attract unique characters. If you get involved
with a team in any capacity, the chances are your personality must be
at least somewhat submerged by the group. Tennis back then, when
it was still catch-as-catch-can, was, as Riordan understood, really
more like boxing than any other sport. So whereas a lot of hardened
sportswriters would look down at the swish country-club game, hold
up a pinkie, and gurgle "Tennis anyone?"* I found it was a veritable
garden of priceless oddballs to write about.

Tinling, though, was in a class by himself. (This time around,
anyway. He firmly believed in reincarnation.) He spoke the English
language perfectly, acutely, stylishly, and wickedly—and I'm sure
his French was just as precise, if only I understood French. He also
seemed to understand the United States—critically, with affection—
as well as all the sociologists and historians who write great volumes

---

*You won't believe this, but that line actually came from a Broadway play—first uttered
onstage by a then unknown bit actor named Humphrey Bogart.

on the subject. I listened carefully. For example: "In America there is this enormous determination to make an identity—a desire to be somebody out of 220 million. That helps explain, I think, why so much emphasis in America is placed on macho body-contact sports. There's a higher accent placed on virility and with more rewards."

I'm sorry, but you don't find those wise, idiosyncratic characters around the old gridiron. Teddy was at least 6-foot-5, with a bald bullet head, and he wore the most outlandish outfits. The 1970s, when I really got to know him, were made for him. Pastels, stripes, high collars, white gunboat shoes, the works. Teddy looked like the world's tallest lollipop.

His day job was as a designer. In 1949, when he stuck a little lace on Gorgeous Gussy's drawers, it was just an afterthought, but it created a sensation, and whereas Teddy had been on track then to possibly run Wimbledon someday, instead the tournament officials summarily threw him out. "You have brought sin and vulgarity to Wimbledon," the chairman told him in high dudgeon. I mean, whatever high dudgeon is, that was one time it was surely present.

As for Gussy, her lace-trimmed panties became so famous that she was immediately hired by Jack Kramer to go on tour with him and Bobby Riggs, playing another dame* in the warm-up act. Jack was the last guy I knew who called women "dames." He was another great character, as good a promoter as he had been a champion. Jack barnstormed. My experience as a writer is that anybody who barnstormed, regardless of the sport, was someone worth talking to. Unfortunately, except for the Globies, nobody barnstorms anymore.

Years later, I asked Gussy whatever had happened to the most famous underpants in history. She said that she'd forgotten all about them, but after her mother died, as she was going through her effects, she came across the lace panties in an old trunk.

---

*Her name was Pauline Betz, and she actually married a sportswriter, Bob Addie of the *Washington Post,* the all-time premier pairing of sportswriter and subject.

"What did you do with them?" I asked (breathlessly).

"I threw them in the trash with the other junk I was tossing out."

I was stupefied. "But they could've gone into the Hall of Fame."

Gorgeous Gussy looked sternly at me. "Is that where you'd like to have your underwear?" she asked.

As for Teddy, he kept on designing tennis dresses, and when the Virginia Slims tour came into being, thanks to Billie Jean and Joe Cullman, Teddy entered the period of his greatest prominence, as he became the circuit's interlocutor, its master of ceremonies. No one in sports ever introduced better than Teddy Tinling. The let's-get-ready-to-rumble boxing emcee is small potatoes compared with Teddy. "I'm often the court jester, someone to tinkle the bells," he explained to me. "I never forget that a large quantity of people have a very dull life. It's terrifying to consider, for example, that when I come back it might be as a Russian, for those people are so horribly dull. It's just such a terrible thing to be dull."

And that was my good fortune. Tennis, which I had stumbled upon, was anything but dull. Of course, even though I knew I'd fallen into the rabbit hole when I started covering the sport, no one could have imagined what a fabulous era lay ahead. Like boxing? You can't be serious. Tennis became much more bizarre than boxing. Who could have conjured up Jimbo and McNasty and Ilie Nastase, Ion Tiriac,* Billie Jean playing Bobby Riggs in the Astrodome, tennis writers coming to blows at a Wimbledon press conference, Renée Richards ("mixed singles"), Czechs defecting, the Ice Lolly, World Team Tennis? It was a writer's buffet.

Now, of course, everybody, man or woman, plays the same type of bloodless game, and all the characters have been squeezed out. Bill Riordan wouldn't be able to get near the game today, and Teddy Tinling, when he comes back, would surely find tennis too dull for his

---

*He ate glass.

taste—whether or not he's a Russian this time. Myself, I don't think I'd like to be playing piano on the modern tour.

"Everything in life," Teddy told me once, "is more so than it was. That is the basic premise we must live under in the world today."

Uh-huh. Fair enough. But more so is not better than.

40

THE MOST AMAZING THING
I EVER SAW AN ATHLETE DO

*It was as if the universe had been turned upside down and dark
was light and up was down and the people below were like stars
sprinkled above in the heavens.*
"The Best vs. the Best," *Sports Illustrated*, 1986

The first thing I want to say about Arthur Ashe is what a good sense of humor he had, what great fun he could be. It's important to get that on the record, because he died so young, so tragically, and because he was so associated with such serious causes that everybody assumes that he must've been, however good a person, terribly deadly as company—sort of a Ralph Nader with a Head racket. Well, yes, he was good, a truly fine man, and really smart and clever and devoted and honest—a whole basket of exceptional qualities—but Arthur was also wonderfully attractive and fun. He had a very distinctive laugh, even if I don't know quite how to characterize it. The only description of laughs that really resonates in print is "belly" and Arthur's was a much higher pitch, rising toward a screech.

His humor inclined toward the wry, and he always had both himself and the world around him in clear perspective. He was, of course, invariably the only black person in a sea of whites, but he certainly could be comfortable whomever he was with. I remember one time, when a bunch of us were standing around with him at a tournament, and he looked up and saw two club ladies approaching, smiles as frozen as their beehives. "Oh God," Arthur said, "here they come to put me at ease. I am at ease. Really, I don't need to be put at ease."

But as much as Arthur was a relaxed, delightful person, I must also say that, in the whole cavalcade of my career, the only time I ever was involved with anything truly consequential that went far beyond the realm of sport itself was when, in November of 1973, I went to South Africa with him. That was when he broke the color line there. I was helping Arthur write a book then—a diary of a year—so I literally lived with him in the house where we stayed in Johannesburg. I think we were cohabiting lawlessly: the white guy and the black guy—well, technically, Arthur would've been classified as "Colored"—sharing a suite.

Being there, covering the sundering of the color line in the most racially divided country in the world, was a matter of real consequence that we sportswriters simply never partake of. While we feared that something dramatic might occur, nothing unexpected actually happened the whole two weeks we were there in South Africa. It was just a matter of Arthur *being there*. And, you see, in the long run, that did count. Why, at that time, you couldn't find anyone in South Africa, white or black, who could see the end of apartheid. That was only a fond hope, a vision somewhere out there on the distant horizon of imagining. Good grief, the government didn't even allow television in the country then, lest seeing something normal elsewhere in the world might foment revolution.

But after Arthur came there as a competitor in the South African Open, and because, well, because a black guy just played some white guys some tennis in public and life went on as before—something of a rent had been opened in the curtain of apartheid, and after that, it simply wasn't possible to close it all the way again. Barely sixteen years later, Nelson Mandela was freed from Robben Island, and four years after that he was president of South Africa. Apartheid is ended. Pigs fly. Cubs win. Hell freezes over.

Now that you're free, Mr. Mandela, what American would you like come and visit you? After thinking it over: "Arthur Ashe."

I'd first met Arthur when he was playing for UCLA, and I was a kid reporter. Because of his race, he already had a certain amount of fame, always toting an apposition along with his rackets: "Arthur Ashe comma the first Negro ever to play [fill in the blank] comma . . ." and so forth. But he was only one of several good young American players. Chuck McKinley and Dennis Ralston were at the top of the tree; even Ashe's roommate at UCLA, Charlie Pasarell, was ranked ahead of him. He was, still, at the time we met, more a racial curiosity than a prospective champion.

But, as I quickly discovered, he was damn good company, and we came to know and like each other. Especially after college when he moved to New York, I got closer to Arthur than to any other athlete I ever covered. One of the things that connected us, in an ironic way, is the fact that so much of my family came from Richmond, his hometown. And Richmond, of course, had been segregated. As nearly as we could figure, one of his relatives had been a maid for a time for one of mine. It gave us a kind of perverse all-American relationship.

I told him that when I was a little boy, I would sit on my grandfather McAdams's lap, and once he brought out a small length of old rope and showed it to me, and told me how, when he was a boy, school had been let out so that all of the (white) boys of Richmond could help tug the new statue of Robert E. Lee down Monument Avenue to where it was being installed. The event was so momentous that when the statue was in place, my grandfather had taken out his pocket knife and cut the particular piece of rope he had pulled on and had saved it all these many years. Arthur liked the story, certainly not because he approved of Confederate lyricism, but because it was so personal and so quaint a piece of history about Richmond, and he was fascinated with history.

Even more interesting, though, would've been the reaction of my grandfather, had I been able to tell him that another statue, up Monument Avenue from General Lee's, would be installed, and it would be, of all things, a statue of a tennis player, and, of all things, a statue of a black man. They erected that after Arthur died of AIDS in 1993.

Actually, I took two trips to Africa with Arthur—the first a State Department tour in 1970. Unlike the historical visit to South Africa, the 1970 trip was mostly fun. Such a trip is always called a "goodwill tour," and I believe this one really was.* We landed in Nairobi and visited six countries, with twenty-five parties in eighteen days. Arthur kept count.

Stan Smith came along as Arthur's opponent in the exhibitions. What was so funny is that Stan then was the better player. For goodness sake, he was the Wimbledon champion—or the "holder" as they say over there—but in Africa, Stan was a nobody, a genuine white shadow. After a while, on those rare occasions when any of the press would bother to ask him a question, Stan learned to reply: "I can only echo what Arthur has already said." Everybody thought that Stan showed great sagacity with this answer.

As we headed to Uganda I convinced Stan to let me take his rackets when we got off the plane and play being him. I thought that would make a neat little bit in my story, and, after all, I was only thirty-one then and could pass for a tennis player . . . as long as I wasn't on the court. Stan agreed to it, too, but as we were taxiing to the gate at Entebbe, he lost his nerve and took back his rackets and went into the terminal, unnoticed once again, the Wimbledon holder, while the dignitaries and press mobbed the black guy.

I coulda been a holder.

As instructive and entertaining as the trip was, Arthur took his responsibilities very seriously. He told me: "We've never had a black athlete in the United States who can do what I've been given the chances to do." He wasn't boasting, but was merely pointing out that he was that rare African-American athlete who played on an international stage . . . and that rare American athlete who cared about the

---

*In fact, it was so successful that Arthur made another journey back to Africa the next year, and on that trip, in Cameroon, he hit against a young player named Yannick Noah and was so impressed that he notified the French Federation of the boy's talent. So was Noah taken to Paris and fame and glory.

international stage. He truly had a worldview. I especially remember him trying to explain to some children in Kenya how, in America, most citizens—including many blacks—still formed their opinions about Africa from Tarzan movies. What was especially intriguing, to both Arthur and me, was the response of the children, looking back with a you-gotta-be-kidding-me expression. "No, really," Arthur said, "really, I mean that."

And then, just as ironically, he laughed at the way so many of the Africans viewed him, cautiously, more as a visiting alien than a long-lost brother. "I'm too light here," he told me, and, shaking his head in mock sorrow, added, "No matter where I am, I'm never the right color."

He pointed out to me once, though, that, actually, he was probably right in the middle of the whole spectrum of human skin color. A decade later, when Carol and I adopted a little girl from the Philippines, and I first spoke to him about Scarlet, I told him, "She's like you; when it comes to color, she's about right in the middle."

"Tell her welcome to the center."

Of course, in a less blithe moment, it was also Arthur who instructed me in a truth so obvious—and yet one that, as a white person, I'd never thought through before. We were discussing how much better things were racially, how much more "equal" blacks had become. He shook his head and told me that, at least in our lifetime, he could never gain true equality with me, simply because a certain amount of his time—any black person's time—must be diverted (wasted, in effect) by thinking about race. "Frank, don't ever forget: you can get up in the morning and just walk outside and start your day. I can't do that. If I walk down the street and pass a white guy, I automatically start wondering if he's looking at me and thinking about my race. It never leaves you completely. So you see, you'll always have an advantage over me."

More famously, later, when he was sick, he made the observation, quite casually, that it was more difficult being a black American than an American with AIDS. For Arthur, it was just an everyday observation, but it infuriated a number of those Americans who, like me, had never walked down the street in his skin, thinking. . . .

People always had a hard time figuring Arthur out, because he was so polite and agreeable, foremost a man of peace and comity, but he came to his own conclusions and sometimes they conflicted harshly with the comfortable image people had formed of him. I remember Harry Edwards, the professor who spearheaded the idea that black athletes should boycott the 1968 Olympics, telling me that when he went to see if he could enlist Ashe in supporting the boycott, and Arthur turned him away, politely but firmly, Edwards had thought to himself, "My God, Arthur Ashe is an Uncle Tom." Only later, Harry said, did he come to appreciate the very opposite, that Ashe was so much more bold and more courageous to stick to his own ways and means even when that attitude was contrary to the popular will of the moment.

Hell, there were even a great many African-Americans who thought it was elitist of Ashe to bother himself with South Africa, with any place other than the United States, when black Americans had enough racial problems at home. Likewise, many South African blacks thought he was being both naive and complicit in coming to play there. I was with him in a hotel room in London when a delegation of blacks and Coloreds, South African exiles, came to make a last-minute appeal for him to call off the trip. "They're using you, Arthur," one of them said, pleading urgently.

"I know that," Arthur replied calmly. A long pause, then: "But I'm using them, too."

So he went.

We lived in a private house in a swank white section of Johannesburg; visited Soweto, the huge black township a few miles away; attended functions; played at being tourists. Arthur met with all sorts of people, from children who viewed him wide-eyed—"Master, I never even *saw* a free black man before," one little boy answered Bud

Collins and me, putting tennis in perspective—to the government officials who had permitted his visit. At one fancy dinner, I committed the ultimate faux paux. To the elegant lady next to me, I casually said, "Are you a native?" Now, in Belgium, say, this would elicit a "Yes," or, say, "No, I moved here from Germany," but there in South Africa, the grande dame looked at me as if I were out of my mind. Natives, to her, were people with bones in their noses. Arthur roared when, back at our rooms, I told him the story.

He did well in the tournament, which was then one of the most prestigious in the world. He won the doubles and got to the singles final, but Jimmy Connors clobbered him there. Connors was just coming into his greatest year, a reign of utter mastery that would, in fact, last exactly until that moment, a year and a half later, when Arthur would upset him in the 1975 Wimbledon final. During the tournament, blacks cheered lustily for the player they had come to call "Sipho," which means "a gift" in Swahili.

Afterward, we traveled about the country. In Cape Town we met Christiaan Barnard, the famous surgeon who had performed the first heart transplant. He was a genial fellow, and one of the rare South African whites who would reveal their true feelings to Arthur. He just baldly told Arthur that blacks were like "children," who needed government help to survive. As they say: We appreciate your candor, doctor.

Our last visit was to a place well off the beaten track called Stellenbosch. I asked Donald Dell, Arthur's good friend and manager, what in particular was taking us way out there. Donald explained that Stellenbosch University was a sort of Harvard for Afrikaners, and that they'd arranged to have Arthur attend a large luncheon there with a professor of anthropology named Christopf Hanekom and three of his rabid Afrikaner students. It was, by all measures, to be a good old-fashioned debate about apartheid.

I just nodded. It occurred to me only later what an extraordinary adventure this was, Daniel in the lion's den. By comparison, playing

Jimmy Connors at the top of his form was a day at the beach. Never since have I been able to think of one single athlete who could do what Arthur Ashe was asked to do this day: to step into a public forum, on enemy turf, to boot, asked to hold his own against not only an expert—the anthropology professor—but some of the expert's brightest acolytes, publicly debating an emotional and very personal political matter. But I held Arthur in such esteem and so respected his command of the subject that at the time it never even crossed my mind how unusual it was for him to confront a situation like this.

At Stellenbosch, we were escorted to a lovely courtyard, in the shade of some grand old oak trees, jacaranda blooming purple all around, tea and finger sandwiches on the table, racial superiority on the agenda. It was terribly civilized, and that, of course, made it all the eerier. Arthur accommodated himself to the genteel atmosphere. So often accused of being too cool for his own good on the court, he was, in this arena, at his dispassionate best—even as, effectively, his race was insulted. And not only his race but his nation as well. "You see, Mr. Ashe," one of the students said archly, "this way we don't have the riots that you suffer in your country."

The invited guests—fifty or more, assembled at tables with clean, pressed white tablecloths—had now finished with the tea and nibbles and were paying full attention to the main event. I couldn't help noticing that besides Arthur there was only one black present—a Colored tennis official I'd met earlier named Conrad Johnson. Professionally, he was a salesman, and he was dressed as well as all the others, in a suit and tie. Johnson and the rest of us waited for Arthur to respond to the student, and when he did, utterly nonplussed, without any expression of anger or even pique, he simply replied: "Perhaps riots are a small price to pay for freedom of expression."

But then, suddenly, he took the offensive, citing how oppression begats violence. Turning quickly to Hanekom, he asked, "Tell me, professor, are you scared?"

Hanekom was thrown back. After a moment, he managed to say, "No," if without much assurance in his voice. He was beginning to understand that the tennis player might be more than he'd bargained for.

"Boy, I'd be if I were you," Arthur replied, though he chuckled a bit to take some of the harshness out of his remark. The crowd was cowed. Arthur began rattling off the well-known instances of white South Africans' brutality toward the minorities, of murder and rape, of executions, of political prisoners sent to Robben Island.

Hanekom was smart enough to lie low for now. One of his students could only counter, weakly, by citing John Kennedy's assassination —and that had taken place a good decade past. Another—a theology student—tried to undercut Arthur with what he intended as a backhanded compliment. "Of course, Mr. Ashe, you're culturally white yourself."

Arthur let that pass, so Hanekom tried to spin things back to the intellectual, to cultures and colonialism, to the path to "voluntary multiculturalism." They do-si-doed to that for a while, the students all trying to get their licks in, until Arthur suddenly brought the whole business back to the here and now, back to the courtyard where the conversation had grown safe and distant, to that point of civility when it becomes merely sterile.

"But one more thing," he said. "All the sophisticated evolutionary arguments aside, all the intellectual and political position papers forgotten, in your heart"—and his eyes swept across his opponents— "in your heart, do you think it's right?"

The three students all dropped their eyes. Hanekom had to be the one to respond, but he could only stumble and back and fill, retreating into more academic jargon—until Arthur interrupted him. "No, wait," he said, and when Hanekom stopped speaking, Arthur pointed down to Conrad Johnson, sitting there, silent and dignified. "Forget all that, professor. Just what about this man? Why can you vote and this man can't? Why are you free and this man isn't?"

Every eye turned toward Hanekom. He had to look at Johnson, and then, as his mind raced, he turned back to Arthur. He was silent for a while, and then, without ado, he gave up the ghost. "Mr. Ashe, that is an ace up your sleeve. I cannot defend that."

The debate was over.

I've never yet seen another athlete throw a touchdown pass or hit a home run or score a goal that was as impressive as what Arthur Ashe did that afternoon, the underdog, all alone, on the road, at a gracious luncheon under the oak trees.

41

RED

It was supposed to be so difficult, but nobody ever told me how easy dying is, when it isn't you. No, the trouble is more afterward; it's the missing that's so hard.

Alex: The Life of a Child, 1983

I'd just returned home from the Seoul Olympics in the autumn of 1988 when the phone rang one evening. It was Arthur. I'd dropped him a note just before I left for South Korea, because he'd had to go back into the hospital again. It was more heart trouble. Nine years before, in the summer of 1979, he'd experienced a heart attack. He'd just turned thirty-six then and was winding down his tennis career, married now to Jeanne, trooping the colors with her. He was so young. Why, barely a month before he was stricken he'd still been seeded seventh at Wimbledon.

It was only about three or four days after that first heart attack when I visited him in the hospital. Typically, he was already optimistic, and, to the amazement of his doctors, fast becoming an authority on his own condition, and on heart ailments in particular. His mother had died of a bad heart when he was only six; he'd known he was vulnerable. His doctors also told me, as they had him, that the severity of his attack was such that it surely would've killed anyone but the thin, fit athlete that he was.

But, of course, it concluded his playing career. He would become captain of the U.S. Davis Cup team—in that capacity, trying to manage Connors and McEnroe together, an impossible task that probably did more damage to his emotional system than any mere heart attack could do to him physically. Eventually, though, in 1983, his heart disease demanded another operation, and when he was recuperating the doctors suggested that, while it was altogether optional, it might hasten his well-being if he had a blood transfusion. Not until a few months later would it be mandated that all donated blood must be tested to see if the donor was carrying—and would then pass along—HIV to the recipient.

So, sadly, that was why he was calling me on the phone in 1988. He had been diagnosed with HIV, the AIDS virus, which he'd contracted from that transfusion. He was forty-five years old, and, given the technology of dealing with the disease at the time, he was probably already, five years on, stretching the limits of life expectancy. I remember literally screaming out over the phone as he explained his condition. When I regained some measure of composure, he made me promise not to tell anyone, except, of course, Carol. Then he requested a favor of me. He asked if, whenever his secret was publicly revealed, I would help write the statement that he would issue to the media. Of course, I agreed.

There were two reasons, he explained, why he wished to keep his illness secret. First, he wanted to protect, as much as possible, his young daughter, Camera. People with AIDS were often treated cruelly then, dismissed as either promiscuous homosexuals or wanton druggies. He didn't want his little girl to hear anything cruel about her father or his disease. Second, Arthur said, he knew that once his condition was revealed, he would, for the rest of his life, be pigeon-holed with another apposition: Arthur Ashe, comma, who is suffering from AIDS, comma. . . .

So, for as long as he could, he wanted to live as normal a life as possible out of the spotlight. He speculated that it might be for a few months, perhaps as much as a year. After all, he knew that people don't keep secrets, especially where celebrities are involved. Somehow it would leak out, for somebody was bound to blow the whistle on the famous Arthur Ashe.

He had no idea how much people cared for him.

I don't know how many friends Arthur let in on the secret. A dozen, perhaps; maybe twenty or more. Enough, but not a whole lot. However many, though, incredibly, somehow the secret held. A year, two. I remember, in 1990, going on vacation with Carol, taking a night flight to Zurich. When we came aboard I saw Douglas Wilder sitting with a friend. I had met Doug, who would become the first African-American governor of Virginia, through Arthur, and in the middle of the flight, he came over to see me, and we moved to a quiet spot and talked. Naturally, the conversation turned to Arthur, and it was clear to me that Arthur had told Doug that he had AIDS. It was just as clear, I'm sure, to Doug, that I knew. Yet, even as we danced around the subject, neither of us let the secret escape. That is the way it was. No one whom Arthur had trusted with his confidence would betray him.

In 1989 I left *Sports Illustrated* to become the editor of the *National*. The very first person I approached was John Feinstein. I considered him among the most talented sportswriters of his generation, as good a reporter as we've ever had. His book on Bobby Knight was, simply, an extraordinary accomplishment, for I don't think any sportswriter has ever managed so effectively, over time, to draw so close to a subject and reveal him with such unsparing work. I call John "the Woody Allen of sportswriting," because, just as Allen annually produces a new movie, so too does John somehow manage to write a major book almost every year.

The proposal that I made to John was that he would cover college basketball and tennis, with time off to work on books. He accepted the offer with such alacrity that, unbidden, I threw in a signing bonus: a new blazer. After all, John did such justice to the word "rumpled" that I thought he could use a new jacket. I was never so thrilled. I had hired the first writer I'd reached out to, and he was famous, respected, and as good as they came. And everything John would do for the *National* was what I expected—first-rate.

We began publishing in January 1990, and sometime that summer, after Wimbledon, John dropped by the office. We greeted each other warmly, but then, almost immediately, he shut the door, sat down before my desk, and, without any preamble, simply said, "Frank, I know about Arthur."

I was absolutely stunned and totally flummoxed, for I suddenly realized what I was betwixt and between. When Arthur had told me his secret, I was but a magazine writer, an independent contractor when it came to keeping silent about off-the-record information from a source. But now, I had a responsibility to a whole newspaper, an enterprise. John was bound by no confidence. He had come up with what was, simply, a hell of a scoop. I had no right to deny him the opportunity to print that story. Did I? Could I, as editor, even try to talk him out of it? In my position wouldn't that be totally irresponsible of me?

Happily, my mind had to spin for only a few seconds. John saw my distress immediately. Before I could even reply, he just shook his head and, very quietly, said, "Don't worry, I'd never do that to Arthur."

And neither would anyone else. Other members of the media had learned the truth by now—and like John were not honor-bound to silence. But they kept the secret to pay homage to the man. How often does that happen in journalism today?

Whenever I would see Arthur, he'd express surprise that the secret held. Late in 1991, I was in Japan, researching my novel about Pearl Harbor, *Love and Infamy,* when Magic Johnson announced that he had AIDS. Arthur was sure that this would let loose the secret. But it didn't. That April, however, what I had come to call with him "the sweet conspiracy" was finally breached, when *USA Today* was tipped. Ironically, the paper's tennis writer was Doug Smith, an African-American from Virginia who'd known Arthur since they were kids. He was distressed at his paper's role in revealing the secret.

Arthur, of course, had long expected this day, so when *USA Today* called to confront him, he didn't deny the news but simply stalled. He wanted to go public with his disease on his own terms. He called me, but Carol and I were at the theater, so I got his message when I returned late that evening. As was typical of Arthur, his voice didn't suggest any urgency. Just: gimme a call when you get a chance. By the time I called back the next morning, learned the news, and rushed over to his apartment, he had already composed a statement. His words were superb; they barely needed any touching up on my part. Instead, I sat there with him, and as the news began to spread, as the calls began to come in—including one from President Bush—he answered calmly and politely. And then—I shall never forget this—at one point he turned to me and said, "Frank, go out and stay with Doug for a while. He feels terrible about this."

Doug, of course, was Doug Smith, whose paper had broken Arthur's story, intruded on his privacy. But Arthur expressed no anger at all. "They didn't do anything wrong," he said. "They just did what they had to."

And so, soon enough, we went downtown to the HBO offices, where Arthur's friend Seth Abraham, the president of HBO Sports, had volunteered the use of the network's offices for his press conference. And then the whole world knew.

And, despite his fears, almost no cruel rumors sneaked out of dark corners. On the contrary, there was only sadness for his bad luck, acclaim for the man. I had been so mad at *USA Today,* but in the months following I changed my mind, and was so glad that the newspaper had forced the secret out, because it was almost as if Arthur had become Tom Sawyer, who got to look in on his own funeral. In the ten months more that he lived, Arthur learned how much the world valued who he was, how beloved he was. In effect, he read his own obituaries. I don't know if ever there was such wide affection displayed for any athlete.

His health continued to diminish, but after all the time he had carried the virus, he appeared to hold up pretty well. Even when he was hospitalized that next January, his condition did not seem to be critical. Certainly, he was sure that he would be going home, because he kept talking about a Valentine's dance that he had planned. It would be just for fathers and daughters. He knew that I would be particularly taken by such an idea, because, of course, I had lost a daughter. Alex had died in 1980, when she was eight. Arthur had been one of the pallbearers who had carried her casket into the church, then outside into the cold, watching with us as she was laid in the earth.

But now I had my new daughter; Scarlet was twelve now. We would be at the dance. That was the only qualification Arthur had for attendance: a father and his daughter. The father might be forty-nine, and the daughter six, as were Arthur and his daughter Camera. Or the father might be ninety and the daughter sixty-five. Never mind, as long as it was a father and his daughter. And one other thing: everybody, Arthur said, had to wear something red.

So, when I visited him in the hospital, late in January, he was anxious for his doctor to release him so he could finish planning his big party. He'd completed work on his autobiography with Arnold Rampersad. The Valentine's dance was his top project for now. And so we chatted, and at one point he actually said to me, "You know, everything in my life is just wonderful now—except for the hospital stuff."

I started to dispute that, perhaps to say, *Come on, Arthur, even you can't dismiss AIDS as mere "hospital stuff,"* but he anticipated me and said it again: "Really, Frank, everything is almost perfect."

A little while later, I told him good-bye and said that I'd see him again soon, when he got home.

"Or at the Valentine's dance," he said.

"Don't worry," I said, "Scarlet and I have both got it on our calendars."

But then, as I headed away, he called after me: "Now don't forget. You gotta wear something red."

Funny, I didn't even look back. I just raised one hand and waggled it, assuring him I'd heard. "Don't worry, Arthur. Scarlet and I'll both be in red."

So the last time I saw him, I had my back to him.

That was because Arthur died a few days later, on February 6, 1993. No athlete was ever so mourned. To this day, you can't imagine how many times I just hear the word "red," and it triggers thoughts of him. Arthur's the only person in my life whom I forever associate with a color—and the best thing is, it has nothing to do with black or white.

42

THE AMATEUR VOICE

To Madison Avenue, a player who made a razor commercial is,
ipso facto, *better than some stiff who is only hitting .335 with 43*
home runs. Why? Because he made a commercial.

"Hot Pitchmen in the Selling Game,"
Sports Illustrated, 1969

I suppose I was in the first generation of sportswriters that did not hold a constitutional antipathy toward our television competitors. Starting with test patterns and Howdy Doody, I had pretty much grown up with television, so it was not the alien force that so many of my older writing colleagues perceived it to be. It's rather ironic, too, because whereas back when I started, the twain—newspaper reporters and television faces—were never supposed to meet, today the prime career goal of most sportswriters seems to be to develop a good enough pair of lungs so that they can get on ESPN and try to shout down other sportswriters.

This is not to say that I didn't have my own pretty little head turned by television. A producer in Boston saw me being interviewed when I was plugging my first novel on the *Today Show*, and asked me to make an audition tape. Nothing came of that, but the tape somehow reached a big television hotshot named Al Primo. He was the guy who had pretty much invented the happy-talk news concept, with dual anchors. Al Primo was the absolute maestro of television news, and one day I picked up the phone and it was Al Primo himself, saying he had seen my tape and was very excited about it and wanted to see me—pronto.

I figured: big-time showbiz. On *my* way. To the top, baby. This was the hottest thing to happen to me since that one day when I'd made the "Who's Where" listing in *Variety*—boldface (and even spelled right, too)! **Frank Deford** in from Gotham."

I put on my best suit, a snazzy Turnbull and Asser shirt, and a knockout tie and pocket handkerchief and went to see Al Primo right there in midtown Gotham. When I entered his office, I could see he was sizing me up, and when I sat down, these were the absolute first words out of Al Primo's mouth: "You know, you're funny looking."

But, as we are constantly being told, the United States of America is a nation that believes in second chances, and so it was, several years later, that I would again get the opportunity to go into television—and radio, too. Both cases were pretty serendipitous.

In the autumn of 1979, National Public Radio, which had started on the air eight years before, introduced its morning-drive program, *Morning Edition*. Today, I firmly believe that NPR has become the American BBC, that as the power of most newspapers and newsmagazines has diminished, NPR has ascended to a position of wisdom, authority, and reach second only to the *New York Times*. However, at that point, in 1979, I'd never even heard of NPR.* But at that time, people at the fledgling network's headquarters in Washington decided that it might be nice to throw sports fans a bone. So out of the blue, they picked a pretty young staffer named Ketzel Levine to find a couple of your sports-type people to bloviate on *Morning Edition*.

Now, Ketzel, who would become an NPR star as the gardening expert, didn't know a thing about sports, but she became, she recalls, "the so-called sports director." That is to say, there were really no sports to direct. But then, if Ketzel had been a real sports director,

*Even now, I still have some people tell me: "I always hear you on PBS."

obviously, she would've had the good sense to go after somebody who was actually *in* broadcasting, as opposed to me, who had no broadcast experience whatsoever.

But first, Ketzel began her search for sports voices by, casually, asking her father for advice. He had been a Brooklyn Dodgers fan, so he suggested she find Red Barber, who had been the Dodgers' fabled "voice" for many years. Ketzel located Red retired in Tallahassee, and he signed up, and would, for many years, spend a few beguiling minutes, once a week, coming on with the *Morning Edition* host, Bob Edwards, presumably to discuss sports—although as often as not they discussed opera or azaleas instead.

Well, that Cinderella fitted into the slipper, so Ketzel started calling around for others and happened upon Jane Gilchrist, a blithe spirit of a sort of PR director at *Sports Illustrated*. I adored Jane. I always wanted to base a character on her because she's the only person I ever knew who, when *she* called you up, would then be totally surprised when you answered. "Hello."

"Oh . . . *Frank?*"

"Yes. Jane, remember: you called me."

Anyway, Jane took Ketzel's bait and invited her to visit *Sports Illustrated*. Coming to a macho male enclave, Ketzel bought a new pair of sexy boots. Jane held a catered lunch for her, which was something we did all the time at Timeink, but which was something totally new for Ketzel. Then, as she remembers it, Ketzel gave "a presentation about 'NPR Sports,' as if such a thing existed." After lunch Ketzel visited my office and liked all the cheap memorabilia I kept around; I was just then starting on my shampoo bottle collection and hadn't moved it home yet. Ah, a woman with an eye for style. Thereupon she officially invited me to be a commentator for the vaunted NPR Sports. And what the hell, even if I hadn't heard about this radio PBS thing, I thought it sounded like a fun thing to do for, oh, a few weeks, maybe three or four months. That was thirty-two years ago.

The great attraction about being able to do a sports commentary on NPR is that I'm talking to a broad audience. Usually, whatever the medium, sports is placed over there somewhere in a discrete corner, where you have to go poking around to find it—the sports pages, sports radio, *Sports Illustrated,* ESPN. It's easy to completely avoid sports if they're not your cup of tea. But on NPR, there I am, right smack in the midst of the news, and even if you can't abide sports, what's a body to do: turn the dial to Howard Stern for three minutes just to avoid me?

This is not to say all NPR listeners are fond of me. The most common criticism is that I rant, which always surprises me, because even if I might sound cockeyed or disagreeable, I really don't rant. But if you don't like somebody with a microphone nowadays, it's fashionable to say he rants. Critics of NPR's Frank DeFord also say I sound "pompous." Now, in all honesty, I'm fair game for that. When you express opinions, you almost have to sound pompous, especially nowadays when subtlety of expression is not heard above the din. So, I plead nolo contendere to pomposity, but I will deny to the death the accusations of ranting.

People often ask me: *Mr. DeFord, how long does it take you to write an NPR commentary?*

The answer is that it is coming up with the idea that takes the time. Remember, the quota is fifty-two a year, year after bloody year. Sometimes I get so desperate for an idea that I hope someone dies. I don't mean anyone in particular, you understand; I just want some dear old jock who always gave 110 percent whom I can eulogize. You see, if you will allow me to feel sorry for myself, not a whole lot changes in national sports. Oh sure, different teams win and lose and so forth, but where's the commentary in that?

Now, if you're doing local commentary, your audience is familiar with the territory, so you can just fire the coach every week or say the manager has to do a better job at changing his relief pitchers. Nationally, though, that kind of stuff is too esoteric.

No, in sports, it's pretty much the same old who-shot-John. Thirty years ago, when I started at NPR, figuring there were just enough subjects for me to vamp for a few months, nobody'd even heard of Iraq or gay marriage or debentures or global warming, so as the years have passed, political commentators have had a whole new flotilla of issues to rant on about pompously, while, about 1,500 commentaries on, I'm still stuck with the Yankees and Cowboys and Olympic idiocy and what a fraud college sports is. And how dreadfully dull soccer is, of course. I play that for all it's worth. Thank God for steroids, Tiger Woods's libido, and the recent discovery that football is actually (goodness gracious!) a violent game.

I created a character called the Sports Curmudgeon, who comes on periodically and rails (not rants, you understand, but just rails) at foolish things in sport, but long ago I started to run out of foolish things for the Curmudgeon to bitch about, so I pretty much retired him. Also, I was starting to get tired of people making a fuss about the Sports Curmudgeon to the detriment of me—much as Sir Arthur Conan Doyle finally had it up to here with Sherlock Holmes. I wanted people to congratulate me on my own sage and trenchant thoughts, but instead all I would hear was: "Mr. DeFord, I love it when you have the Sports Curmudgeon on PBS."

When I was writing my latest novel, *Bliss, Remembered,* wherein I, the narrator, am an old woman talking about love, I got so into being in a female mode that I created an old lady for my NPR sports commentary, too. She is named the Duchess, but I don't do falsetto. That'd be too over the top for such a serious enterprise as NPR. Instead, I have it that the Duchess writes me letters, in a cursive hand, on personal stationery, as in olden times, and then I read them in my own dulcet tone. Unlike the Curmudgeon, who is disagreeable, the Duchess is more of a fussbudget. She wants to see more grace in sports. Like less spitting in baseball. That sort of thing. I haven't gotten jealous of the Duchess. Yet.

People lump radio and TV together, naturally enough, because these are both broadcast media (or "platforms" as people are wont to say now). The truth is, though, that writing for radio is much more like print than like writing for TV. At least that's so with writing for NPR. It's just a matter of me reading to you what I wrote, as opposed to having you read it yourself. Oh, the sentence construction has to be simpler on radio, and you have to go easy on the unfamiliar words, and stay away from the French and Latin folderol, but otherwise it's not a whole lot different from print. On the other hand, television is so absolutely visual that writing there—such as what I do for *Real Sports with Bryant Gumbel*—is more akin to turning out greeting cards. All you ever have to know about what matters to television is that "talking heads"—that is, human beings actually shown speaking—are to be avoided at all costs.

But it is indeed a real privilege having a spot on NPR, and the surprising thing to me is that people say I have a very distinctive voice. I never knew that before, but there've been actual instances when someone has heard me talking and, without any knowledge of what I look like, has asked if I wasn't Frank DeFord. Myself, I really don't think I have any familiar accent. I think mine might be called the domestic version of a mid-Atlantic accent. Maybe it's because I was never trained in radio, so when Ketzel got me on the radio I had an amateur voice and I didn't know how I was *supposed* to try to sound, so I sound different from trained throats.

Carol and I went to the White House once, because I had written an HBO documentary on women's sports, and Hillary Clinton had been prevailed upon to do the introduction, so the Clintons held a black-tie reception. This was the time Eleanor Holm hit on the president. In the receiving line, I told Carol that I thought the president would probably recognize me, because he was a sports fan and I'd written a long, touching story on Nolan Richardson, the basketball coach at Arkansas, but when the Marine officer said, "Mr. President, Frank DeFord," President Clinton didn't know me from jack.

So, crestfallen, I turned to the first lady and said, "Mrs. Clinton, I'm Frank Deford."

And immediately, she said, "Oh, Frank, I'd know that voice anywhere. You wake me up every Wednesday morning."

Of course, it is also true that as mysteriously distinct as my voice may be and as consistently brilliant as my sporting observations are, I come on pretty early at most NPR stations, and so people are just up and multitasking. Thus, they can manage only to lend me an ear as they brush their teeth or otherwise perform their morning ablutions.

I was speaking at one swanky eastern college, and at the reception beforehand, the president entered the room. She was very pretty, very vivacious, and also very loud. Spotting me across the room, she called above the crowd, "Oh, Frank, this is the first time I've ever heard you with my clothes on."

Heads turned. Gasps gasped.

Actually, lots of people—especially women—tell me that they don't really know much about sports, but having started out as a captive audience, they have come to actually listen attentively to me. That's very flattering, of course, but a friend, Michael Mewshaw, the novelist, made this trenchant observation: "Frank, do you realize that in your career you've written mostly about people who don't read— athletes—and spoken on the radio mostly to people who don't know what you're talking about?"

Well, as the expression goes: just spell my name right.

Only, of course, no one does that either.

And, too, my experience on the air taught me that sports broadcasters are admired no more than sportswriters. Because I tape my commentaries in Connecticut and rarely get to NPR headquarters in Washington, I really have very little contact with the NPR higher-ups. But one time about ten years ago, Ellen McDonnell, who is the executive director of news programming, called me up to say that despite the fact that some captious, unenlightened listeners thought I ranted, I was, in the big picture, a positive member of the NPR team, and was there anything I might ask for?

Well, I don't normally beg, but, given this very generous opening, I figured what the hell: in for a penny, in for a pound. Would it be possible, I asked Ellen, for NPR to nominate me for a Peabody Award? That's the sine qua non of broadcasting, a consummation devoutly to be wished. I promise, too: it's the only award I've ever lobbied for. Ellen could not have been nicer, saying that NPR would be delighted, that it was even a little embarrassing that she had needed to be prodded to seek this recognition for such a stalwart voice as I.

Unfortunately, then I was embarrassed to discover that getting a Peabody Award is not like just being *recognized* by the experts who dole out the honor. You would think they'd simply turn on the radio Wednesday mornings and decide for themselves if I was worthy. I'm very visible to the ear. But that's not the way it works. Rather, it turns out that winning a Peabody is more like applying for a job. Letters of recommendation (including one from Hillary Clinton, who was nice enough to take the time) had to be procured. A lengthy dossier was completed. I believe blood samples and PIN numbers were also required. I began to realize that a Peabody does not recognize excellence in broadcasting so much as it does excellence in hoopla.

But eventually, Ellen called me up and told me that despite all the yeoman efforts, above and beyond, that NPR had devoted to hyping me, somebody from the Peabody Award had called her to say that the organization wouldn't give me one. OK, fine. Nowhere is it written that I deserve a Peabody. What the hell, I'd gotten Frank DeFord Day in Buffalo hadn't I? But this is what stung: Peabody's spokeswoman told Ellen, "You should've nominated Daniel Schorr for politics."

The late Mr. Schorr was the distinguished political commentator on NPR—and as far as I was concerned, they could've given him a Peabody each and every year. But the idea that his work talking about politics merited recognition simply because of the subject matter, while mine in sports disqualified me—well, yeah, that upset me. I'm sorry, but every now and then I take umbrage.

It still fascinates me that the Pulitzers award one of their precious prizes every year to a cartoonist. Hey, I love political cartoonists. But how many of them are there left? What? Two dozen? And how many newspaper sportswriters are there? Thousands. And for them, the Pulitzer people deign to give out one to a guy at the *New York Times* every generation or so.

OK, so I'm ranting now. Let me rant a little more on behalf of my neglected profession. The University of Missouri Journalism School is at the top of the tree, and every year it hands out a few Distinguished Service to Journalism Awards, and in 1987 I was very honored to be granted one. That year I was in fine company with people like Flora Lewis, William Raspberry, and Ted Turner, and I keep the award, proudly, in a credenza, visible, right there in my office.

Then, a few years ago, I read that John Walsh, an old friend, the one person who had made ESPN a respectable news organization, had been chosen, very deservedly, to receive one of the Missouri awards that year. Happy for John, but curious, I idly looked up the all-time list of winners. There have been 394 individuals so honored in the eighty years since the Missouri awards were inaugurated in 1930. Two, Bob Broeg and Jack Buck, both St. Louis sports journalists, had been chosen as sort of favorite Show-Me State sons. Otherwise, only three people in sports journalism—about 0.7 percent of the total number celebrated—had been selected. John Walsh remains the only person in sports broadcasting to be honored. Edgar Scherick, Roone Arledge, Dick Ebersol, Howard Cosell, Red Barber, Jim McKay, Vin Scully, Bob Costas, Al Michaels—not one of them was up to snuff. No sports photographers at all. Red Smith in 1976 was the only person, writer or editor, from the newspaper sports pages ever to be chosen. I mean, come on: never mind Jimmy Cannon and Jim Murray, but they also missed Grantland Rice? And I was the only sports person from magazines.

I know I'm whining, and it's certainly awfully nice to be paired alone with Red Smith as a sportswriter, but I'm sorry, I can't apologize for pointing out what slights we in the profession so regularly receive. Sports journalism has been such a crucial economic part of the daily press that it ought to be recognized more, if only because it's kept a lot of newspapers in business. And yeah, I know, it's the toy shop. But some toys are very well made.

Really, we aren't the pole dancers of journalism.

43

THE BEST I EVER WAS FIRED

In TV, there are only two types of people. One is a bad guy. The other is not a bad guy.
"Promo Wiz in Kidvid Biz," *Sports Illustrated*, 1977

Not long after I started doing commentaries at NPR, Ted Turner started to crank up the Cable News Network, a project that all the wise guys laughed at. Ted hired Bill MacPhail to run the sports division, because unlike NPR, CNN really did have a sports division. Bill had once headed up CBS Sports, back in its heyday when it had the exclusive contract with the NFL. He and Pete Rozelle were bosom buddies and also, more functionally, drinking buddies. Unfortunately, unlike Rozelle, who could really hold his booze, Bill developed a genuine drinking problem, and CBS put him, as they used to say then, "on the beach." After Bill dried out, Turner was the one who picked him up out of the sand dune and gave him another chance.

To fill up the endless time, which was 24/7 before that became a cliché, CNN decided to hire a multitude of expert commentators to rant on about a veritable plethora of subjects. Bill asked me to be the sports commentator, and I accepted. The pay was $50 per piece and I was booked for three a week—each about a minute long, but nobody much minded if you went over because that helped fill the endless void, 24/7/52.*

---

*Although, if you notice, everybody always says, incorrectly, "24/7/365."

The CNN bureau in New York was in the lobby of one of the World Trade Center towers.* And let me tell you, that was *the* CNN showcase, because the headquarters in Atlanta were themselves located in a faux antebellum mansion on the outskirts of town. Still, even in the World Trade Center, CNN's Big Apple operation was a pretty spare enterprise. Much of the equipment was the television equivalent of army surplus. Even worse, when I did commentaries in London, I would go over to a one-room office that was passed off as a "bureau," and the office didn't even own a stand for the camera. The little office manager would stack up a bunch of books, and then she'd try to hold the camera steady atop the highest volume.

It was all very quaint, and I will forever hold the distinction of being the first talking head to appear on CNN from New York when it opened on June 1, 1980. Then too, because it was so embryonic, I could mess around with impunity in my commentaries. For example, tennis players were starting out younger and younger at that time, so one day I brought my daughter Scarlet, when she was about two, down to the studio, and pretended to interview her as if she were the new Virginia Slims star. William "the Refrigerator" Perry was the hot football player, so I interviewed the refrigerator in the bureau kitchen.

I guess it was the equivalent of blogging on the Internet today. Nobody was watching, and there was hardly a week when I went down to the World Trade Center that there wasn't a rumor that the whole thing was going under. I was absolutely amazed whenever people would tell me that they had actually seen me on TV.

The sports correspondent for the New York bureau was named Debi Segura. She was, as the name suggests, a woman; this was quite revolutionary for sports at that time. Then one day there was a new sports guy there, because, I learned, Debi had fallen in love with Lou Dobbs, the business anchor, and they had gotten married. Her replacement was a kid barely out of Cornell named Keith Olbermann.

*CNN had moved uptown long before the Towers were destroyed in 2001.

Very soon, everybody told me exactly the same thing, that he was absolutely brilliant, but a handful. *Plus ça change, plus c'est la même chose.*

Because I would tape the week's three commentaries all at the same time, I would bring two extra ties with me in an effort to fool the CNN faithful into thinking that I was in different, fresh regalia each time I aired. Bella Abzug was one of the political commentators, but she was busier than I was, so she'd come in only about every two or three weeks and do a whole slew of her commentaries all at once. That's the great thing about political journalism. Once you've taken a side, you can do essentially the same stuff over and over. Bella would wear one of her signature hats each time, of course, but to create the impression that her material wasn't stale, the staff asked Bella if she wouldn't bring some extra blouses, like my extra ties, so—as if anybody cared—she too could appear to be in a different outfit for each commentary.

So Bella would bring a bunch of blouses, and take them to the desk in the World Trade Center lobby, where she taped, and after she'd do a commentary, she'd just take her blouse off right there before God and the lobby wayfarers and put another one on, sit back down, and tape another commentary.

Such was life at the new CNN. Keith Olbermann left for bigger and better things, and lots of the commentators gave up the ghost. A radio guy named Larry King was hired to do an interview show at nine PM that had been hosted by a lady named Sandi Freeman. About once a year Bill MacPhail would call me up from Atlanta and tell me I was doing fine, and once he gave me a raise to $75 per piece. The equipment began to improve.

Then, one fine day in 1986, MacPhail called me up. "Hey, Bill," I said, "good to hear from you."

"Well, Frank," he said, in a very sprightly manner, "I've got some news for you."

"Yeah, what's that, Bill?"

"Ted just bought MGM."

That took me aback for a moment. "He did, huh?" I said.

"Yeah, Ted bought MGM."

"That's great, Bill, but why are you telling me?"

"Well, you see, it took so much money, we have to let you go."

So it goes in big-time entertainment: one day you own Frank DeFord, the next day MGM.

44

NAKED SLEPT
THE COMMISSIONER

Most coaches adore automobiles and have no rapport with women.
That is not to say they don't like sex; it is to say they tolerate women
because women provide sex. But they don't enjoy the company of
women. They don't like them around. On the other hand, American
coaches are nuts about cars. Cars count. The most important thing
to coaches is to get a courtesy car to drive around town in. This is
the sign of being a successful coach.
"The Depression Baby," *Sports Illustrated*, 1976

I've always enjoyed the difficult people. Give me Howard Cosell, for openers. Give me Billy Martin. Or Bobby Knight. Red Auerbach. Give me Jimmy the Greek. A. J. Foyt. Pancho Gonzales. Jimmy Connors. Geno Auriemma today.

These are the best characters to write about, largely because so many people flat-out don't like them or are at least dubious about them, so it's a challenge to surprise or even upset the reader with the unexpected. Also, I think, because I'm rather restrained, unlike those outspoken, even rude characters, I imagine there's a part of me that admires their guts. You always hear about the comedian who wants to play Hamlet. I think writers are probably something like that too. What fun is it for Frank Deford to write about a guy like Frank DeFord?

One of my most treasured compliments came when I read an interview with John McEnroe. The reporter asked him if there wasn't *any* writer he liked, and, after thinking it over, McEnroe named me. Why? "Because he asked me why are you such an asshole on the court? I liked that. See, he was honest." Or maybe I was just confounded.

Or Earl Weaver, the McEnroe for baseball umpires. I can still see Weaver after a game, in his baseball underwear, beer in one hand, cigarette in another, chastising an uninitiated writer who asked how the Orioles, in the midst of a little losing streak, could get their momentum back. "Momentum," Earl snapped. "Momentum? This ain't fucking football. It's baseball, and momentum is a new starting pitcher every day."

Al Davis. No matter what he was telling you, even if it was just that he wanted a ham sandwich for lunch, it was always spoken in this southern accent he'd grafted onto his tongue sometime after he left Brooklyn—but with a very conspiratorial tone. As if the ham sandwich was going to be an all-pro. Still, Al's most identifying characteristic (well, besides his pompadour) was that he didn't appear to have a body temperature like other people. My lasting vision of him: we were watching the Raiders scrimmage the Cowboys in August outside Dallas, and it was about 120 degrees on the field, and everybody else was in shorts, and Al was wearing his heavy white Elvis sweat suit. And he never sweated. I don't think he ever shivered, either.

When Al was commissioner of the American Football League, he really was responsible for forcing the NFL to merge with the AFL, but Pete Rozelle is always given credit. Look, Pete did a lot of brilliant things to take the NFL to the top, but it was Davis who forced the NFL to sue for peace. Davis simply outsmarted Rozelle. Pete was an old PR man,* but Davis was an old coach, and he outcoached him. I don't think Pete ever forgot that—even when history made him the hero.

---

*Perhaps the most interesting scoop I unearthed was that Pete never wore monogrammed shirts. He didn't want you to see the "PR" and remember that it was a PR man you were dealing with.

Years afterward, when I was doing a profile on Rozelle, once, late at night down in Philadelphia, after dinner when we shared a couple of rusty nails, he pleaded with me not to interview Davis. That was incredible. Rozelle knew the press better than anybody else, and you simply don't ask a writer *not* to talk to someone about you. In fact, this was the only time I ever remember that happening to me, and to think that it came from Pete Rozelle, who was so savvy about the media. But rusty nails are powerful —Drambuie and Scotch—and Al Davis drove him crazy—cantankerousness and stubborness.

The irony was that when I did reach Davis, he didn't have much of anything interesting to add about Rozelle, and years later, when Pete was near death, and I called Al again, he said he didn't think it would be appropriate for him to say anything about his old adversary, who was dying. I think that would have amazed Rozelle.

Before the merger, before Davis took the measure of Rozelle, Pete really was the last emperor of American sport. He was proof of that old saw about the best form of government being a benevolent dictator. It's quite amazing to look back on that time, to understand what unilateral powers he had. When, for example, Paul Hornung was found to have bet on pro football games, Rozelle summoned him personally over the phone. Not only that, Paul told me that Rozelle made it absolutely clear that "I want this to be a very clandestine meeting."

So without questioning the order, without even thinking about any counsel, Hornung promptly took the next plane to New York and waited, like a little boy, to be summoned to the principal's office. He did precisely as Rozelle ordered and told no one why he was in Manhattan, but just spent the next couple of days hanging out with Frank Gifford at places like Toots Shor's or Mike Manuche's. When he finally heard the call from on high and went to the throne room, he got a talking-to from Rozelle, who then summarily handed down an indefinite suspension. Hornung accepted it without dispute, obsequiously thanked the commissioner, and left to go back home, where, as Vince Lombardi told him, he was "to stay at the foot of the cross" in the hope that Rozelle would someday be moved to reinstate him (which Rozelle eventually did, just as capriciously as he had suspended him in the first place).

"I took my medicine, Frank," Paul told me, "and I think I was better for it. You know, litigation with lawyers—as far as players were concerned, that was not in vogue whatsoever."

That's the way it was in those days.

Avery Brundage had the same sort of assumed authority over the Olympic *movement,* but the funny thing is that, as common as he was, I found out, to my utter surprise, that Brundage took his biggest hit unfairly. When the Israeli athletes were murdered at the Munich Olympics, the American press pilloried Brundage for his callousness toward Israel and Jewry for not calling off the Games. Twelve years later, I went to Israel to do a story for NBC about the massacre, and there I discovered that, to a person, the families of the murdered athletes—wives, parents, and children—all agreed with Brundage. They believed that even to have postponed the Games would have given the terrorists a victory.

Coaches tend to be interesting characters. However, the different sports throw up different types. Generally speaking, baseball managers and basketball coaches are more attractive than football coaches, who are valued more for their organizational skills than for their personalities. Football coaches coach practice. They watch film. They order people. They watch more film. A lot of them (like a lot of ESPNian fans) are one-track zombies; the Germans have the best word for them: *Fachidioten*—specialty idiots. They watch the same film over and over. Football coaches never call it "movies." Movies are fun. Film is football.

Baseball managers and basketball coaches are, instead, swept up in the real games that rush at them and are then swept along by the media they can't escape, let alone control. Lou Piniella told me, ever so wisely, that if he ran a baseball organization, every manager would have to take classes in dealing with journalists, because that's as important to the job as filling out the lineup card or making double switches.

I'm sure that it generally works the other way, too: that the writers who cover baseball and basketball are, say, different sorts from football writers. After all, most sportswriters eventually end up covering the sport they like best, so even if they're hard-nosed journalists, there is always an emotional attachment to the game they love.

But then, go easy on us: political writers like politics and movie critics are crazy about movies. And people choose dogs that suit their personalities.

Anyway, you figure baseball managers will at least accept you as a necessary evil. But most football coaches this side of Rex Ryan are not necessarily that accommodating to the prying eyes from the fourth estate. Maybe that's the reason that the best story I ever wrote about football was about a coach who was dead. Also: nobody outside rural Mississippi had ever heard of before. He had been known as Bull Cyclone Sullivan—so tough he had to have two nicknames. His former players adored him, even if he had been a martinet, and they overwhelmed me with anecdotes. Football players love coaches who are mean to them, because, I suppose, you've got to be mean to play football, and they're looking for an arche-type to lead them. Football players are always saying that their adored coaches "love them as people, too," as if that is a hallmark of goodness, to actually treat people as human beings.

The sappiest thing college coaches like to say is that Coach So-and-So isn't really a coach; he's a teacher. Every famous coach, living or dead, is complimented in that fashion by other coaches. When they're paid like teachers I'll believe it.

Incredibly, when Billy Martin made me, the strange writer, his confidant I had hardly met him. During the first game I watched him manage, he got mad at a rookie umpire named Rich Garcia (who would go on to become tops in his profession). So, when I came into Martin's office before the game the next day, he greeted me right away: "Whatdya think o' this? I go out to give the lineup card, I call that Garcia a spic."

You're not supposed to get personally involved in a story you're writing, but I was so taken aback that I naturally demurred. "I don't know, Billy," I said, tentatively.

"Why not?" he snapped back at me. "They called me a dago. Let's see what the sonuvabitch is made of."

I sympathized with his having suffered such slings and arrows, but suggested that although he'd had to endure passing personal ethnic insults, umpires were, well, authority figures. Perhaps Billy might want to run this idea by someone else before trotting it out. He mulled that over, and ultimately he decided not to slur Garcia.

Bear Bryant was the coach who, inadvertently, got me into the most trouble. He was going for the record for most all-time victories. He was old, the Bear; in fact, he'd be dead in only another few months. He was tired, and he didn't mind admitting to me that his assistants were doing most of the real coaching. He was weary of writers, too, and I understood that. How many times do half-bright young reporters have to show up, and how many times do you have to answer the same old goddamn questions like how you got the name Bear and what Joe Namath was like?

But the Bear was perfectly polite to me, just uninterested. He also had to pee all the time. Now, this is hardly a stop-the-presses revelation among old men.* The vast preponderance of commercials on the six-thirty news seem to be concerned with this affliction. But when, in my article, I mentioned it (and, for God's sake, just in passing), the entire great state of Alabama came down on me. How dare I reveal that Alabama's demigod, who could walk on water, had bodily functions just like the rest of us? Petitions were sent in, demanding I be fired. I received one letter from a Methodist minister, and to give the devil his due (aha!) he wrote it on church stationery and signed it the Reverend So-and-So. It was very terse and to the point. "Dear Mr.

---

*Especially now that I'm one myself.

DeFord," it read. "Whenever your parents would like to get married, I would be delighted to perform the ceremony."

Worse, when another writer for the magazine, John Papanek, went down to cover the game in which Bryant set the record, the good citizens from the Heart of Dixie cursed him and one actually spit on poor John, even as a state trooper looked away, rather like an accessory to the crime. And, as I understood it, the Bear himself thought the whole thing was a tempest in a teapot. As I said, he was weary. And the truth was that he did have to pee all the time, and he didn't make any bones about it.

But as Paul Harvey would've intoned, there was the rest of the story, too. Coaches, like sportswriters, are a tight fraternity. After all, it's a high-risk job; you get fired all the time; you sympathize; maybe you're next. They always call each other "Coach," using the honorific, something usually otherwise reserved in our society only for military officers and the clergy. Coach Bryant. Coach Jackson. Nobody says Teacher Brown. Or Insurance Agent Green. Or Writer DeFord. Or, thank God, nor do they even say Manager Piniella in baseball. But a few months after Alabama threw its hissy fit about me, I called up Coach Dean Smith at Chapel Hill and told him I'd like to do a story on him. I'd known Dean for almost twenty years, and we'd always enjoyed cordial relations.

He got right to the point. "I'm sorry, Frank, but I won't talk to you."

Flabbergasted, I managed to gasp, "Why?"

"I didn't like the way you treated Coach Bryant in that article."

Well, that got my back up. Practically speaking, too, I knew that Dean was a man who did not easily give himself away. He was not waiting for me to come along so that, at last, he could unburden himself. No matter how much he talked to me, I was not, from his lips, going to uncover the Real Dean Smith, the Dean Smith Nobody Knows. It really wasn't all that much a loss that I would not hear his nasal tones. So I told Dean—excuse me: Coach Smith—that I was sorry, I understood his position, but I had a job to do, and I was going to write the story anyway. And he replied, simply, that he understood my job.

Now, in most circumstances like this, the affronted party would immediately send out an alert that a rotten writer was trying to do a number on him, and whatever you do, don't say a word to him. But not Dean. He held to his belief that I had been rude to Bryant in an article, and so he would not allow me to interview him. But he did not force that opinion upon a single other person. Also, he was able to separate the inconsiderate writer from the person he had known. Indeed, every day I was at Chapel Hill, I was graciously welcomed into his office, where we would exchange pleasantries, and then I would proceed to interview his assistants, his players, even his good friend the university chancellor. What a weird experience. But, in counterpoint, I too honored Dean's stand; I never asked him to change his position.

I've seen him occasionally in the years since the story came out. Poor Dean is suffering from dementia now, but up until the last time I spoke with him, our personal relationship remained exactly as it was before he thought I'd slighted Bear Bryant; it was as if that episode had never happened.

Doing a piece on Bobby Knight was exactly the opposite experience, for he didn't originally want to do the story with me, and so there had to be a lot of prenuptial negotiations. Bobby was mad at *Sports Illustrated*, and when I mentioned that I'd *personally* never criticized him before, he actually remembered one lousy throwaway negative line I'd written about him in a movie review from years ago and he tossed that back into my face to prove that we were all lying snakes.

But finally I convinced him that I really could approach him with an open mind, and he accepted my word and agreed to do the story, and when we did meet he was charming and fascinating, as he can be, and we stayed up at his house talking about the Civil War till one o'clock in the morning. Bobby knows a great deal about the Civil War, and may have been impressed that I knew a little. After all, as he said once, "The best time in every sportswriter's life were the three years he spent in second grade." But then, don't ever forget that an interview is two people on a high school date, and it's not just the reporter who's doing the flirting.

Years later, I had become a correspondent on *Real Sports with Bryant Gumbel,* where I happily do, in many respects, the same sort of pieces for television that I had written for *Sports Illustrated.* It's simply storytelling in another medium—the main difference being that on TV, the producers take care of me and handle all the nasty details I used to have to take care of by myself on the road. Once again, I just have to carry the guide-on.

Anyway, sure enough, I did another piece on Knight. He had sort of grabbed at a player he was mad at, and everybody was hysterical, saying he'd choked the kid, but I thought it was terribly overblown just because somebody caught it on camera. If it had been a football teacher absolutely manhandling a player, nobody would've blinked. And, in the end, I thought, altogether, that we put together an objectively fair piece.

After it was shown, though, as I was chatting in that on-air epilogue we correspondents do with Bryant, he started in on what a creep he thought Knight was. Now, the irony here is that while Knight is often misunderstood, so too is Bryant. Most people think he must be a real hard-ass. I'm sure this reputation developed when he was on the *Today Show,* where he would be paired with sweetie pies like Jane Pauley and Katie Couric, so by comparison, to some people, Bryant seemed like . . . well, like Bobby Knight. It is also the truth that Bryant is the best interviewer, ever, on television. And he can be brutal.

The day that the *National* debuted, it was such a big deal that I was scheduled on all three network morning shows—the trifecta. First I do Harry Smith on CBS, then Charlie Gibson on ABC, and both were not only respectful but obviously hopeful that this wonderful new journalistic venture might succeed. Then I go see my dear pal Bryant at NBC, and we're chatting over old times during the commercial. But as soon as the red light comes on, he turns to me, and without so much as a how-do-you-do, he gives me this coyote smile and says something like: "What makes you think a thing like this has any chance?" And after that it really got tough. Chewed me up and spit me out.

But, off camera, Bryant is friendly and generous. All the makeup ladies and the camera guys on the floor love working with him—and this is the real mark of a celebrity's character, that he doesn't put on airs with the enlisted men and women. The producers like working with him, too, even if they also, affectionately, mock Bryant's squeaky voice behind his back. So he is, in fact, a very nice gentleman, at odds with the no-nonsense prosecutor that most viewers see. Of course, all that aside, Bryant is opinionated. And one opinion he has is that he can't abide Bob Knight, as he made absolutely crystal-clear in our little on-air sidebar after I had finished presenting, immaculately fairly, the two sides of Coach Knight.

About two months later, I was walking down Sixth Avenue, and who should be heading directly toward me but Mr. and Mrs. Robert Knight. I was immediately uncomfortable, because Bobby had already let me know, in a telephone call at eight o'clock sharp the morning after the Gumbel interview ran, what precisely he thought of that conversation in general and Mr. Gumbel in particular and, by the by, also what he thought about my being a cretinous unwitting tool of said Mr. Gumbel. But, here we are on Sixth Avenue amid the passing throng, so Bobby is at his most civil. To his wife, he says: "You remember my friend Frank DeFord."

"Sure," she says straightaway. "With friends like that, you don't need any enemies."

This put a damper on things.

I didn't run across Bobby for several more years, until I gave a speech at Texas Tech, where he was now bivouacked after being dismissed at Indiana. And damn if he didn't completely surprise me and come out to the little dinner that they gave me before the speech, and we had a delightful time. I'm glad he quit coaching, though. He's too intense to do that at his age. I'm sorry, but coaching ain't just teaching.

Athletic directors used to be old football coaches kicked upstairs, but now with so much money in the athlete-student league, athletic directors at the big-time sports conglomerate-universities tend to be rah-rah businessmen. I think I understand them pretty well—it's as if they're running a high-class escort service for the alumni—all except why they let the guys who run bowl games bugger them. That utterly confounds me.

University presidents ought to be ashamed of themselves for selling out to the NCAA, but then, I appreciate that they have a very difficult job all around, so I pretty much excuse their duplicity. I wonder sometimes, though, if the presidents let their hair down when they get together and admit to one another what a horrible fraud they're perpetuating upon higher education.

One time, two presidents I knew came up to me at a Knight Commission meeting where I was the invited speaker. The Knight Commission is a glossy-résumé, happy-meal group, mostly of educators, who assemble periodically with a lot of weeping and wailing and gnashing of teeth to discuss how terrible college athletics are. Then they make all sorts of gauzy recommendations that nobody pays any attention to. But it makes the members of the Knight Commission feel better about themselves. If I were still in high school, I would call it a circle jerk.

Anyway, these two presidents asked *me*, when I spoke, to please emphasize, gently, to one of the most distinguished presidents of a high-toned private school that his college was just as guilty as all the big state universities, so stop putting on airs. They wanted me to do their dirty work. So, no, I don't think even the presidents can bear to level with one another.

The Southeastern Conference is really a hoot, isn't it? They turn so many tricks down there it makes your head swim. Y'all have to hand it to the good ole SEC.

Professional sports commissioners are very much a mixed bag. Their only constituency is the team owners, so, in a way, the czars, so called, usually reflect the group personality of the magnates, so called. Of course, that's not always true. Bart Giamatti was much too attractive to represent baseball owners, and Fay Vincent didn't have a baseball pedigree. Most of the football owners had no idea who Pete Rozelle was when they picked the kid, in desperation, to break a deadlock. The most telling artifact I ever spotted in a commissioner's office was in Bud Selig's. Posted proudly on his wall was the cheap certificate you can send away for for a few bucks attesting to your having duly made *Who's Who in America.* Here Selig is the lodestar of the national pastime, and he has to advertise that he's made it in the Yellow Pages of people? But the owners love him; he's their kind, only they all think they're all just a little bit smarter than Buddy is.

One time I did a story on the four extant team commissioners—at the time: Rozelle, football; Bowie Kuhn, baseball; Walter Kennedy, basketball; and Clarence Campbell, hockey. My idea was simply to present them as personalities, sans issues. I wanted, if possible, to humanize commissioners. Three of them made the cut.

There used to be a tabloid columnist named Sidney Skolsky, who did puffy little celebrity profiles. Skolsky's gimmick was to end each sketch by asking the star what clothing, if any, he or she slept in. All the nuggets that I read always concluded with the stars going along and happily revealing their sleeping attire. So I thought it would be cute to end my ante-Facebook summaries with this information. Rozelle, Kennedy, and Campbell were all very amused and quickly revealed this deep, dark bedroom secret. Old Campbell, in particular, was tickled pink to let the hockey world know that its czar slept bare-ass naked. But Bowie Kuhn was beside himself with indignation that I had dared make such a raw personal inquiry. He flat-out refused to answer the question about what he slept in, and took me to task for prying. I assumed he must've slept in a stuffed shirt.

Subsequently, Bowie did, however, make the Hall of Fame at Cooperstown, if for no good reason whatsoever.

45

TABOO

For a man like The Greek, the ups and downs have been so steep
and jagged that life loses its everyday proportions.
"The Line on Jimmy The Greek," *Sports Illustrated*, 1980

Jimmy The Greek Snyder was always a character, always on the edge, and if he was famous for a long time, he didn't become notorious until late in his life, when he made some unfortunate racial observations on television. I knew why Jimmy said what he did, and although he didn't mean to be racist, I knew immediately that most people would take it that way, and that he would suffer terribly for it, which he did for the last eight years of his life. As he was wont to say, he died that day, when he tried, artlessly, to explain why African-Americans tend to dominate so many sports: "The slave owner would breed his big black with his big black woman so he could have a big black kid."

In the same brief interview, Jimmy also praised the black athlete for being so accomplished and for working harder than the white athlete. Race is not a taboo subject, but if you make just one mistake, factually or stylistically, in talking about race, there is no forgiving and there are no explanations. Then, what you meant as merely racial is automatically deemed racist. So, I knew The Greek for the last eight years that he was alive after I did a story on him in 1980, and then I also knew him for the next eight, when he was dead.

At first, I didn't want to do that story. That was not a good year for me, 1980. That was the year my daughter Alexandra died of cystic fibrosis, on January 19, when she was eight years old.

Nobody ever told me, but I did read that some people thought that after this, I became more preoccupied with death in my writing. Perhaps. After I wrote a book about my own daughter, I let myself do one more story about a child dying—the daughter of Nolan Richardson, the Arkansas basketball coach—but no more. Maybe I did find more morbid subjects, but then, don't people always think more about death as they grow older?

Anyway, death and dying aside, I'd always tried to plumb the psyches of the people I wrote about. I'd heard that some people called me "Frank DeFreud," which I thought was pretty funny, and fair enough. That surely traced back to the most Freudian piece I ever wrote, which was about Jimmy Connors, his mother, and his grandmother and was entitled "Raised by Women to Conquer Men." Jimmy was so furious with the article that he punished me by refusing to talk to all other media at the U.S. Open, but his mother, Gloria, sent me a Christmas card, with a personal note saying, "Hope you have a super year." Later, a friend of Gloria's and mine told me that she had indeed gained some wisdom about herself and her relationship with Jimmy from my article, which had painted her so harshly. So you never know.

The Greek, I would discover, contained a deep repository for conflicts and phobias, but there was only one reason that I didn't want to do the profile on him, and that was because he too, like me, was a father who had lost a child to CF. Jimmy, in fact, had already seen two daughters die of the disease, and his oldest son, Jamie, would also fall to CF a few years later—buried on an unforgivably torrid summer's day in Las Vegas, with a parade of white stretch limos making up the desert's funeral cortege.

There, of course, is where Jimmy had made his mark—in a way, made gambling fashionable for middle America—and there is where he had raised Jamie: Vegas. I was also present in 1996 when they buried Jimmy himself, but that was a chilly spring day way up on a hill in Steubenville, Ohio, the rusty river town from which Dimetrios Georgios Synodinos had fled, thereupon to invent Jimmy Snyder. In Vegas.

Gil Rogin, who had done the first national article on The Greek, was the managing editor of *Sports Illustrated* in 1980, and he was the one who broached the idea that I, the bereaved father, connect with the man more experienced in that sorrow. Gil and I both knew that Jimmy had never opened up about that part of his life. "That's history," he would say, putting inquisitors off about almost anything of the gauzy past that he didn't want to touch on. Finally, I decided to take on the story. What the hell? Because I was on the board of the Cystic Fibrosis Foundation, I'd talked with all sorts of other parents who had lost children, and I thought maybe Jimmy could use the opportunity to open up to someone who was in the same sad fraternity.

It wasn't easy. Cystic fibrosis is a genetic disease: both parents contribute a faulty carrier gene to produce a child who is born with CF. The odds are immutable, and yet Jimmy, the oddsmaker to the nation, tried not to concede that. He would talk about his wife Joan's "sick genes," as if, unsaid, his side of the family—he—really had nothing to do with it. But, at the end of the day, that sort of ignorance lay at the heart of Jimmy's insecurity. He hadn't even completed high school and for all his native intelligence, all his success, and all his fame, he forever felt insecure around more educated people.

I was with him once at Duke University, when James Barber, the eminent presidential scholar, asked him to join a panel on the upcoming election, to discuss the odds and probabilities of the vote. The Greek was absolutely ecstatic, so honored was he to be placed in that esteemed company. He, who blithely went on national television all the time, was so terribly nervous that he was out of sorts for days leading up to his academic appearance. When Barber publicly complimented him on his contributions to the panel, he burst his buttons, like a kid who'd succeeded at a piano recital.

Jimmy really was an open book: the uneducated fellow who'd come up from nowhere, who'd found success in something of an unsavory profession, but who longed for respectability. "Don't put a cigar in my mouth," he would wail, even as he invariably, grandiloquently referred to himself in the third person and wore gold chains that screamed out: Gambler! Tackpot! Vegas! But gold signified wealth, and since he did not possess the other more genteel displays of success, that was The Greek's outward and visible sign. He talked about money all the time.

In fact, I found out that there were two kinds of money in his life. "Gambling money" might as well have been altogether different from the sort of legal tender that you and I and Jimmy use to buy groceries with. If you didn't think of currency in those bifurcated terms, you couldn't take the risk, you couldn't make it at the tables or betting the line.

But for all the wealth he had made with the gambling money and then with his celebrity, The Greek always felt vulnerable, and he would try to sound smarter than he was, to compensate; that is why he finally came a cropper expounding, out of his league, on culture and genealogy. He was just showing off, that was all, poor guy. People said to me: he must've been drunk. They had no idea that, the gold chains aside, there really were considerable parts of Jimmy that didn't fit the stereotype. He barely ever took a drink, and when he did, of all things, he preferred Harvey's Bristol Cream.

Yeah, imagine: Jimmy The Greek and Harvey's Bristol Cream.

We did occasionally talk a little about what we shared, that fatal gene, which took our children, but, by and large, he felt uncomfortable with the subject, with the idea he really didn't want to admit, that, as he had given life to his six children, so had he helped to pass on the curse of an early death to three of them. Of course, all of us who had a child with CF can never really ignore that reality, but most of us learn to face it as irony, rather than guilt. But as Jimmy had managed to run away from Steubenville and that desperate past, he couldn't ever escape from his genes, and he suffered terribly for it.

So, we didn't talk about cystic fibrosis a whole lot. We did go to the races a few times. He was more comfortable at a track than anywhere else. One day, we were at Belmont. It was a perfectly beautiful afternoon, and not only that, but, with his gambling money, Jimmy hit the trifecta on the last race. He wheeled the four-and-six with all the other horses, and it came in, so he won $1,400.

In the limousine, going back into the city, Jimmy suddenly asked me about my son, Alex's older brother, Chris. "How's the kid doing?"

"Watching his sister get sicker and die, Jimmy—you can imagine. Like how Jamie and Stephanie must've felt when Tina died."

He nodded, but quickly turned the other way, and I realized that The Greek, the big tough Vegas guy, was fighting back tears. When he turned back his eyes were just clouding up. "What's his name? Your boy?"

"Christian. Chris."

"Yeah. What's he like to do?"

"Well, you know, he's twelve. He plays Little League baseball. Rides his bike. Swims. He's a pretty good tennis player."

"Yeah?" The Greek brightened up a little. "What's a tennis racket cost?"

"Oh, I guess a good one is $75 or $100."

Right away, then, The Greek reached into his pocket and pulled out his roll of gambling money, of which there was a lot there from hitting the trifecta. He peeled off a hundred. "I wanna give him this to get a new racket," he said.

Now, if there is one taboo in journalism that is undisputed, it is that no writers ever take money from someone they're doing a story on. In our business, that is the law of the Medes and the Persians. And there was Jimmy the Greek starting to hand me, the writer working on the Jimmy the Greek story, $100.

In my mind, there were three responses that quickly popped up. The first was to explain very bluntly that I appreciated it, but taking money from him was strictly out of the question.

The second was that I would just say to hell with all the rules and take the money. For the best rationalization purposes, you see, after all, it wasn't real money, just gambling money.

The third thing that occurred to me was that I would take the hundred and give it to the Cystic Fibrosis Foundation, and then I would go out myself and buy Christian a tennis racket and tell him it came from The Greek.

And all this is going through my mind, and The Greek is pushing the bill on me, so what do you think I did?

I went for number two. I just took the damn money.

Never mind the taboo; it just seemed to me to be the right thing to do. Sometimes, even when you are a sportswriter, you're not. This seemed to be such a time. We were a couple of fathers who'd lost children to a disease. A hundred dollars was going to make any more difference? What the hell. "Thank you, Jimmy," I said. "Chris will really appreciate this." I put the bill in my pocket.

"The kid lost a sister," Jimmy said, and then the tears began to drip from his eyes. He put his hand—curiously, as big a man as The Greek was, he had dainty little hands—to his forehead and began to dab at his eyes. At first he seemed a little ashamed that he was crying, but he couldn't help himself, and so he just kept shaking his head and crying some more. I put my hand on his shoulder and held it there for quite a while.

"Yeah," I said.

"Yeah, I know," said The Greek.

46

LAST CALL

Nobody knew it at the time, but Toots was dying to tell the awful
truth. He rasped: "No one goes out anymore. Never mind the
Hemingways that used to come in here every night. Forget that. But
it used to be every midnight there would be fifteen sportswriters at
the bar. Every midnight, at least fifteen sportswriters. Where are
they now? None of them, night after night. Nobody."
The next week, Toots Shor's closed down.
"Show Biz Has Always Been a State of Mind,"
Audience, 1972

Today, of course, with the Internet, sportswriting is being squeezed
again, just as television pressured us back when The Kid first appeared
on the scene. Notwithstanding, I think there are more good sportswriters doing more good sportswriting than ever before. But I also
believe that the one thing that's largely gone out is what made sport
such fertile literary territory—the characters, the tales, the humor,
the pain, what Hollywood calls "the arc." That is: stories. We have, all
by ourselves, ceded that one neat thing about sport that we owned.

Of course, it can never ever be quite the way it was when I
came aboard. That door closed long ago. In fact, I was, I am sure,
the last writer in all the world to have been chosen over television,
head-to-head.

Back in the 1960s, the NBA didn't even have a national television contract, but during the playoff finals, for the Sunday afternoon
games, one of the networks would show up, cherry-picking on the

cheap. So it was that when the Celtics beat the Lakers again to win another championship, a little production assistant rushed down onto the court and buttonholed Red Auerbach.

I had already left my seat at the courtside press table and was standing there with Auerbach, as he brandished his victory cigar for the crowd. Breathlessly, the TV boy asked Red to come up to the television booth immediately. Red looked down on the kid, and disdain filled his face. "Where were you in February?" he asked, waving him off with his cigar.

The little fellow was speechless, totally discombobulated.

"I said," Red went on, more stridently, "where the fuck were you in February?" Then, gloriously, he threw his other arm around me. "I'm going with my writers," he declared, and we marched off the court that way, Red and I, together.

It was the last hurrah for the press. After that, it was the media.

ACKNOWLEDGMENTS

Obviously, because so much of my life revolves around things I have written, some of what is found on these pages was referenced earlier in various other books of mine and publications. Bits and pieces from *Sports Illustrated* articles pop up throughout, but the only sustained repetition from *SI* is from the March 29, 2010, issue, "Sometimes the Bear Eats You"—an article suggested by the magazine's managing editor, Terry McDonell, to whom I express special appreciation, inasmuch as that piece was the genesis of this book.

Much of the material about Dan Sachs comes from a eulogy I wrote about him in 1967 in the *Princeton Alumni Weekly*, but the only chunk of direct self-plagiarism is found in the chapter on Baltimore, which appeared in the January 2007 issue of *Smithsonian* as "Bleeve It, Hon." Some other thoughts found herein were originally offered in the 2010 Red Smith Lecture in Journalism at Notre Dame, and some are from various of my NPR commentaries over the many years.

I am indebted to Bill Bradley for allowing me to print his youthful tribute to Dan Sachs, to David C. Morton for telling me so much about DeFord Bailey in his book about him, and to Charles Fountain and William A. Harper for their exhaustive biographies of Grantland Rice. The best bar bill I ever picked up was for Mark Kram Jr., listening to him remind me of stories about his father. My thanks, too, to Ketzel Levine for explaining to me how in the world I came to come to NPR, to Irv Muchnick for his dogged reporting on Vince McMahon, and to my brother Gill and his wife, Laura, for digging up much of the family genealogy. Michael MacCambridge's fine history of *Sports*

Illustrated helped bring back some forgotten recollections, and many other old friends were kind enough to refresh a flagging memory.

I didn't ask my wife for any help at all, which is why we still love one another.

Frank Deford
Westport, Connecticut
August 28, 2011